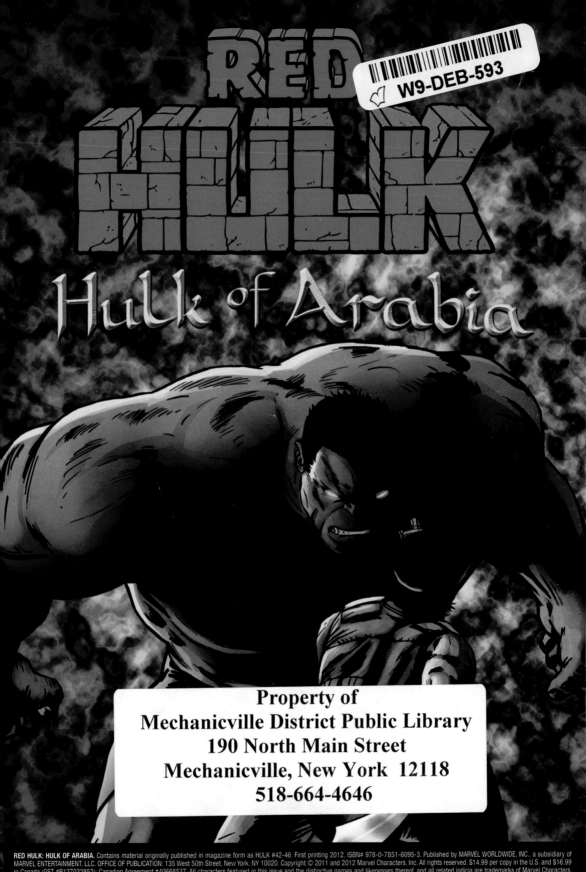

RED HULK

Hulk of Arabia

RED HULK: HULK OF ARABIA. Contains material originally published in magazine form as HULK #42-46. First printing 2012. ISBN# 978-0-7851-6095-3. Published by MARVEL WORLDWIDE, INC., a subsidiary of MARVEL ENTERTAINMENT, LLC. OFFICE OF PUBLICATION: 135 West 50th Street. New York, NY 10020. Copyright © 2011 and 2012 Marvel Characters, Inc. All rights reserved. $14.99 per copy in the U.S. and $16.99 in Canada (GST #R127032852); Canadian Agreement #40668537. All characters featured in this issue and the distinctive names and likenesses thereof, and all related indicia are trademarks of Marvel Characters, Inc. No similarity between any of the names, characters, persons, and/or institutions in this magazine with those of any living or dead person or institution is intended, and any such similarity which may exist is purely coincidental. **Printed in the U.S.A.** ALAN FINE, EVP - Office of the President, Marvel Worldwide, Inc. and EVP & CMO Marvel Characters B.V.; DAN BUCKLEY, Publisher & President - Print, Animation & Digital Divisions; JOE QUESADA, Chief Creative Officer; DAVID BOGART, SVP of Business Affairs & Talent Management; TOM BREVOORT, SVP of Publishing; C.B. CEBULSKI, SVP of Creator & Content Development; DAVID GABRIEL, SVP of Publishing Sales & Circulation; MICHAEL PASCIULLO, SVP of Brand Planning & Communications; JIM O'KEEFE, VP of Operations & Logistics; DAN CARR, Executive Director of Publishing Technology; SUSAN CRESPI, Editorial Operations Manager; ALEX MORALES, Publishing Operations Manager; STAN LEE, Chairman Emeritus. For information regarding advertising in Marvel Comics or on Marvel.com, please contact

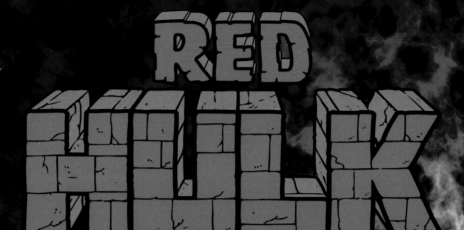

RED HULK

Hulk of Arabia

WRITER: **JEFF PARKER**

ARTIST: **PATCH ZIRCHER**

COLORIST: **RACHELLE ROSENBERG**

LETTERER: **ED DUKESHIRE**

COVER ARTIST: **PATCH ZIRCHER**

WITH **BOO COOK, VAL STAPLES & ANDY TROY**

ASSISTANT EDITOR: **JAKE THOMAS**

EDITOR: **MARK PANICCIA**

COLLECTION EDITOR & DESIGN: CORY LEVINE
ASSISTANT EDITORS: ALEX STARBUCK & NELSON RIBEIRO
EDITORS, SPECIAL PROJECTS: JENNIFER GRÜNWALD & MARK D. BEAZLEY
SENIOR EDITOR, SPECIAL PROJECTS: JEFF YOUNGQUIST
SENIOR VICE PRESIDENT OF SALES: DAVID GABRIEL
SVP OF BRAND PLANNING & COMMUNICATIONS: MICHAEL PASCIULLO

EDITOR IN CHIEF: AXEL ALONSO
CHIEF CREATIVE OFFICER: JOE QUESADA
PUBLISHER: DAN BUCKLEY
EXECUTIVE PRODUCER: ALAN FINE

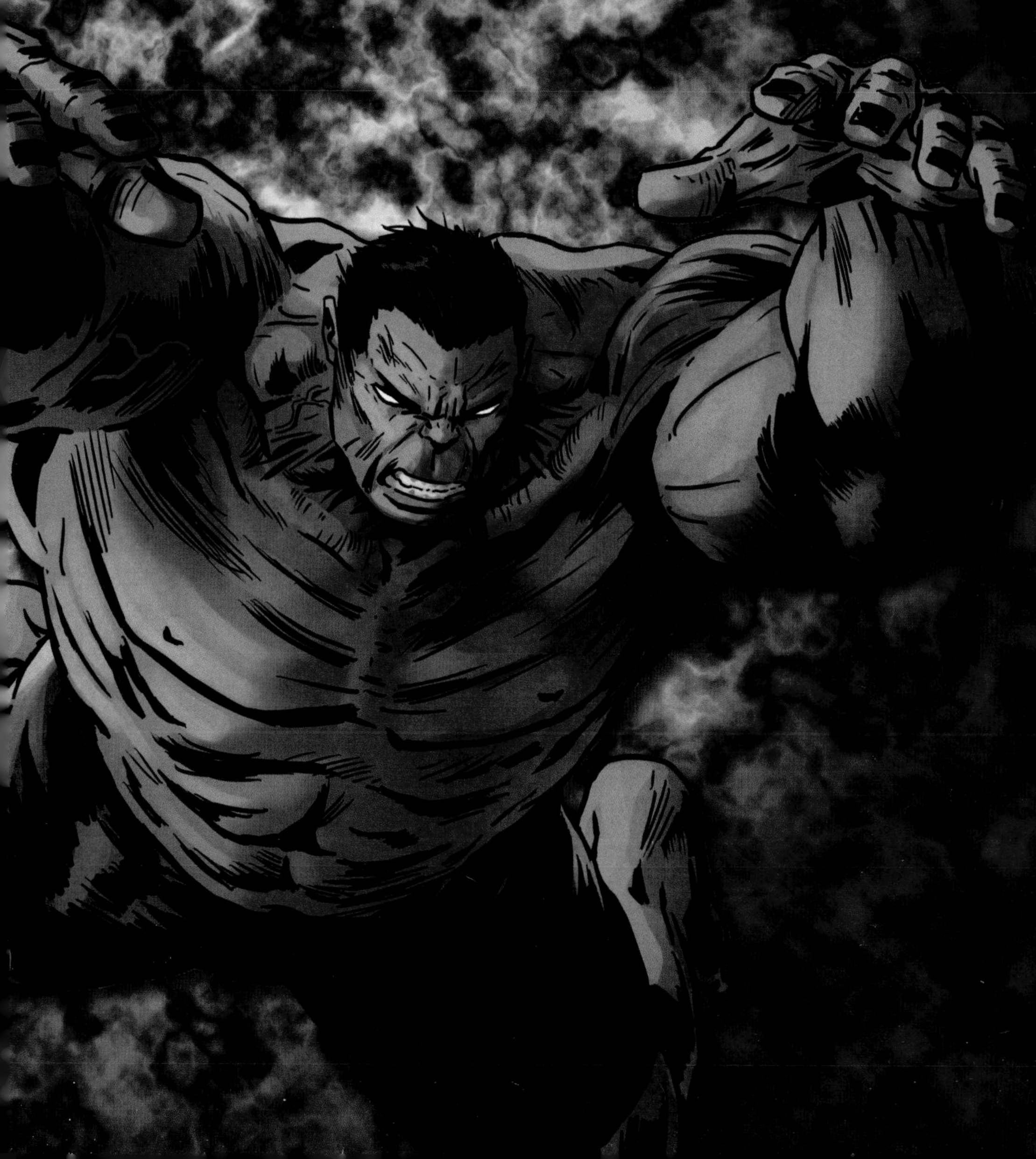

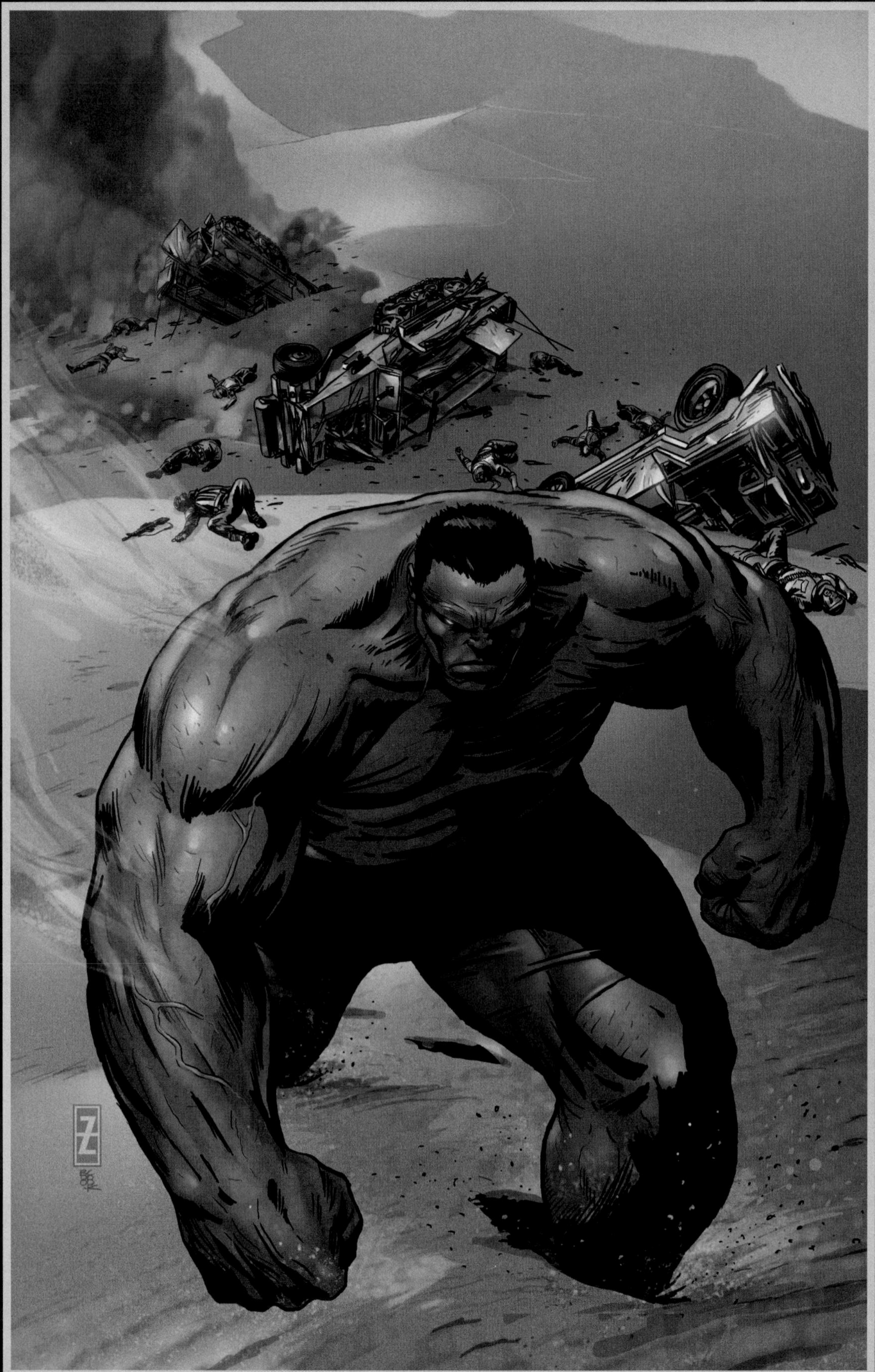

HULK #42

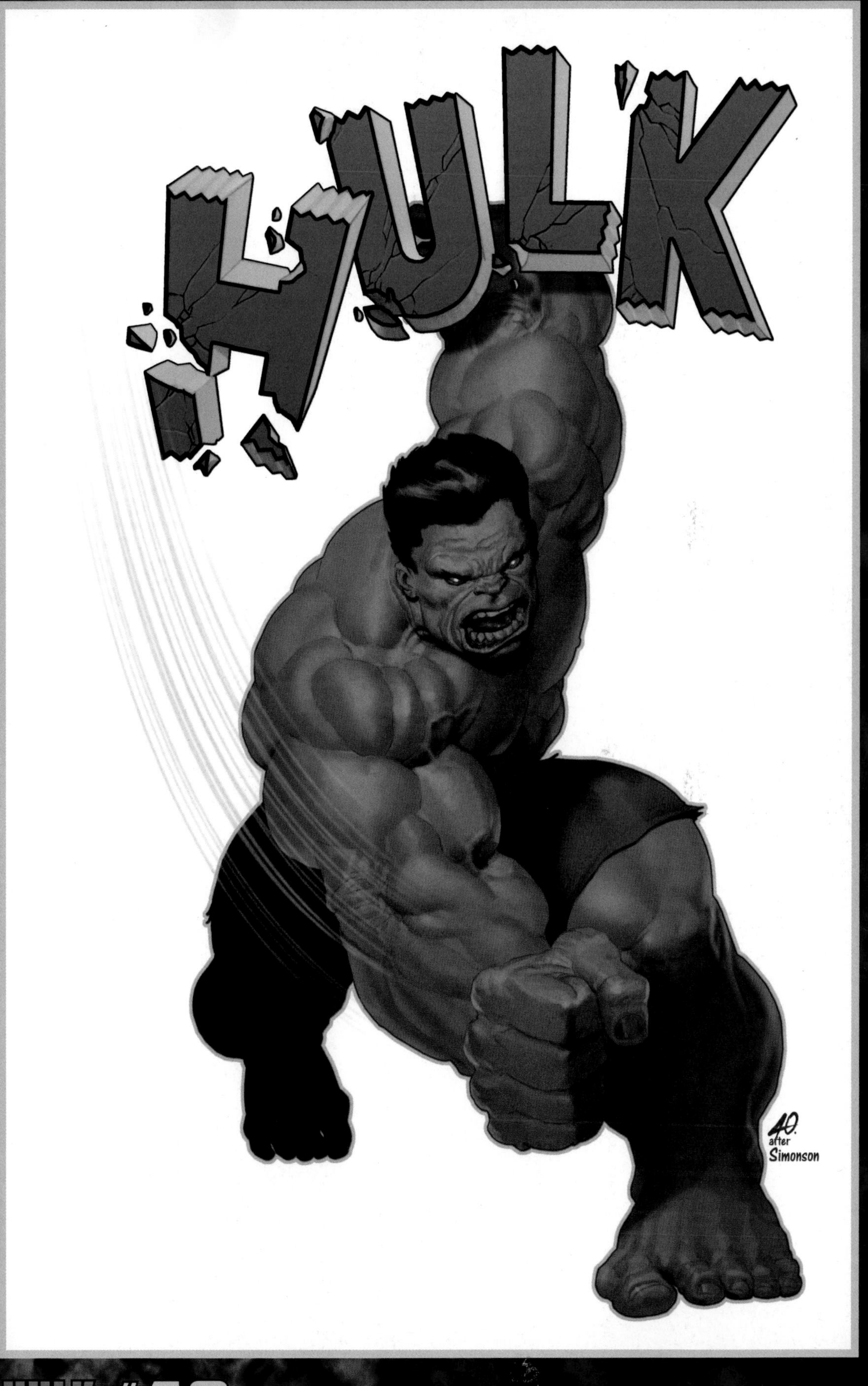
HULK
after
Simonson

HULK #42 MARVEL 50TH ANNIVERSARY VARIANT BY ARIEL OLIVETTI

Previously...

General Thaddeus "Thunderbolt" Ross faked his own death and gave up his identity to become the Red Hulk through a deal with a sinister group of villains. He wanted the power to stop his nemesis Bruce Banner (a.k.a. the Hulk), but all he got was tragedy, defeat and loss. Unable to resume his old life, Ross now atones for the sins of his past under the watchful eye of Steve Rogers. Penance for so many wrongs is hard to come by, but doing the hard thing is what General Ross built his life around, and exactly the kind of thing you call in a HULK to do.

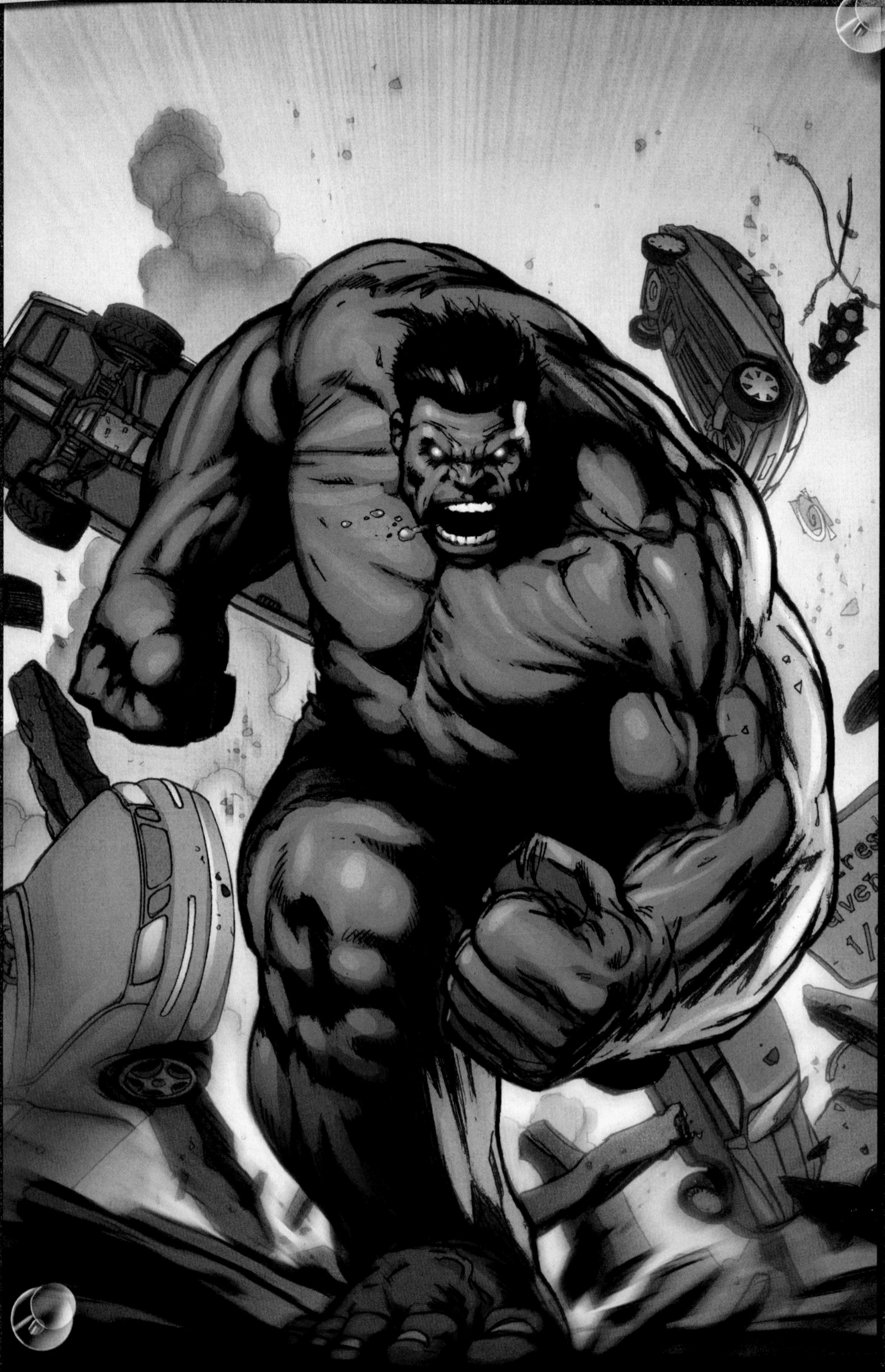

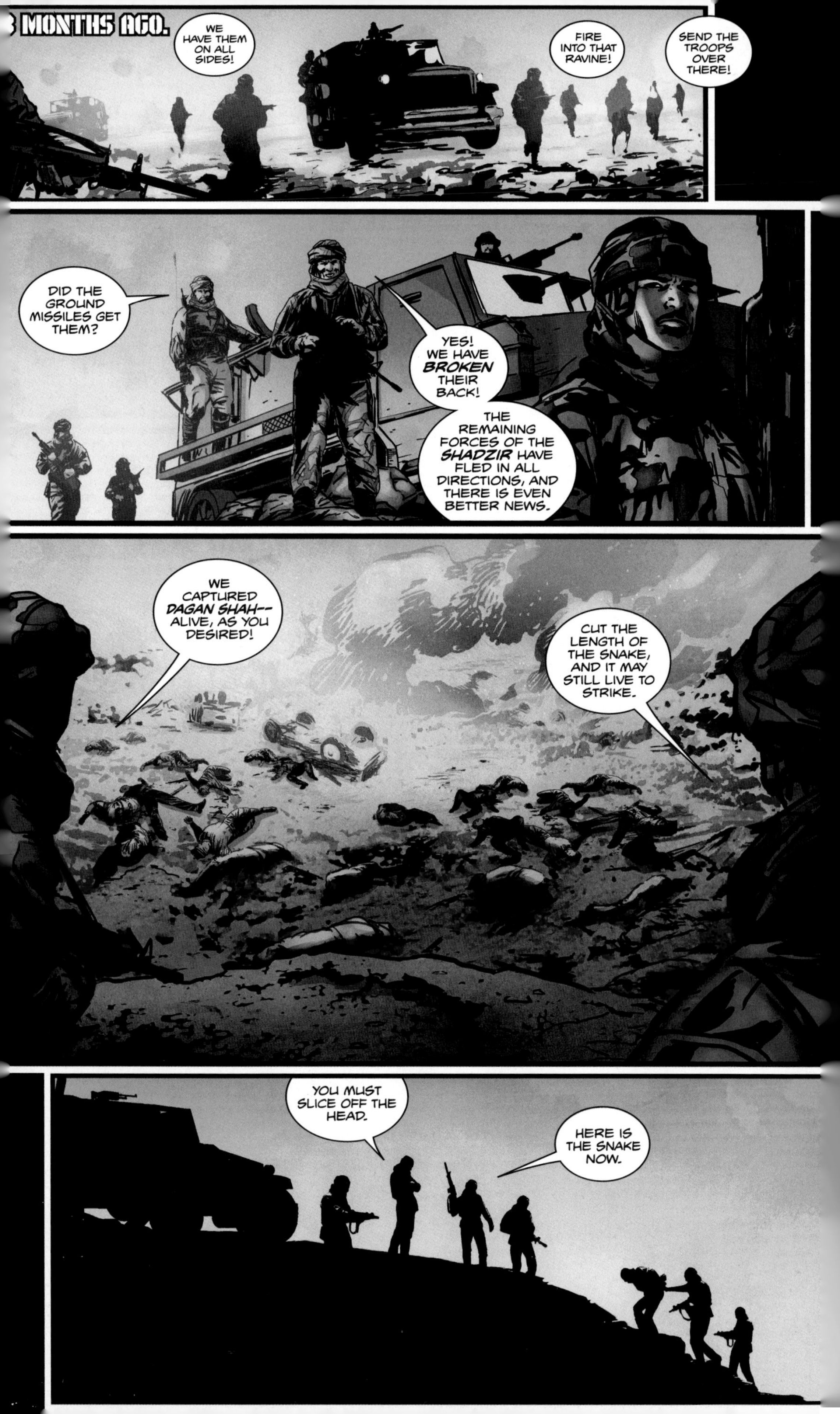
3 MONTHS AGO.
WE HAVE THEM ON ALL SIDES!
FIRE INTO THAT RAVINE!
SEND THE TROOPS OVER THERE!
DID THE GROUND MISSILES GET THEM?
YES! WE HAVE BROKEN THEIR BACK!
THE REMAINING FORCES OF THE SHADZIR HAVE FLED IN ALL DIRECTIONS, AND THERE IS EVEN BETTER NEWS.
WE CAPTURED DAGAN SHAH--ALIVE, AS YOU DESIRED!
CUT THE LENGTH OF THE SNAKE, AND IT MAY STILL LIVE TO STRIKE.
YOU MUST SLICE OFF THE HEAD.
HERE IS THE SNAKE NOW.

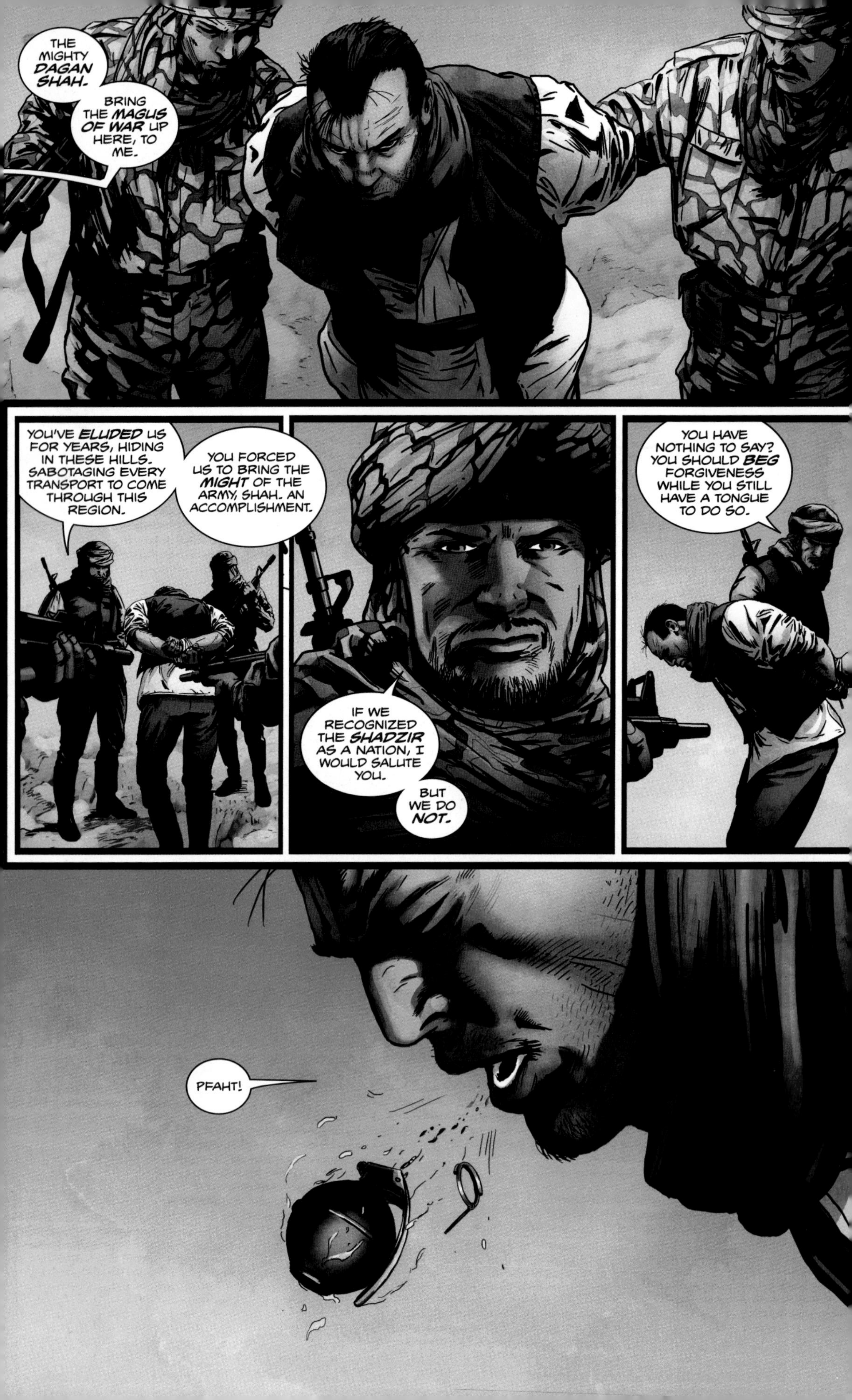

THE MIGHTY DAGAN SHAH.
BRING THE MAGUS OF WAR UP HERE, TO ME.
YOU'VE ELUDED US FOR YEARS, HIDING IN THESE HILLS. SABOTAGING EVERY TRANSPORT TO COME THROUGH THIS REGION.
YOU FORCED US TO BRING THE MIGHT OF THE ARMY, SHAH. AN ACCOMPLISHMENT.
IF WE RECOGNIZED THE SHADZIR AS A NATION, I WOULD SALUTE YOU.
BUT WE DO NOT.
YOU HAVE NOTHING TO SAY? YOU SHOULD BEG FORGIVENESS WHILE YOU STILL HAVE A TONGUE TO DO SO.
PFAHT!

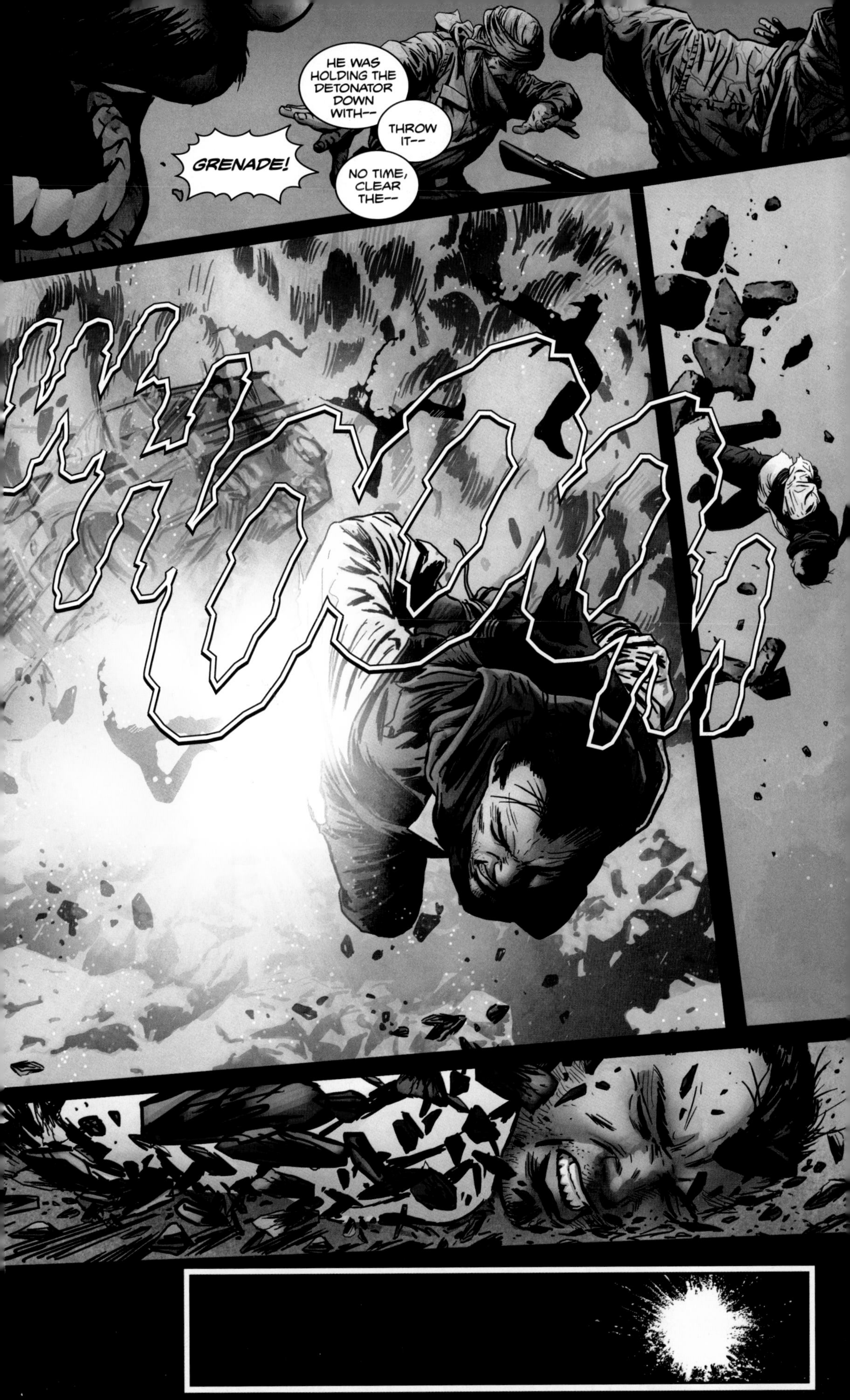
HE WAS HOLDING THE DETONATOR DOWN WITH--
GRENADE!
THROW IT--
NO TIME, CLEAR THE--
WHOOOM

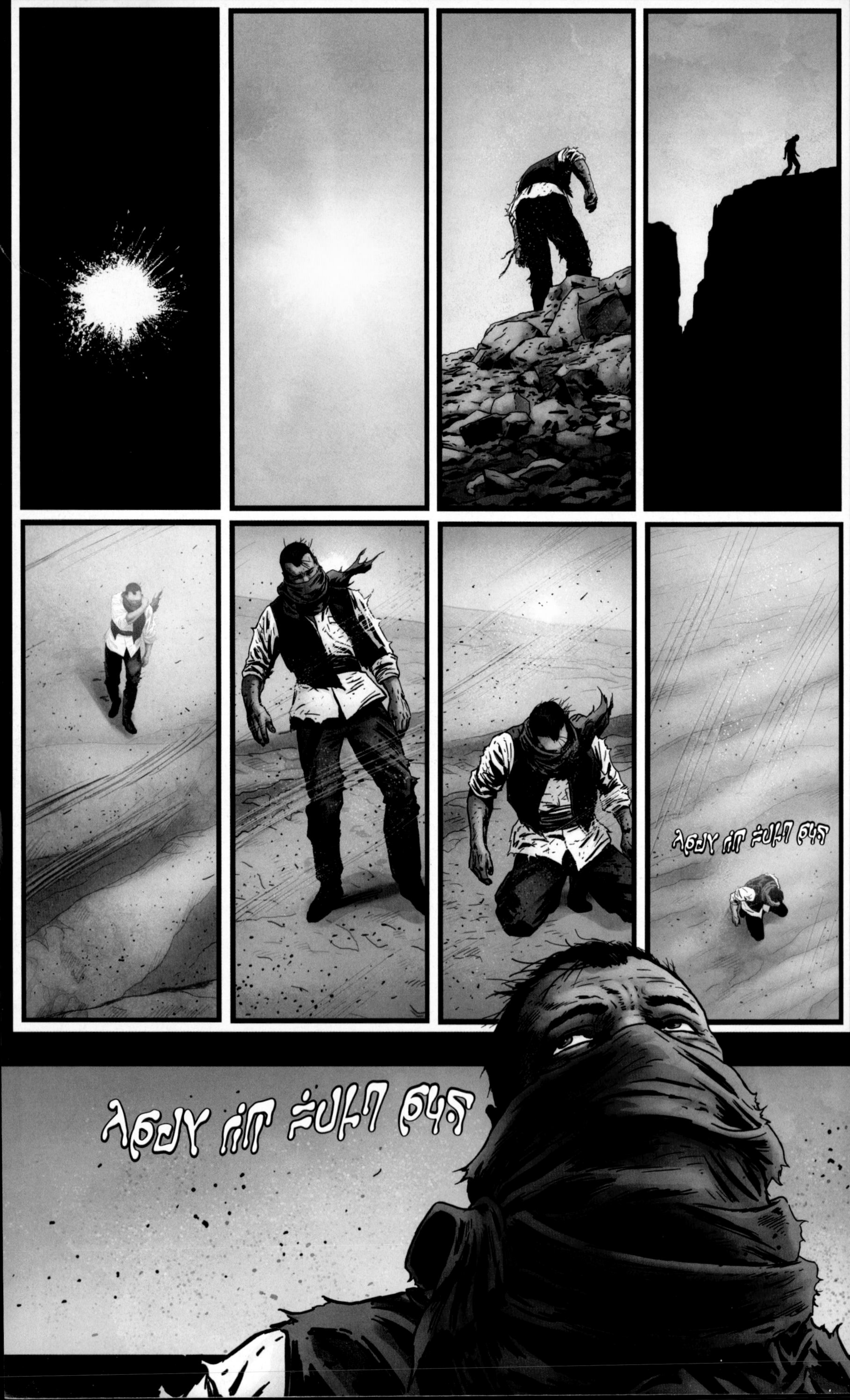

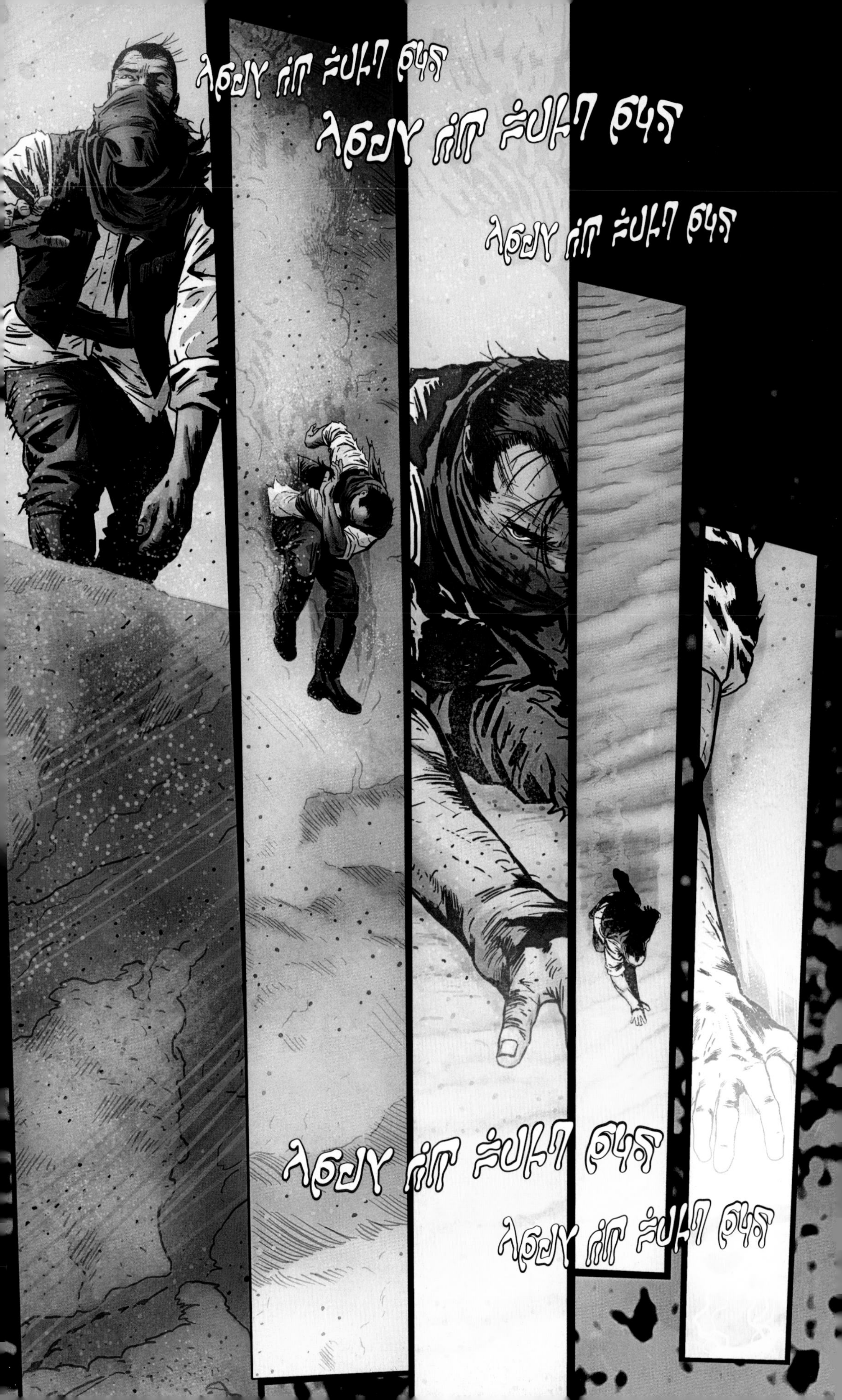

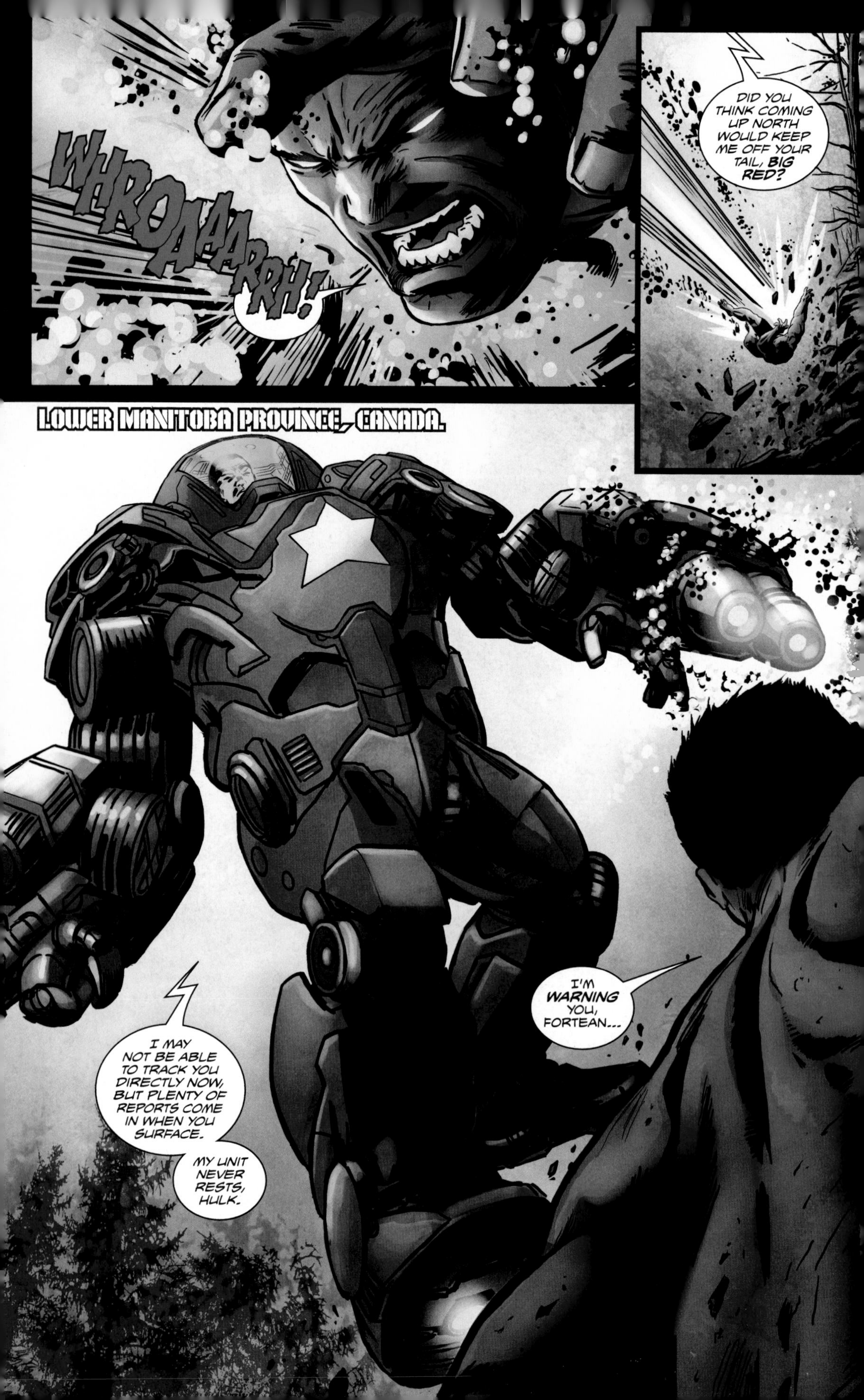
WHROAAARRH!
DID YOU THINK COMING UP NORTH WOULD KEEP ME OFF YOUR TAIL, BIG RED?
LOWER MANITOBA PROVINCE, CANADA.
I'M WARNING YOU, FORTEAN...
I MAY NOT BE ABLE TO TRACK YOU DIRECTLY NOW, BUT PLENTY OF REPORTS COME IN WHEN YOU SURFACE.
MY UNIT NEVER RESTS, HULK.

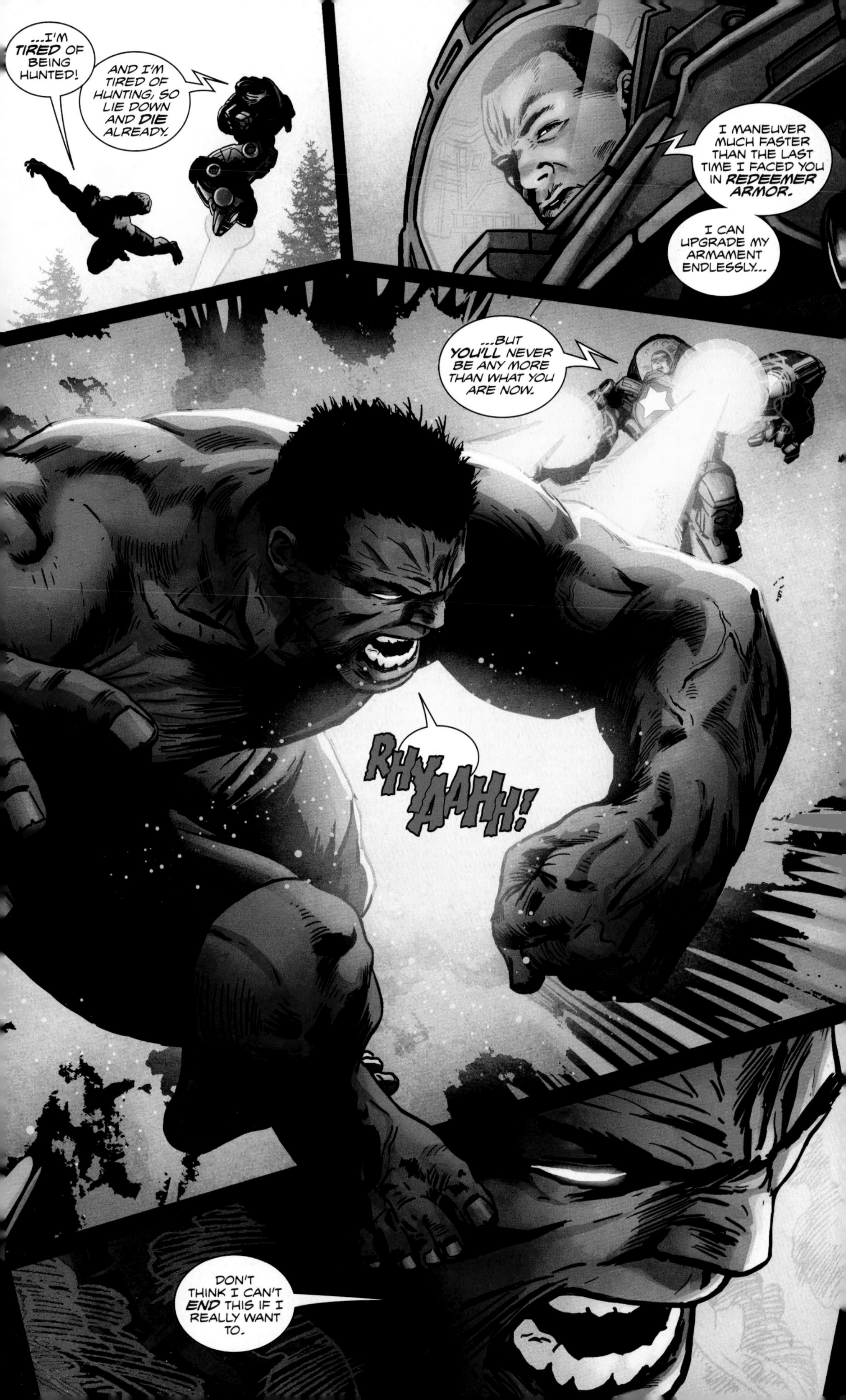
...I'M TIRED OF BEING HUNTED!
AND I'M TIRED OF HUNTING, SO LIE DOWN AND DIE ALREADY.
I MANEUVER MUCH FASTER THAN THE LAST TIME I FACED YOU IN REDEEMER ARMOR.
I CAN UPGRADE MY ARMAMENT ENDLESSLY...
...BUT YOU'LL NEVER BE ANY MORE THAN WHAT YOU ARE NOW.
RHYAAHH!
DON'T THINK I CAN'T END THIS IF I REALLY WANT TO.

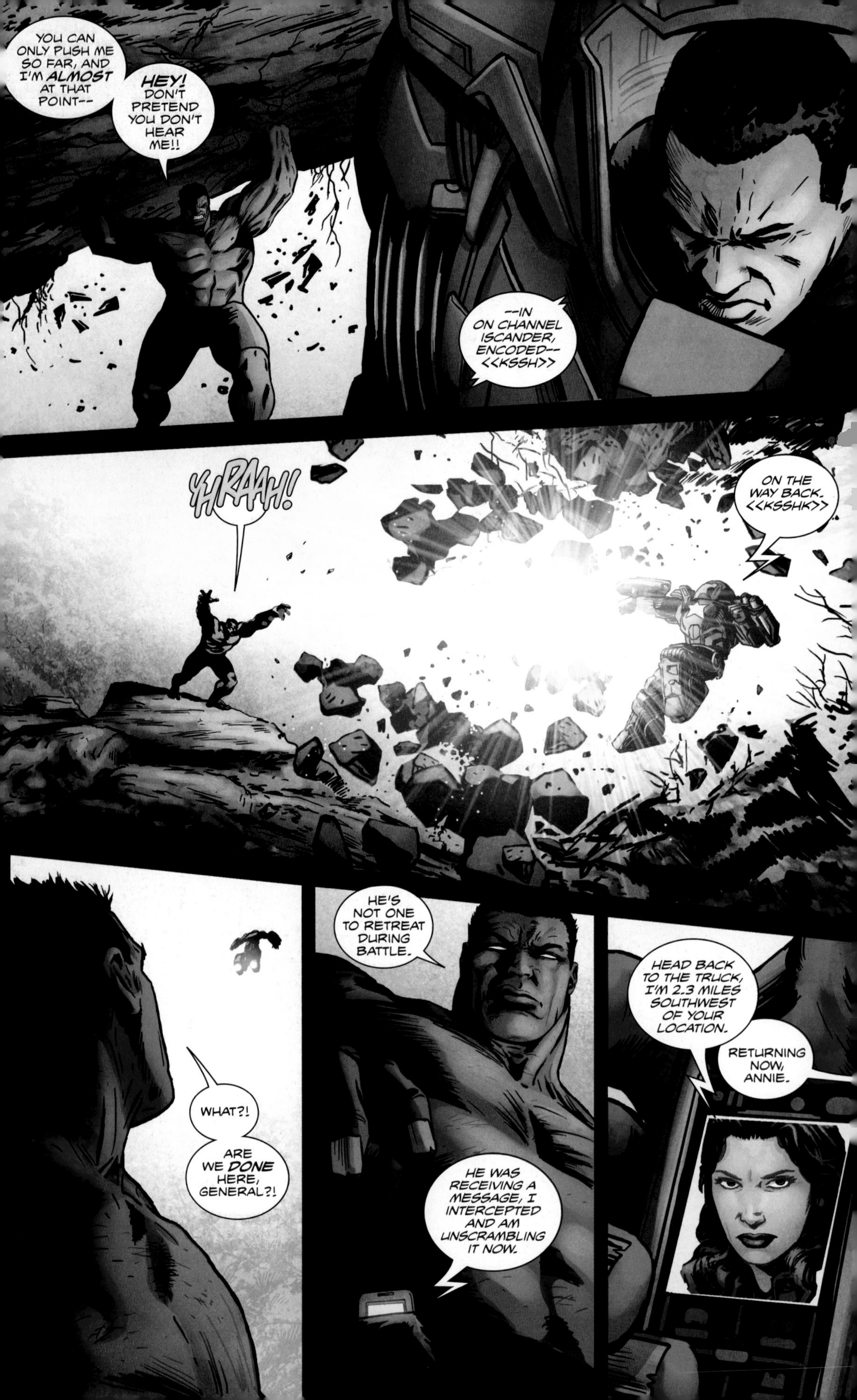
YOU CAN ONLY PUSH ME SO FAR, AND I'M ALMOST AT THAT POINT--
HEY! DON'T PRETEND YOU DON'T HEAR ME!!
--IN ON CHANNEL ISCANDER, ENCODED-- <<KSSH>>
YHRAAH!
ON THE WAY BACK. <<KSSHK>>
WHAT?!
ARE WE DONE HERE, GENERAL?!
HE'S NOT ONE TO RETREAT DURING BATTLE.
HE WAS RECEIVING A MESSAGE, I INTERCEPTED AND AM UNSCRAMBLING IT NOW.
HEAD BACK TO THE TRUCK, I'M 2.3 MILES SOUTHWEST OF YOUR LOCATION.
RETURNING NOW, ANNIE.

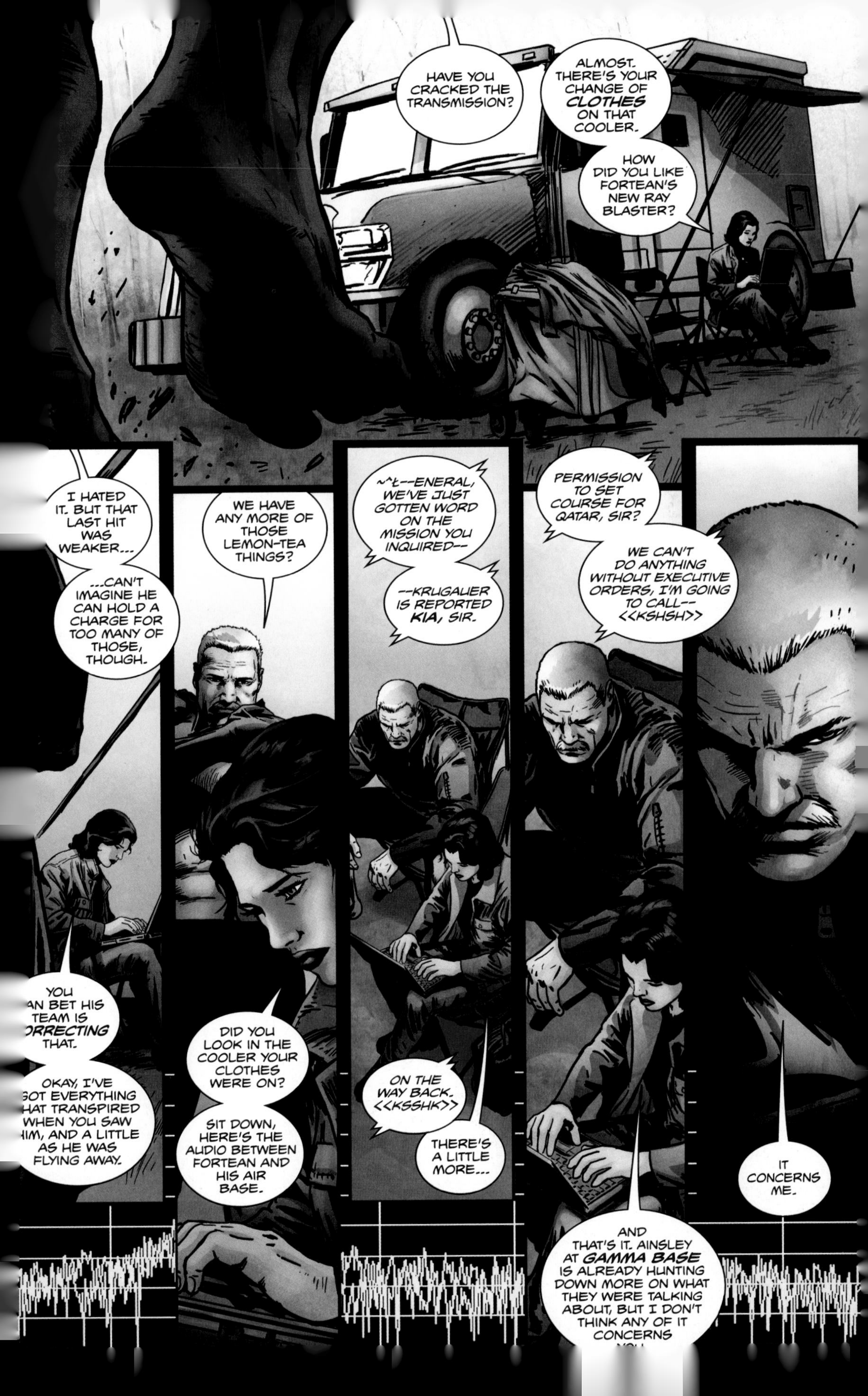
HAVE YOU CRACKED THE TRANSMISSION?
ALMOST. THERE'S YOUR CHANGE OF CLOTHES ON THAT COOLER.
HOW DID YOU LIKE FORTEAN'S NEW RAY BLASTER?
I HATED IT. BUT THAT LAST HIT WAS WEAKER...
...CAN'T IMAGINE HE CAN HOLD A CHARGE FOR TOO MANY OF THOSE, THOUGH.
YOU AN BET HIS TEAM IS ORRECTING THAT.
OKAY, I'VE GOT EVERYTHING HAT TRANSPIRED WHEN YOU SAW HIM, AND A LITTLE AS HE WAS FLYING AWAY.
WE HAVE ANY MORE OF THOSE LEMON-TEA THINGS?
DID YOU LOOK IN THE COOLER YOUR CLOTHES WERE ON?
SIT DOWN, HERE'S THE AUDIO BETWEEN FORTEAN AND HIS AIR BASE.
~^t--ENERAL, WE'VE JUST GOTTEN WORD ON THE MISSION YOU INQUIRED--
--KRUGAUER IS REPORTED KIA, SIR.
ON THE WAY BACK. <<KSSHK>>
THERE'S A LITTLE MORE...
PERMISSION TO SET COURSE FOR QATAR, SIR?
WE CAN'T DO ANYTHING WITHOUT EXECUTIVE ORDERS, I'M GOING TO CALL-- <<KSHSH>>
AND THAT'S IT. AINSLEY AT GAMMA BASE IS ALREADY HUNTING DOWN MORE ON WHAT THEY WERE TALKING ABOUT, BUT I DON'T THINK ANY OF IT CONCERNS
IT CONCERNS ME.

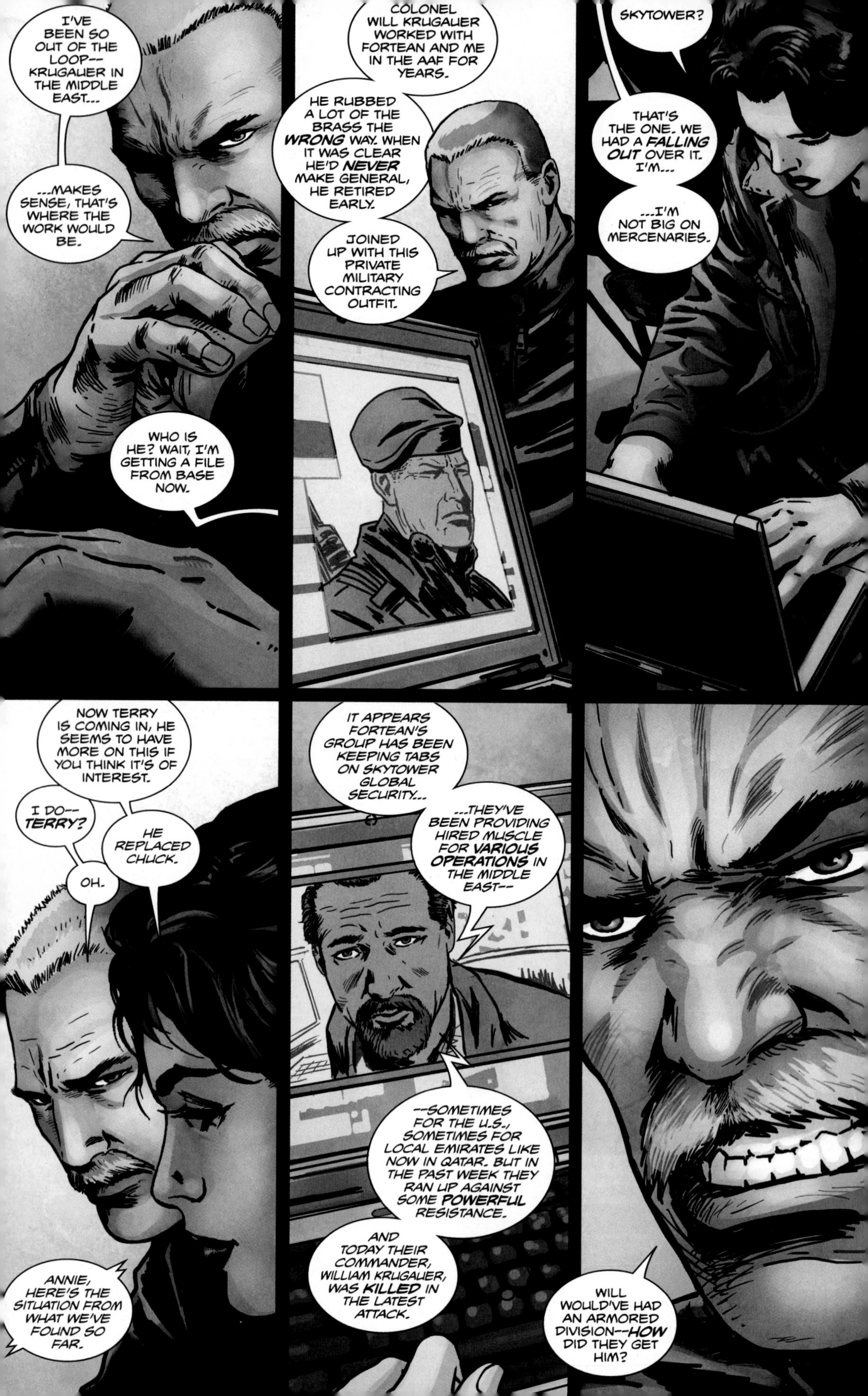

I'VE BEEN SO OUT OF THE LOOP-- KRUGAUER IN THE MIDDLE EAST...
...MAKES SENSE, THAT'S WHERE THE WORK WOULD BE.
WHO IS HE? WAIT, I'M GETTING A FILE FROM BASE NOW.
COLONEL WILL KRUGAUER WORKED WITH FORTEAN AND ME IN THE AAF FOR YEARS.
HE RUBBED A LOT OF THE BRASS THE WRONG WAY. WHEN IT WAS CLEAR HE'D NEVER MAKE GENERAL, HE RETIRED EARLY.
JOINED UP WITH THIS PRIVATE MILITARY CONTRACTING OUTFIT.
SKYTOWER?
THAT'S THE ONE. WE HAD A FALLING OUT OVER IT. I'M...
...I'M NOT BIG ON MERCENARIES.
NOW TERRY IS COMING IN, HE SEEMS TO HAVE MORE ON THIS IF YOU THINK IT'S OF INTEREST.
I DO-- TERRY?
HE REPLACED CHUCK.
OH.
ANNIE, HERE'S THE SITUATION FROM WHAT WE'VE FOUND SO FAR.
IT APPEARS FORTEAN'S GROUP HAS BEEN KEEPING TABS ON SKYTOWER GLOBAL SECURITY...
...THEY'VE BEEN PROVIDING HIRED MUSCLE FOR VARIOUS OPERATIONS IN THE MIDDLE EAST--
--SOMETIMES FOR THE U.S., SOMETIMES FOR LOCAL EMIRATES LIKE NOW IN QATAR. BUT IN THE PAST WEEK THEY RAN UP AGAINST SOME POWERFUL RESISTANCE.
AND TODAY THEIR COMMANDER, WILLIAM KRUGAUER, WAS KILLED IN THE LATEST ATTACK.
WILL WOULD'VE HAD AN ARMORED DIVISION--HOW DID THEY GET HIM?

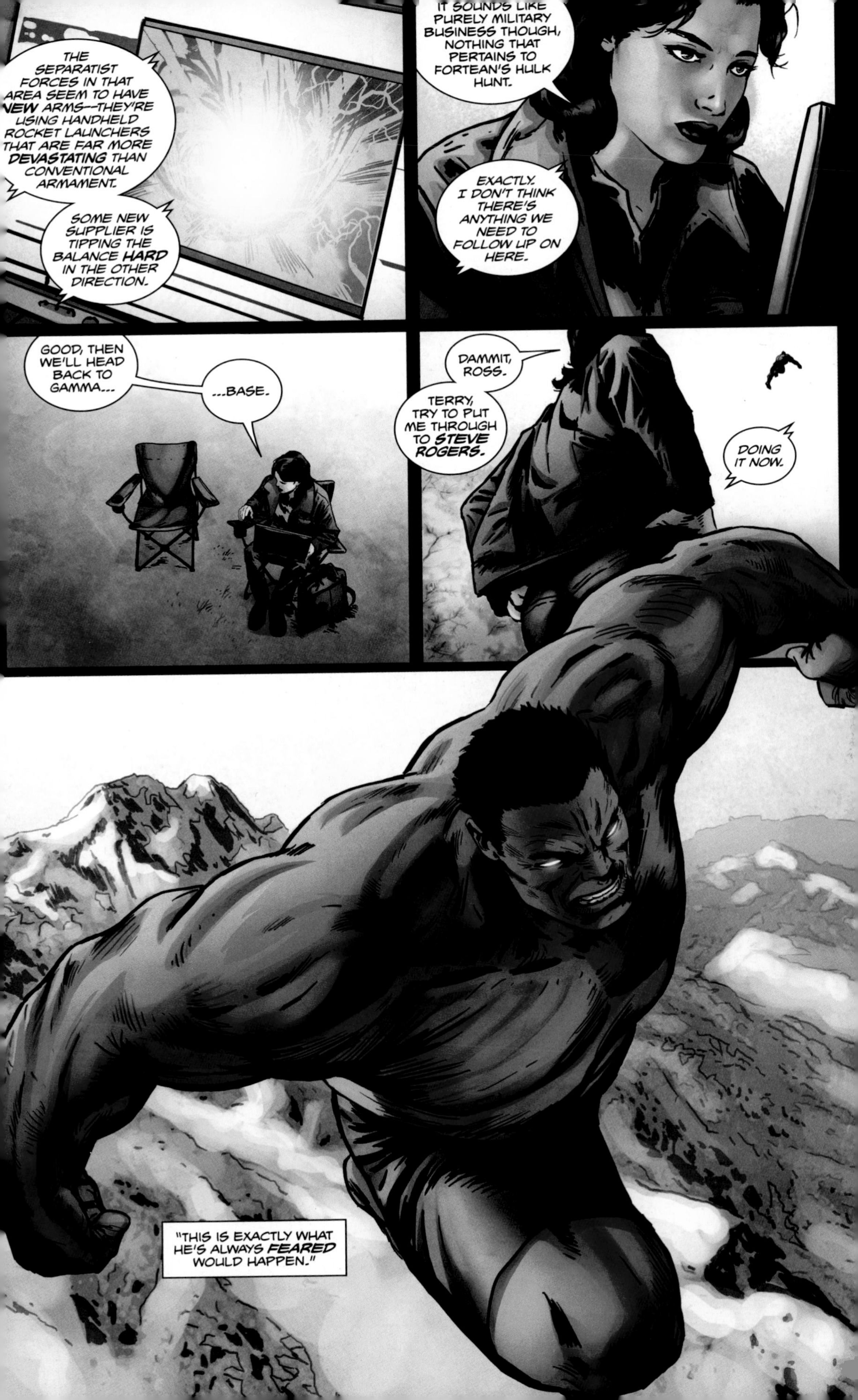
THE SEPARATIST FORCES IN THAT AREA SEEM TO HAVE NEW ARMS--THEY'RE USING HANDHELD ROCKET LAUNCHERS THAT ARE FAR MORE DEVASTATING THAN CONVENTIONAL ARMAMENT.
SOME NEW SUPPLIER IS TIPPING THE BALANCE HARD IN THE OTHER DIRECTION.
IT SOUNDS LIKE PURELY MILITARY BUSINESS THOUGH, NOTHING THAT PERTAINS TO FORTEAN'S HULK HUNT.
EXACTLY. I DON'T THINK THERE'S ANYTHING WE NEED TO FOLLOW UP ON HERE.
GOOD, THEN WE'LL HEAD BACK TO GAMMA...
...BASE.
DAMMIT, ROSS.
TERRY, TRY TO PUT ME THROUGH TO STEVE ROGERS.
DOING IT NOW.
"THIS IS EXACTLY WHAT HE'S ALWAYS FEARED WOULD HAPPEN."

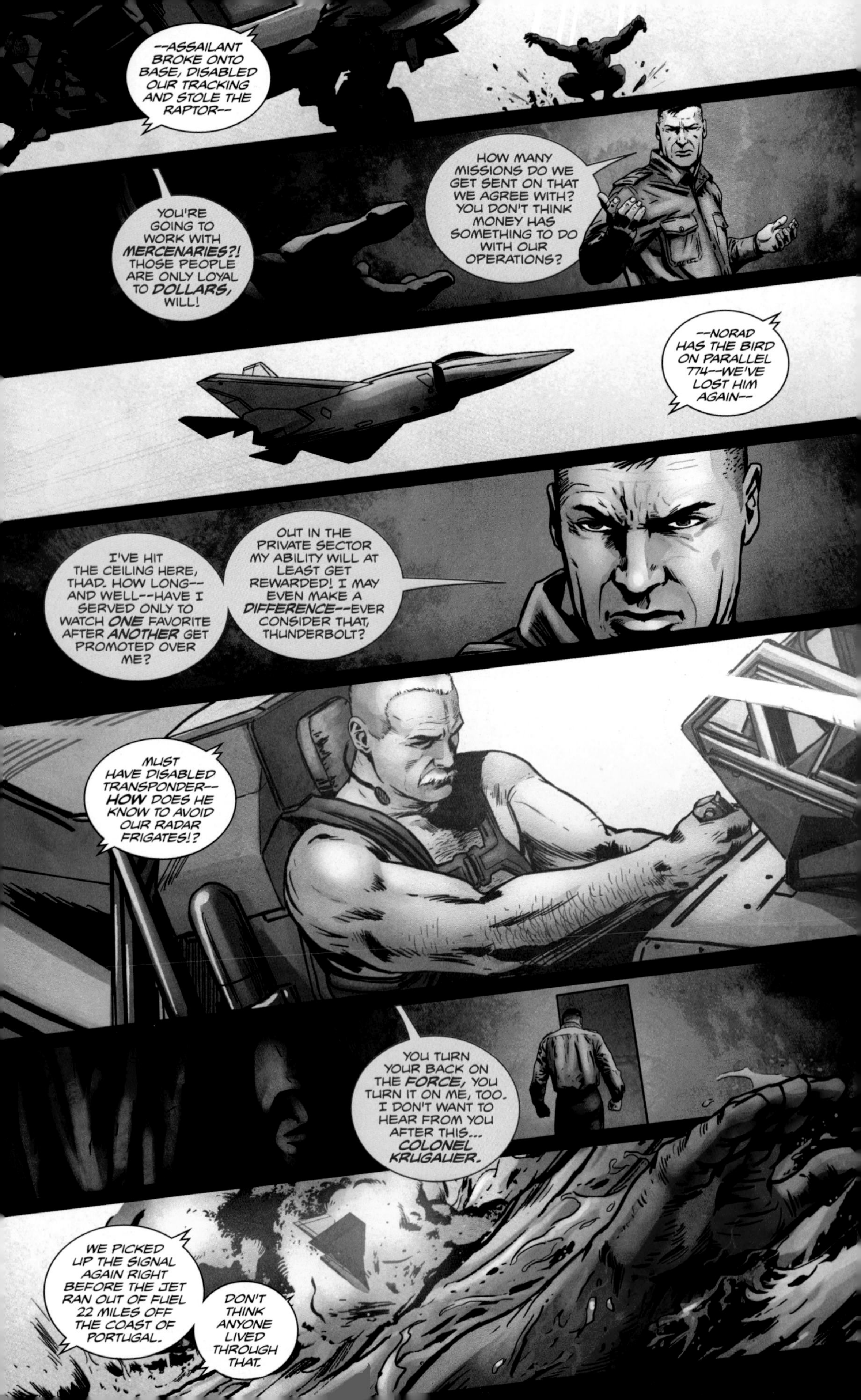
--ASSAILANT BROKE ONTO BASE, DISABLED OUR TRACKING AND STOLE THE RAPTOR--
YOU'RE GOING TO WORK WITH MERCENARIES?! THOSE PEOPLE ARE ONLY LOYAL TO DOLLARS, WILL!
HOW MANY MISSIONS DO WE GET SENT ON THAT WE AGREE WITH? YOU DON'T THINK MONEY HAS SOMETHING TO DO WITH OUR OPERATIONS?
--NORAD HAS THE BIRD ON PARALLEL 774--WE'VE LOST HIM AGAIN--
I'VE HIT THE CEILING HERE, THAD. HOW LONG--AND WELL--HAVE I SERVED ONLY TO WATCH ONE FAVORITE AFTER ANOTHER GET PROMOTED OVER ME?
OUT IN THE PRIVATE SECTOR MY ABILITY WILL AT LEAST GET REWARDED! I MAY EVEN MAKE A DIFFERENCE--EVER CONSIDER THAT, THUNDERBOLT?
MUST HAVE DISABLED TRANSPONDER--HOW DOES HE KNOW TO AVOID OUR RADAR FRIGATES!?
YOU TURN YOUR BACK ON THE FORCE, YOU TURN IT ON ME, TOO. I DON'T WANT TO HEAR FROM YOU AFTER THIS... COLONEL KRUGAUER.
WE PICKED UP THE SIGNAL AGAIN RIGHT BEFORE THE JET RAN OUT OF FUEL 22 MILES OFF THE COAST OF PORTUGAL.
DON'T THINK ANYONE LIVED THROUGH THAT.

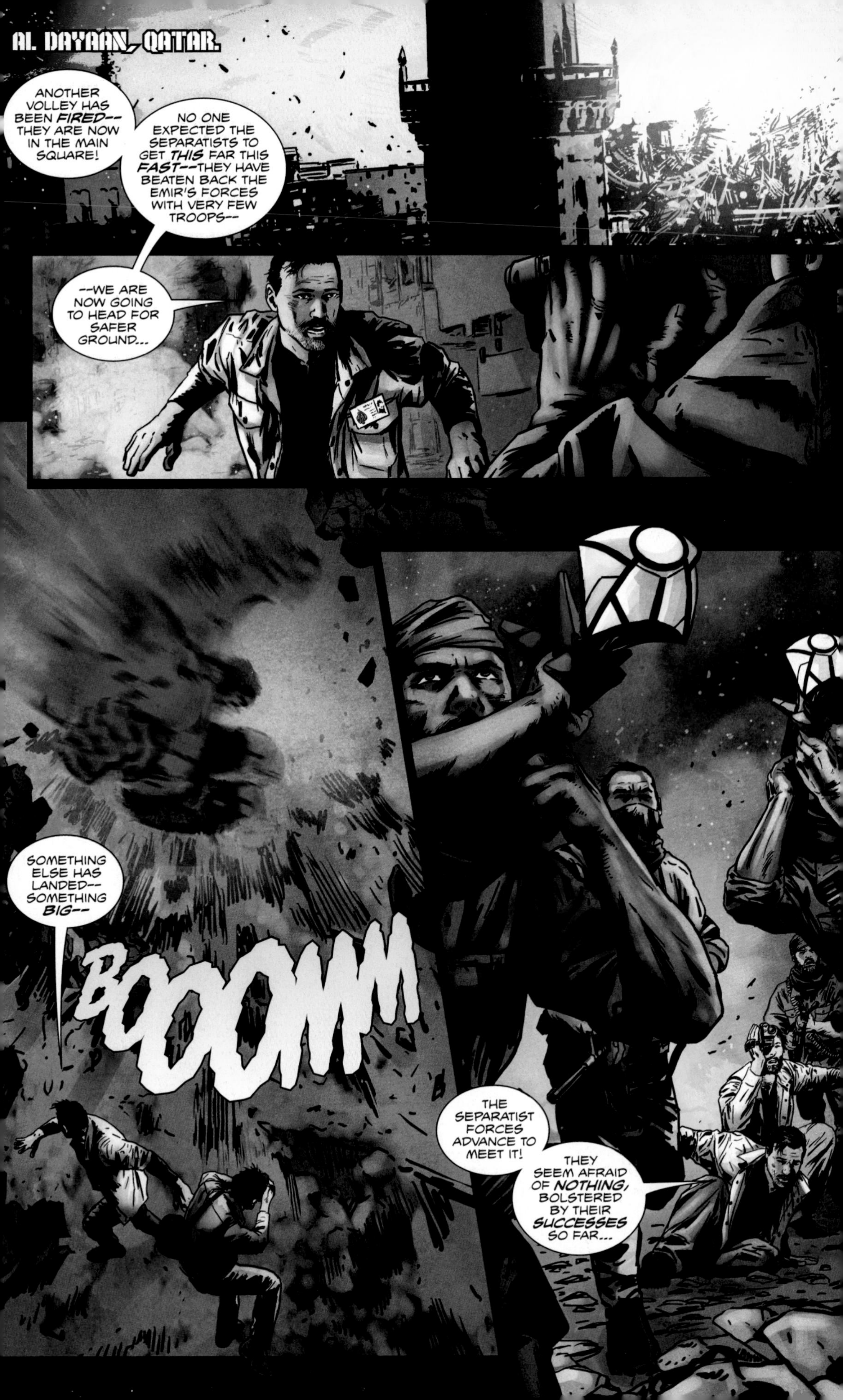
AL DAYAAN, QATAR.
ANOTHER VOLLEY HAS BEEN FIRED-- THEY ARE NOW IN THE MAIN SQUARE!
NO ONE EXPECTED THE SEPARATISTS TO GET THIS FAR THIS FAST--THEY HAVE BEATEN BACK THE EMIR'S FORCES WITH VERY FEW TROOPS--
--WE ARE NOW GOING TO HEAD FOR SAFER GROUND...
SOMETHING ELSE HAS LANDED-- SOMETHING BIG--
BOOOMM
THE SEPARATIST FORCES ADVANCE TO MEET IT!
THEY SEEM AFRAID OF NOTHING, BOLSTERED BY THEIR SUCCESSES SO FAR...

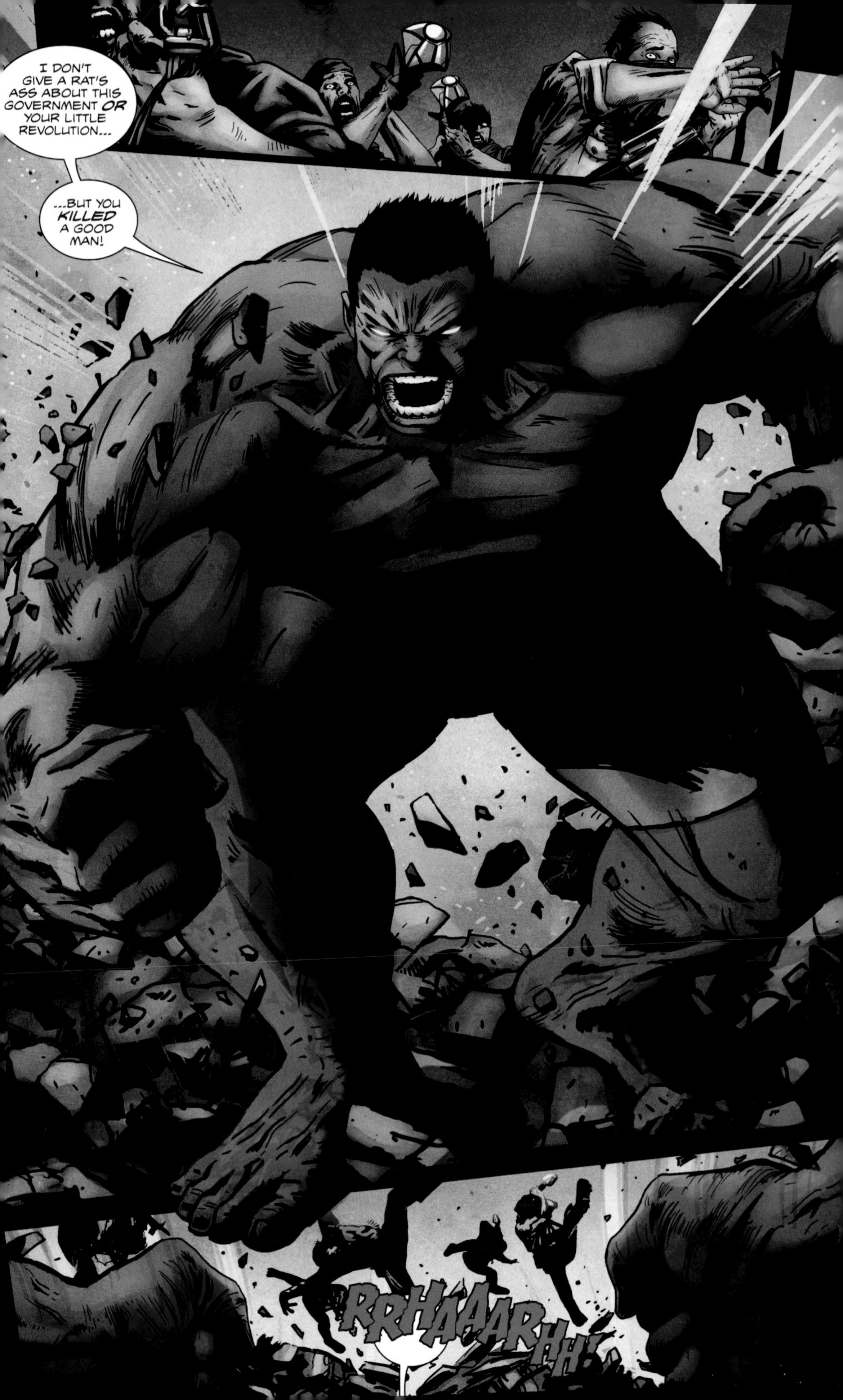
I DON'T GIVE A RAT'S ASS ABOUT THIS GOVERNMENT OR YOUR LITTLE REVOLUTION...
...BUT YOU KILLED A GOOD MAN!
RRHAAARHH!

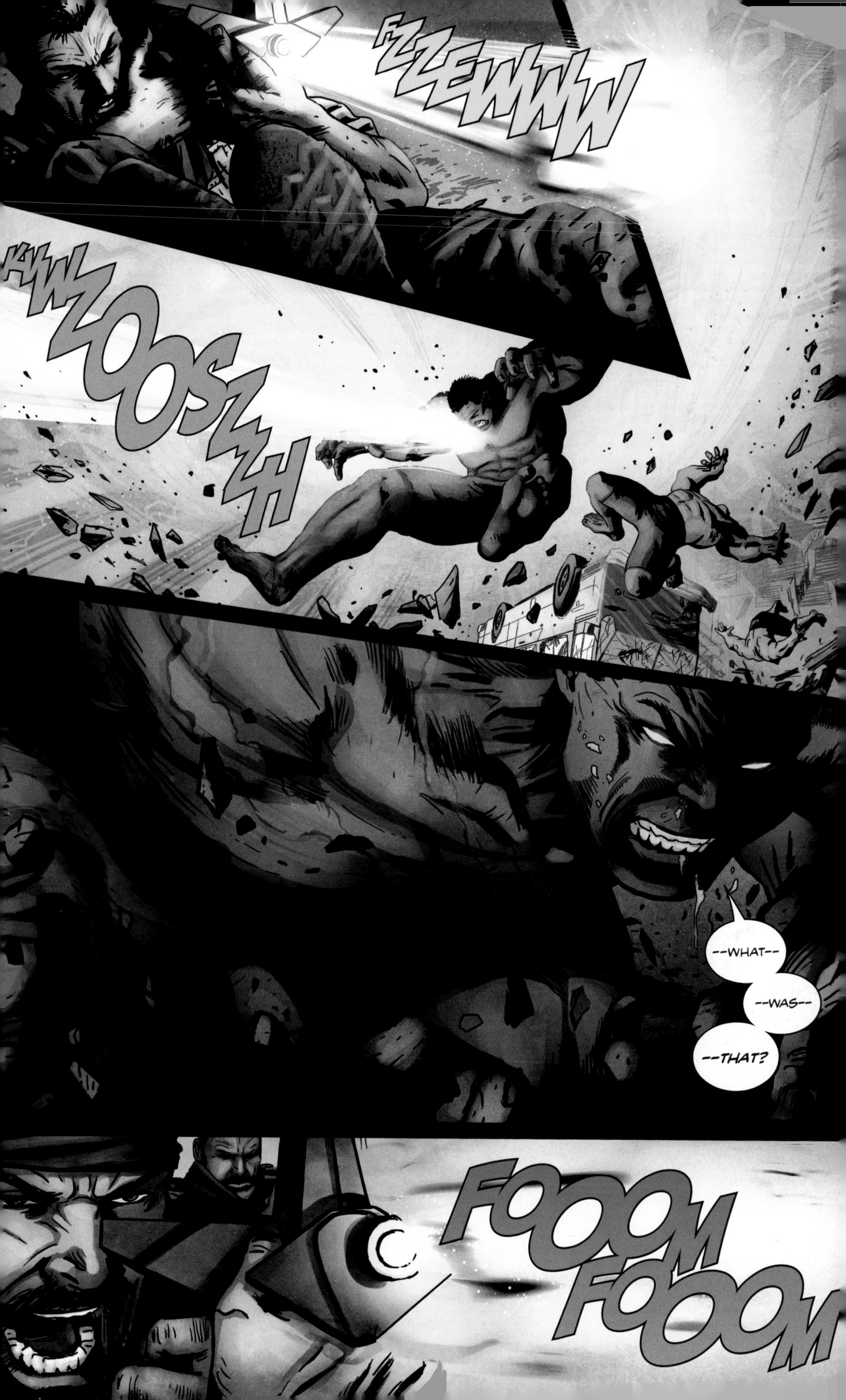
FZZEWWW
KWWZOOSZZHH
--WHAT--
--WAS--
--THAT?
FOOOM
FOOOM

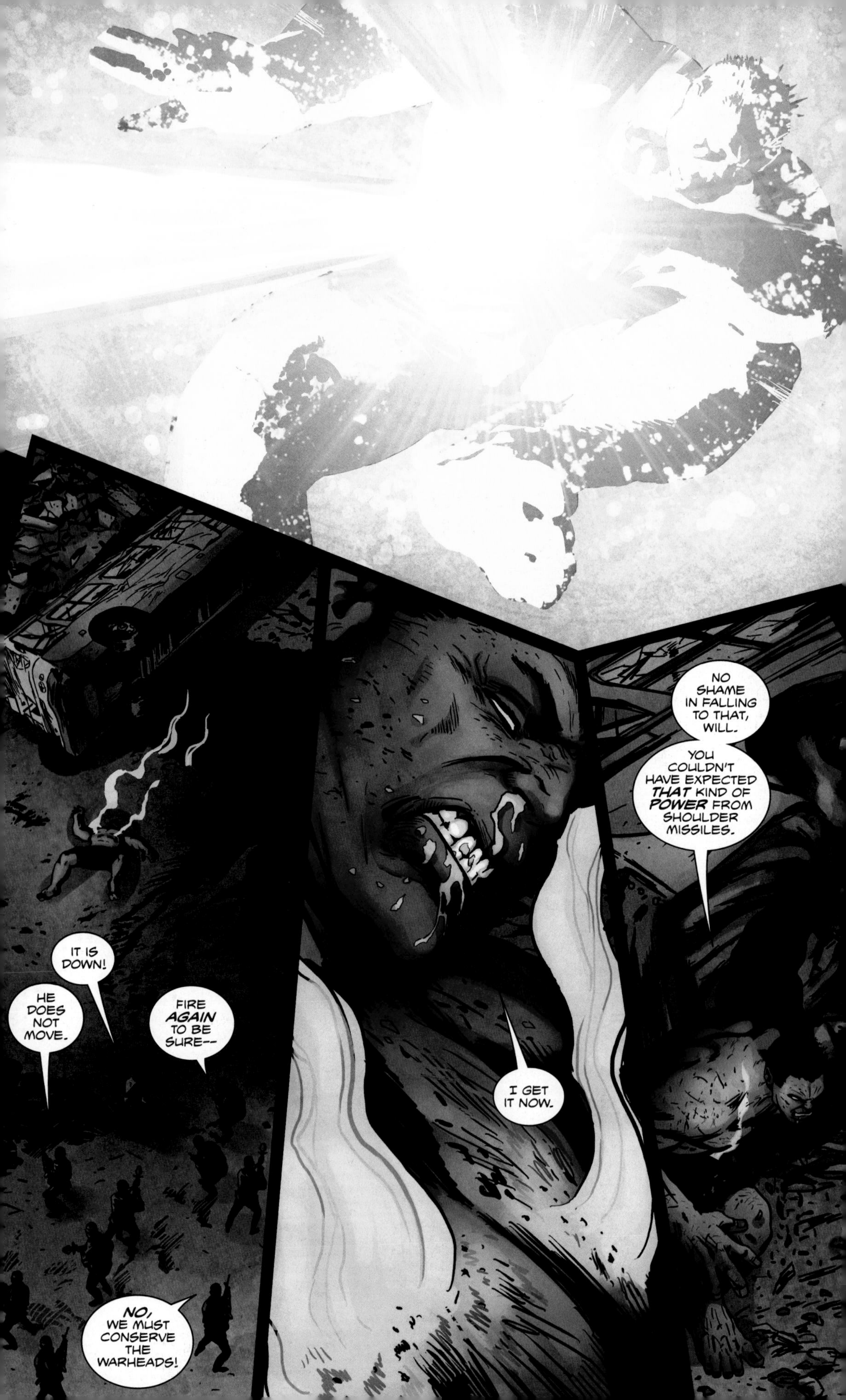
IT IS DOWN!
HE DOES NOT MOVE.
FIRE AGAIN TO BE SURE--
NO, WE MUST CONSERVE THE WARHEADS!
I GET IT NOW.
NO SHAME IN FALLING TO THAT, WILL.
YOU COULDN'T HAVE EXPECTED THAT KIND OF POWER FROM SHOULDER MISSILES.

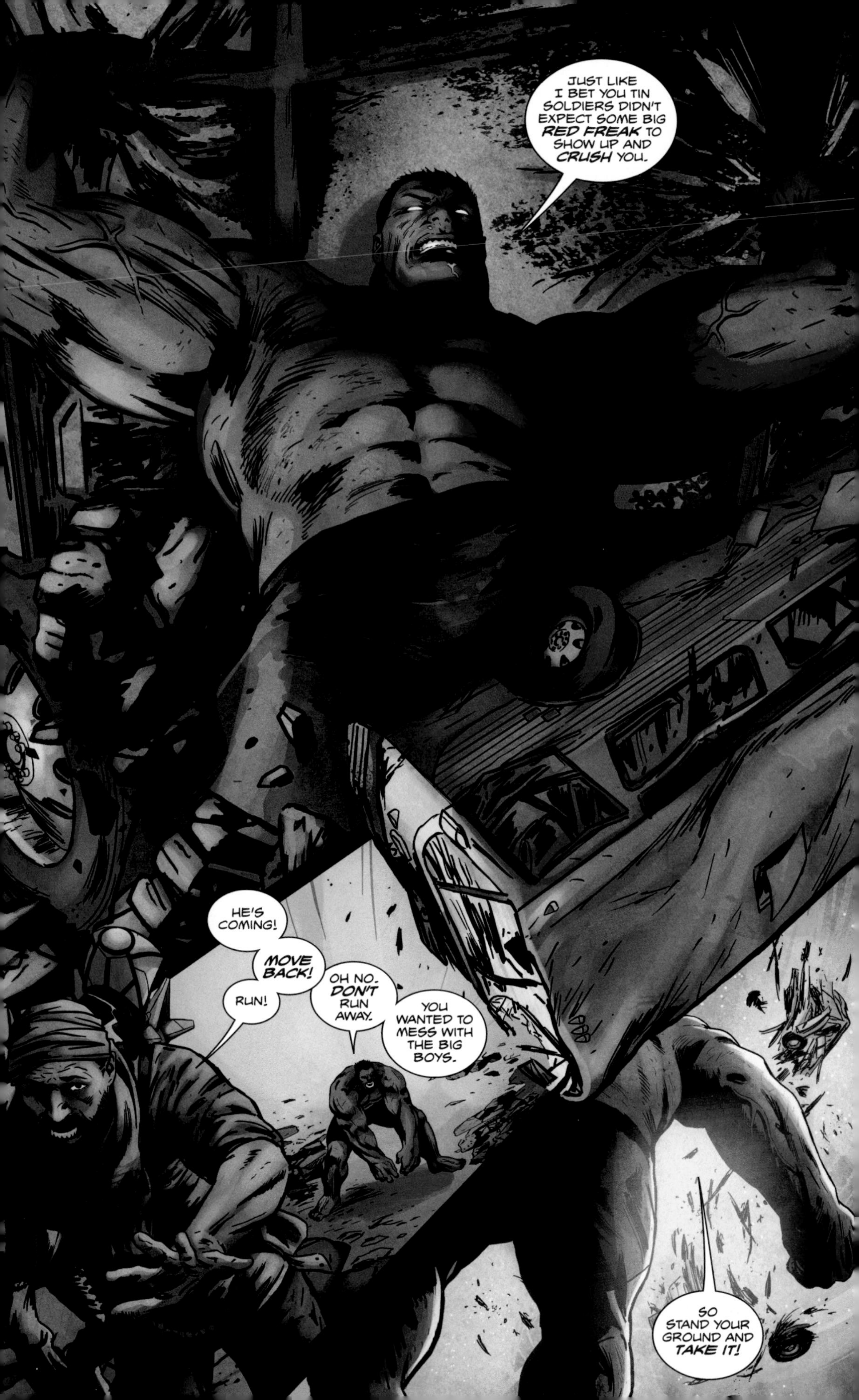
JUST LIKE I BET YOU TIN SOLDIERS DIDN'T EXPECT SOME BIG RED FREAK TO SHOW UP AND CRUSH YOU.
HE'S COMING!
MOVE BACK!
RUN!
OH NO. DON'T RUN AWAY.
YOU WANTED TO MESS WITH THE BIG BOYS.
SO STAND YOUR GROUND AND TAKE IT!

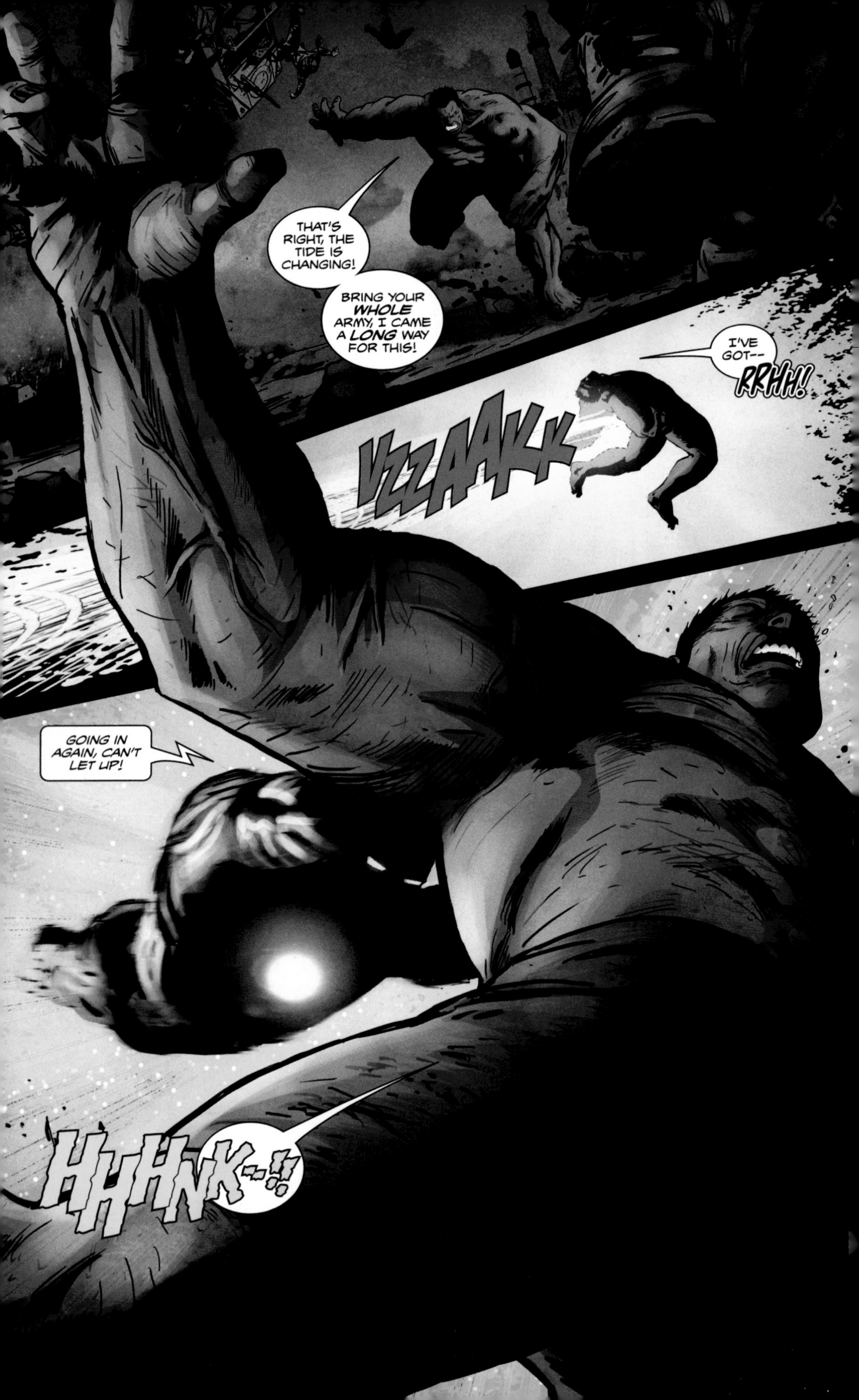
THAT'S RIGHT, THE TIDE IS CHANGING!
BRING YOUR WHOLE ARMY, I CAME A LONG WAY FOR THIS!
I'VE GOT-- RRHH!
VZZAAKK
GOING IN AGAIN, CAN'T LET UP!
HHHNK--!!

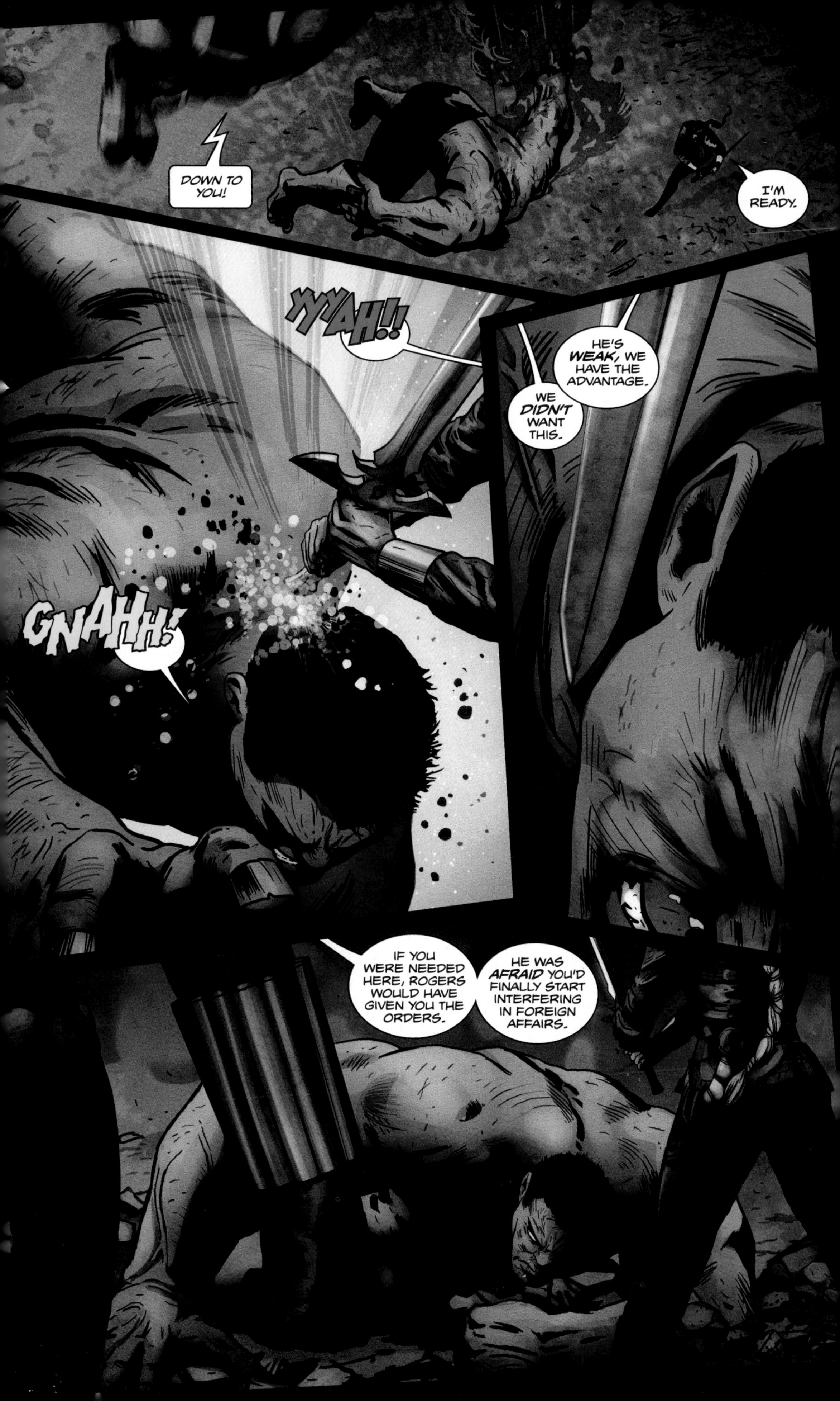
DOWN TO YOU!
I'M READY.
YYYAH!!
GNAHH!
HE'S WEAK, WE HAVE THE ADVANTAGE.
WE DIDN'T WANT THIS.
IF YOU WERE NEEDED HERE, ROGERS WOULD HAVE GIVEN YOU THE ORDERS.
HE WAS AFRAID YOU'D FINALLY START INTERFERING IN FOREIGN AFFAIRS.

THAT'S *NOT* YOUR JOB.
IT'S OURS. THAT'S WHAT THE *SECRET AVENGERS* ARE FOR.
HULK OF ARABIA

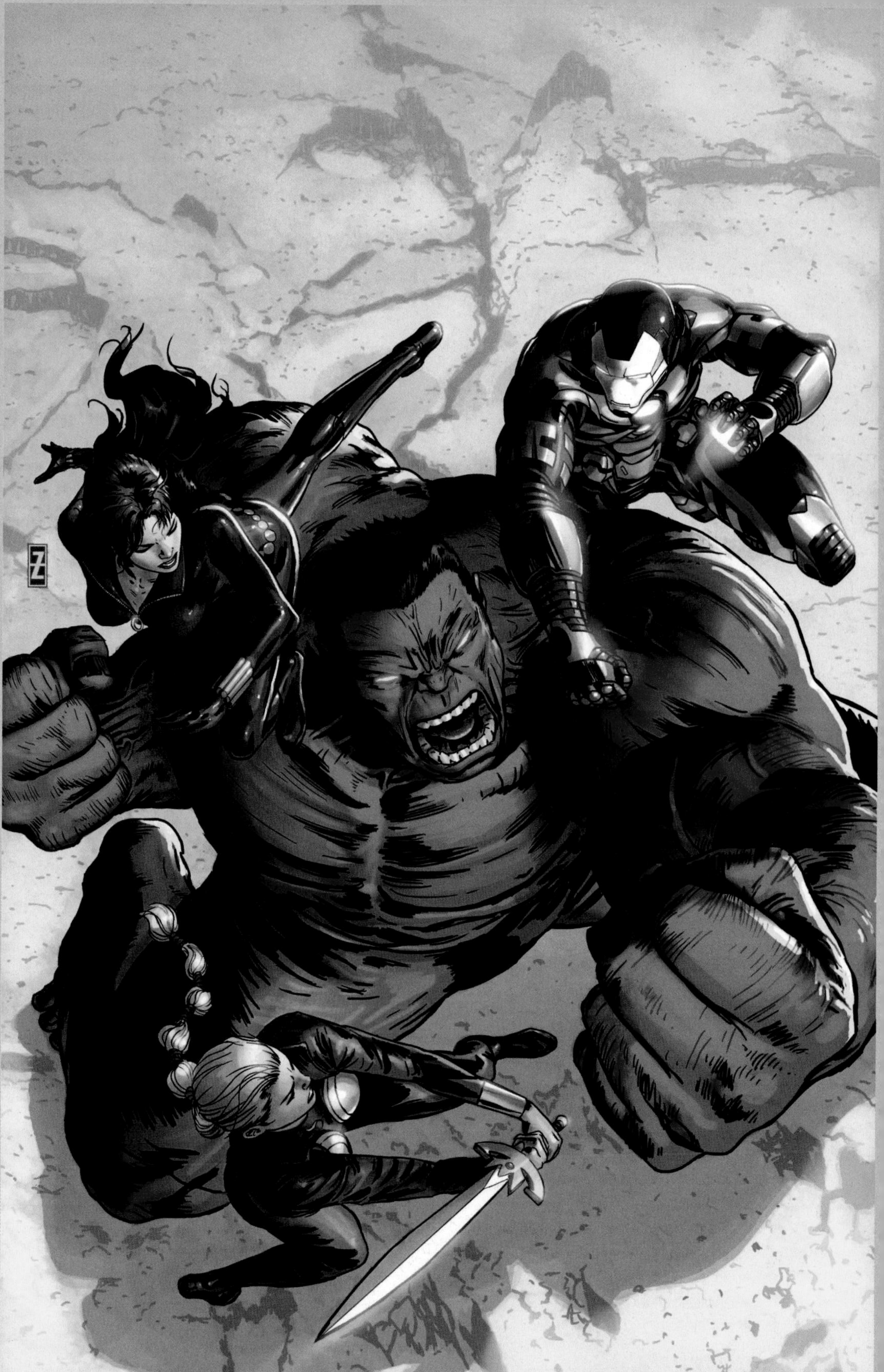

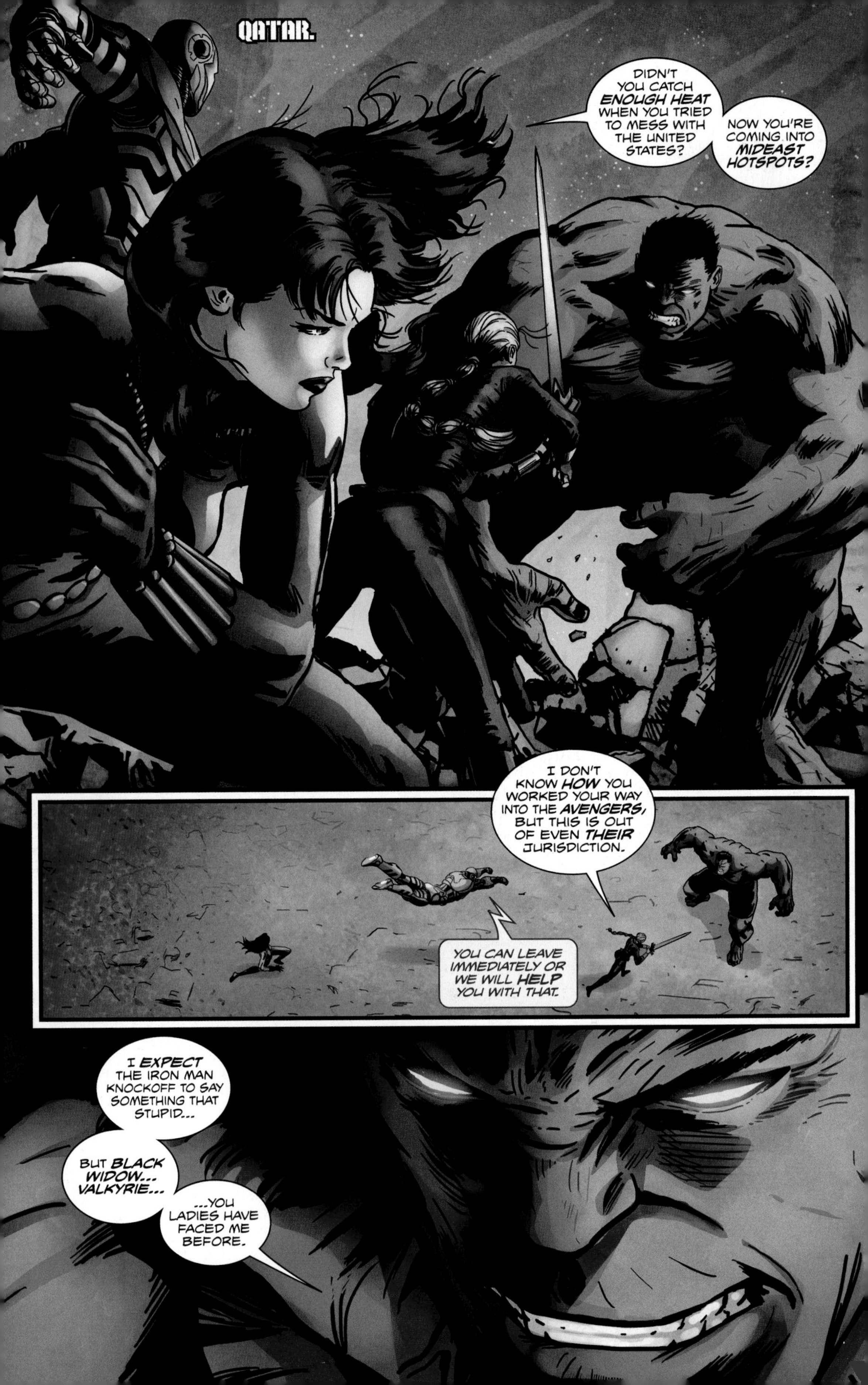
QATAR.
DIDN'T YOU CATCH ENOUGH HEAT WHEN YOU TRIED TO MESS WITH THE UNITED STATES?
NOW YOU'RE COMING INTO MIDEAST HOTSPOTS?
I DON'T KNOW HOW YOU WORKED YOUR WAY INTO THE AVENGERS, BUT THIS IS OUT OF EVEN THEIR JURISDICTION.
YOU CAN LEAVE IMMEDIATELY OR WE WILL HELP YOU WITH THAT.
I EXPECT THE IRON MAN KNOCKOFF TO SAY SOMETHING THAT STUPID...
BUT BLACK WIDOW... VALKYRIE...
...YOU LADIES HAVE FACED ME BEFORE.

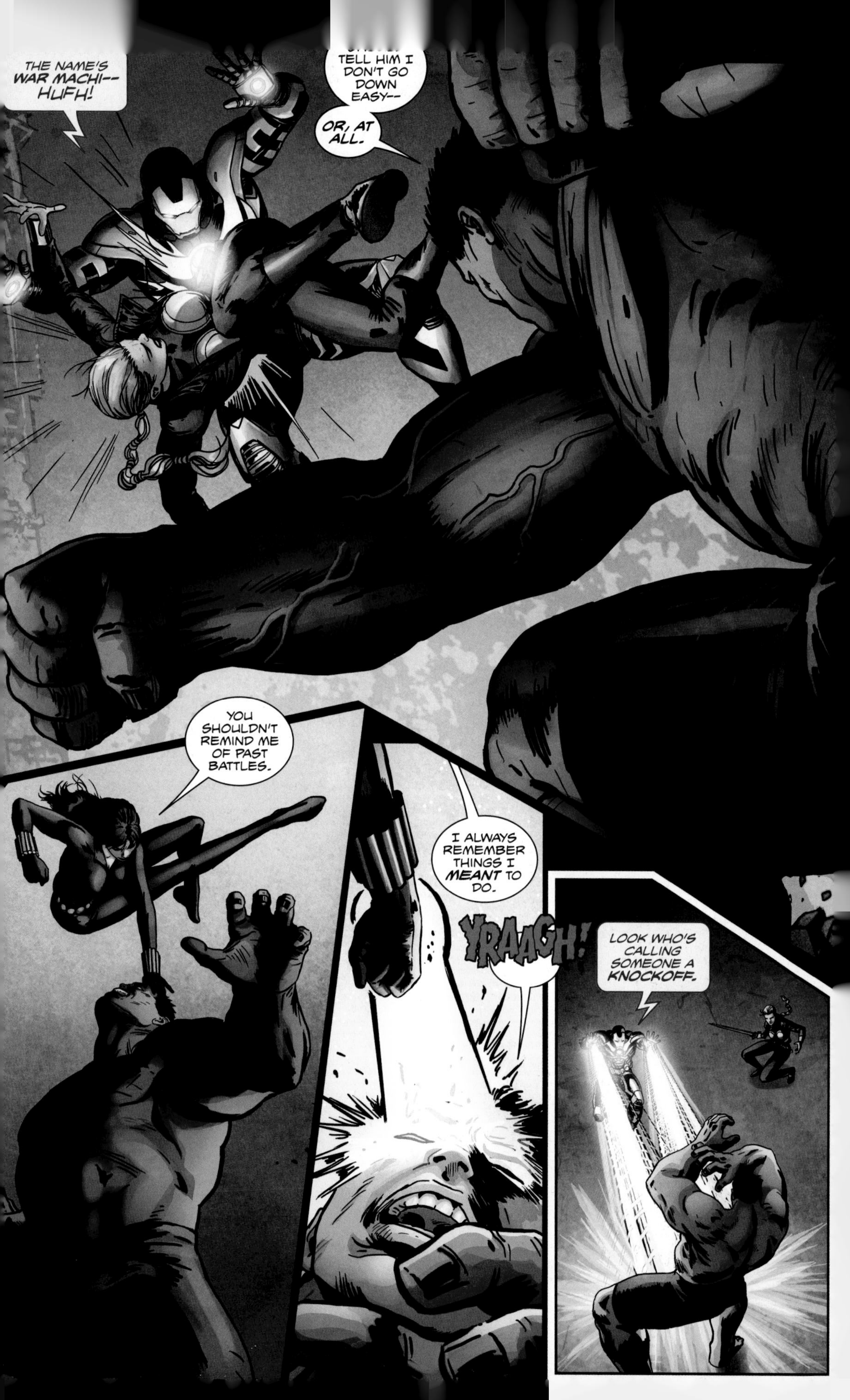
THE NAME'S WAR MACHI-- HUFH!
TELL HIM I DON'T GO DOWN EASY--
OR, AT ALL.
YOU SHOULDN'T REMIND ME OF PAST BATTLES.
I ALWAYS REMEMBER THINGS I MEANT TO DO.
YRAAGH!
LOOK WHO'S CALLING SOMEONE A KNOCKOFF.

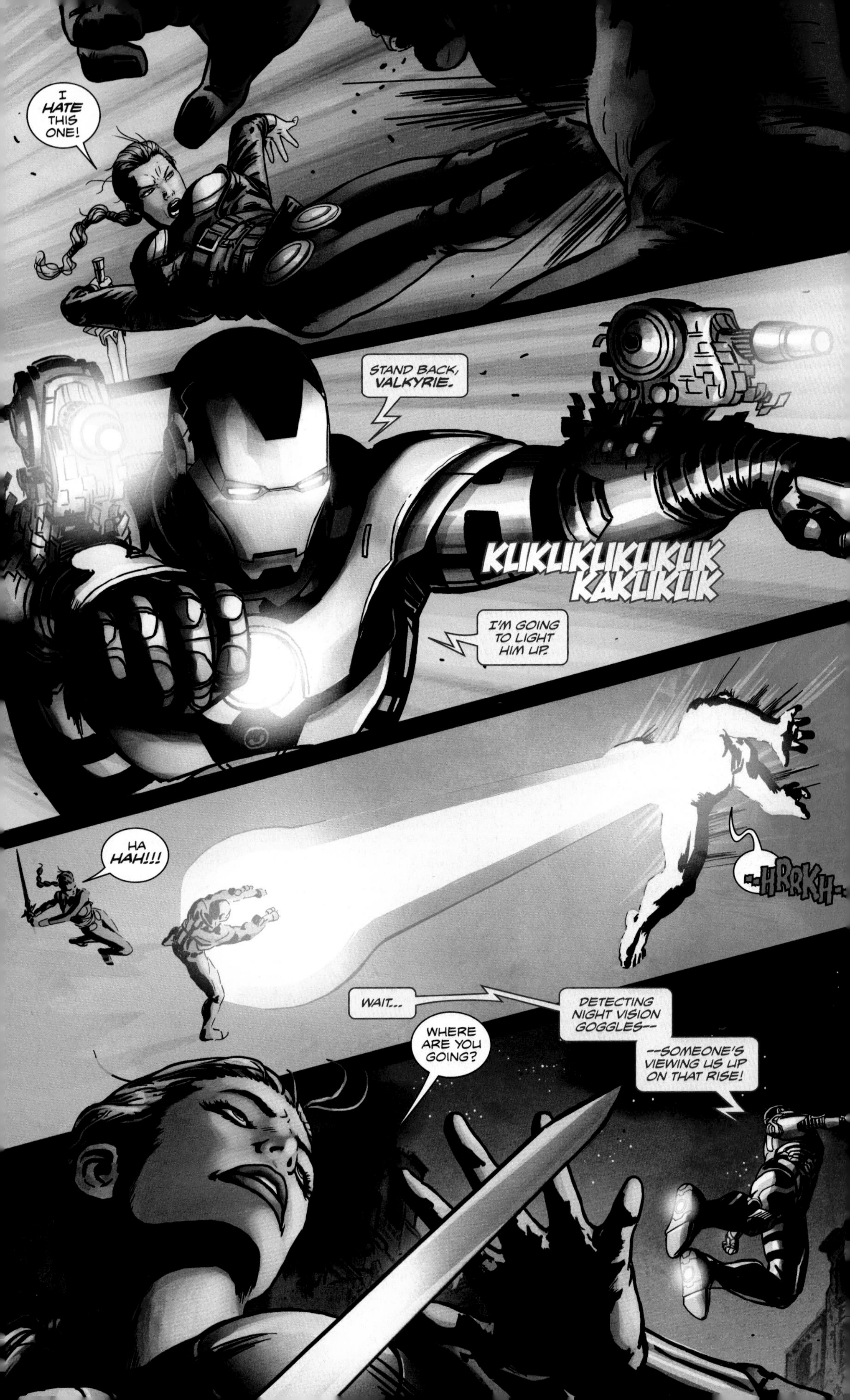
I HATE THIS ONE!
STAND BACK, VALKYRIE.
KLIKLIKLIKLIKLIK KAKLIKLIK
I'M GOING TO LIGHT HIM UP.
HA HAH!!!
--HRRKH--
WAIT...
DETECTING NIGHT VISION GOGGLES--
--SOMEONE'S VIEWING US UP ON THAT RISE!
WHERE ARE YOU GOING?

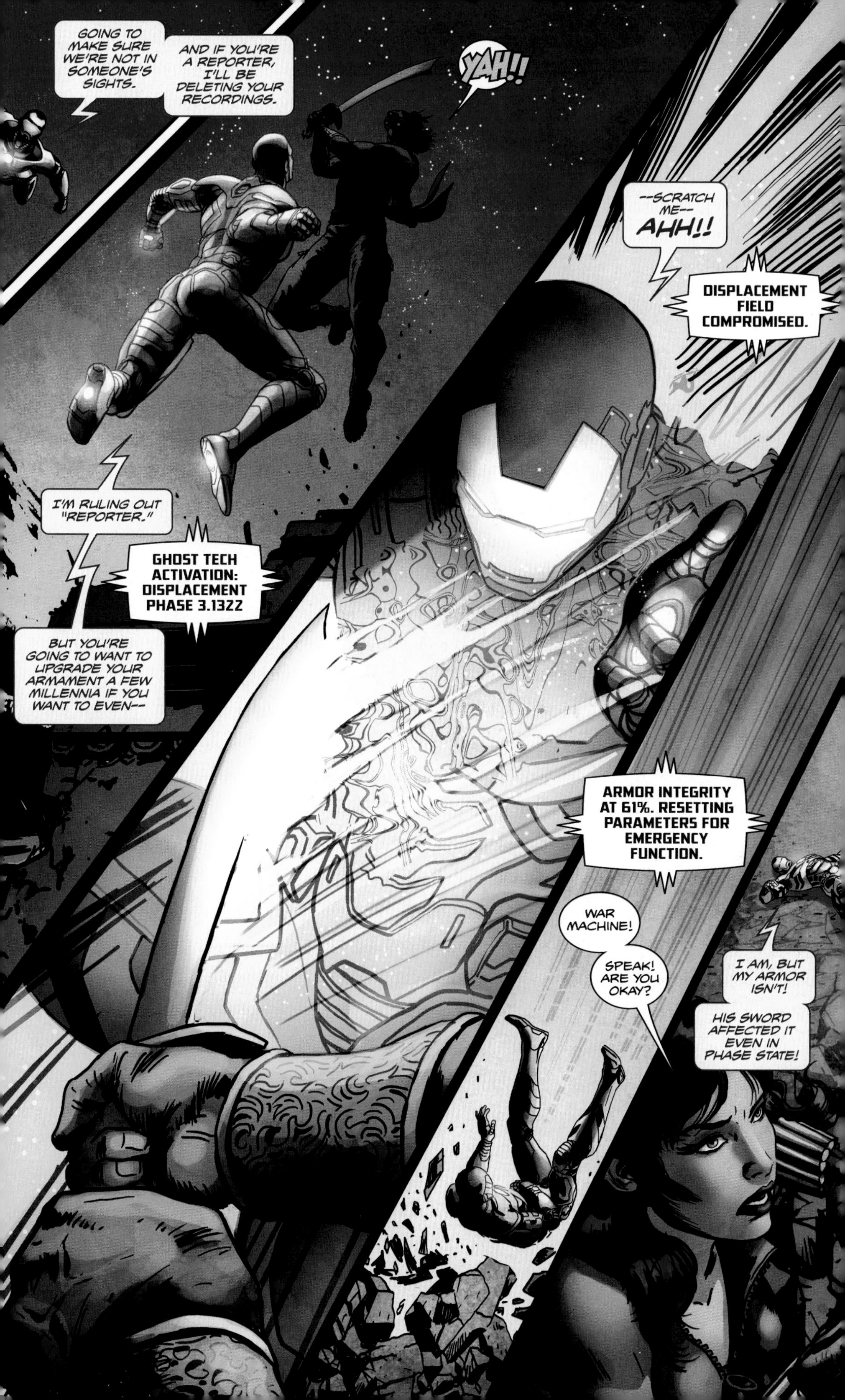
GOING TO MAKE SURE WE'RE NOT IN SOMEONE'S SIGHTS.
AND IF YOU'RE A REPORTER, I'LL BE DELETING YOUR RECORDINGS.
YAH!!
I'M RULING OUT "REPORTER."
GHOST TECH ACTIVATION: DISPLACEMENT PHASE 3.1322
BUT YOU'RE GOING TO WANT TO UPGRADE YOUR ARMAMENT A FEW MILLENNIA IF YOU WANT TO EVEN--
--SCRATCH ME-- AHH!!
DISPLACEMENT FIELD COMPROMISED.
ARMOR INTEGRITY AT 61%. RESETTING PARAMETERS FOR EMERGENCY FUNCTION.
WAR MACHINE!
SPEAK! ARE YOU OKAY?
I AM, BUT MY ARMOR ISN'T!
HIS SWORD AFFECTED IT EVEN IN PHASE STATE!

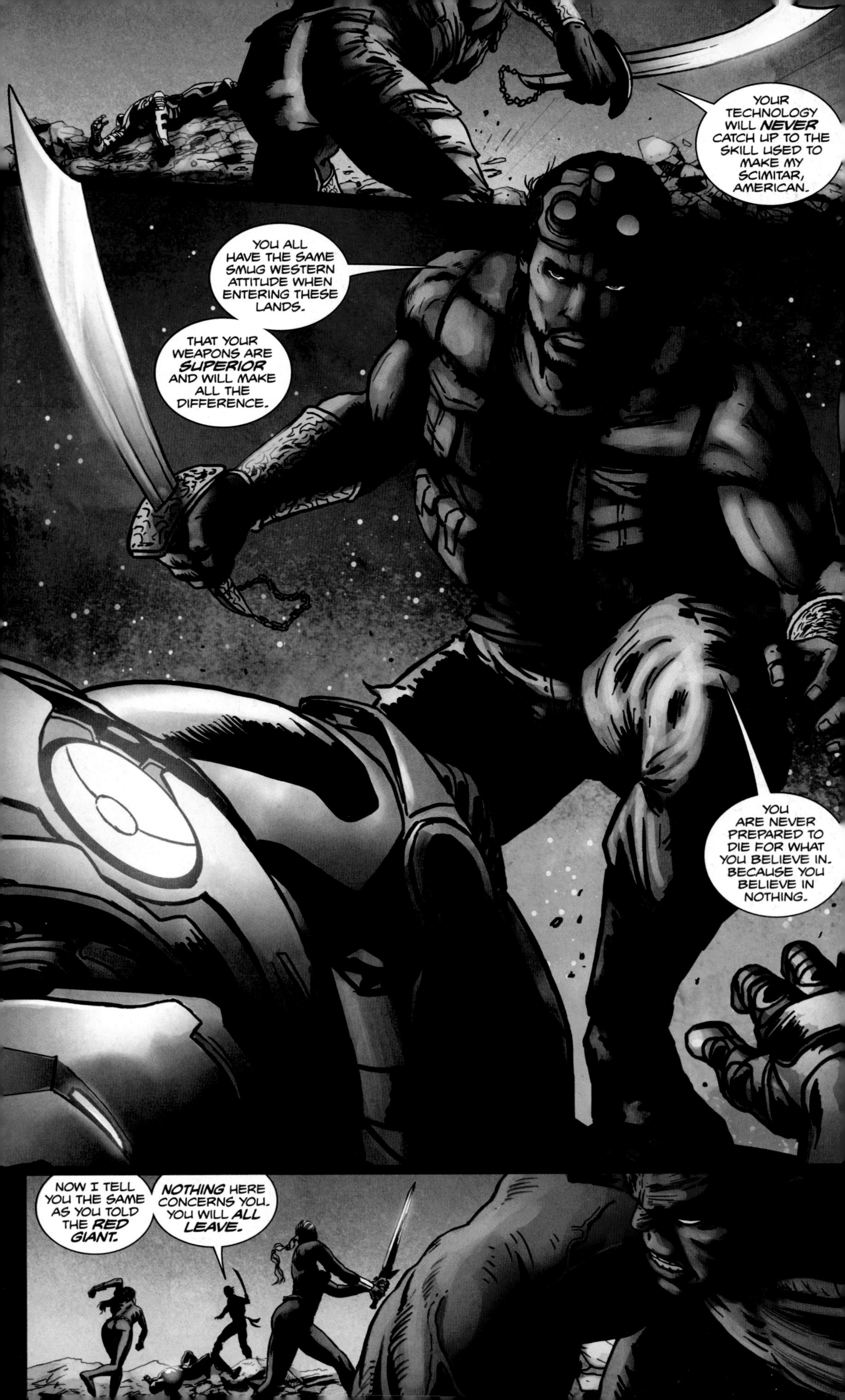
YOUR TECHNOLOGY WILL NEVER CATCH UP TO THE SKILL USED TO MAKE MY SCIMITAR, AMERICAN.
YOU ALL HAVE THE SAME SMUG WESTERN ATTITUDE WHEN ENTERING THESE LANDS.
THAT YOUR WEAPONS ARE SUPERIOR AND WILL MAKE ALL THE DIFFERENCE.
YOU ARE NEVER PREPARED TO DIE FOR WHAT YOU BELIEVE IN. BECAUSE YOU BELIEVE IN NOTHING.
NOW I TELL YOU THE SAME AS YOU TOLD THE RED GIANT.
NOTHING HERE CONCERNS YOU. YOU WILL ALL LEAVE.

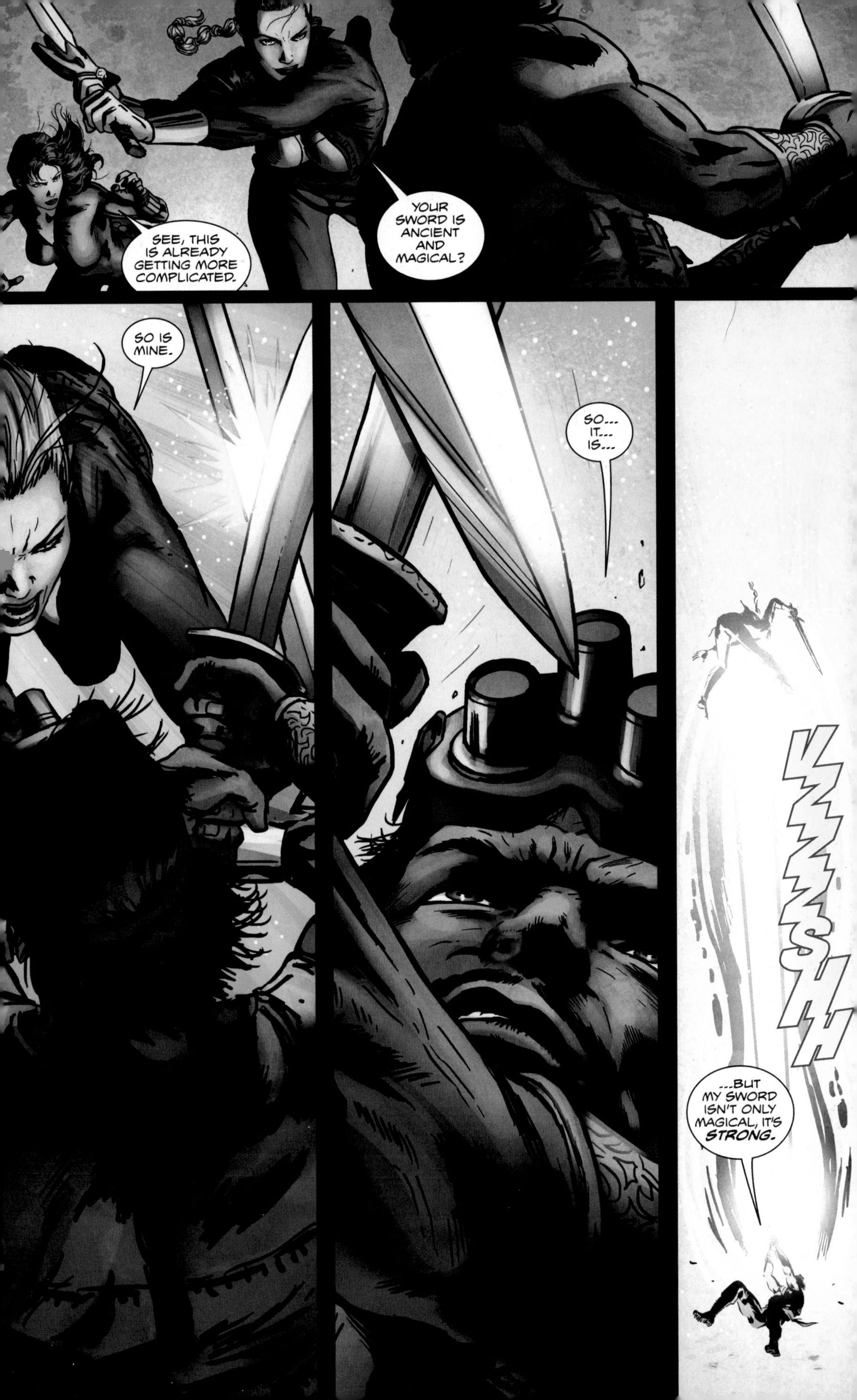
SEE, THIS IS ALREADY GETTING MORE COMPLICATED.
YOUR SWORD IS ANCIENT AND MAGICAL?
SO IS MINE.
SO... IT... IS...
VZZZSHH
...BUT MY SWORD ISN'T ONLY MAGICAL, IT'S STRONG.

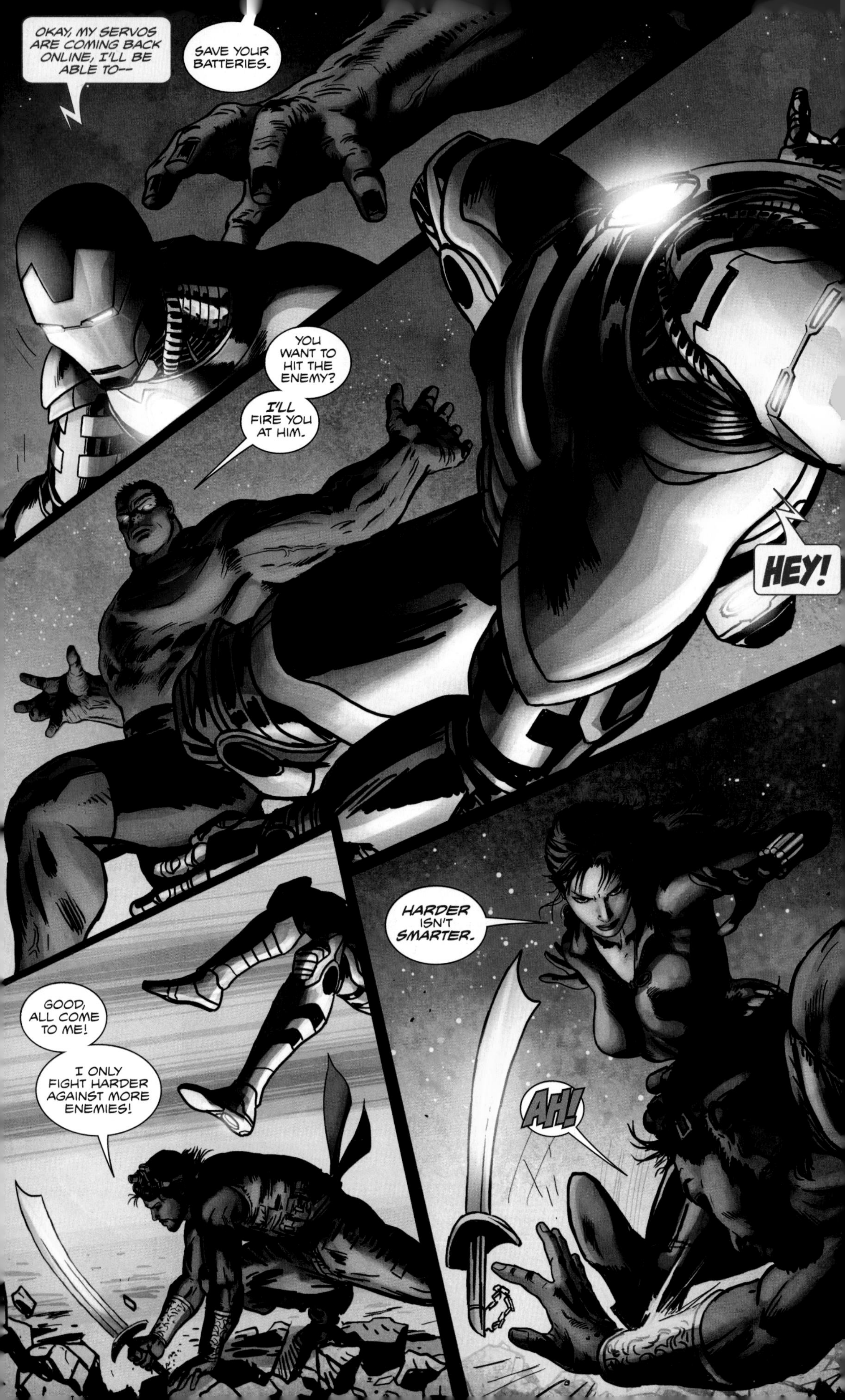

OKAY, MY SERVOS ARE COMING BACK ONLINE, I'LL BE ABLE TO--
SAVE YOUR BATTERIES.
YOU WANT TO HIT THE ENEMY?
I'LL FIRE YOU AT HIM.
HEY!
GOOD, ALL COME TO ME!
I ONLY FIGHT HARDER AGAINST MORE ENEMIES!
HARDER ISN'T SMARTER.
AH!

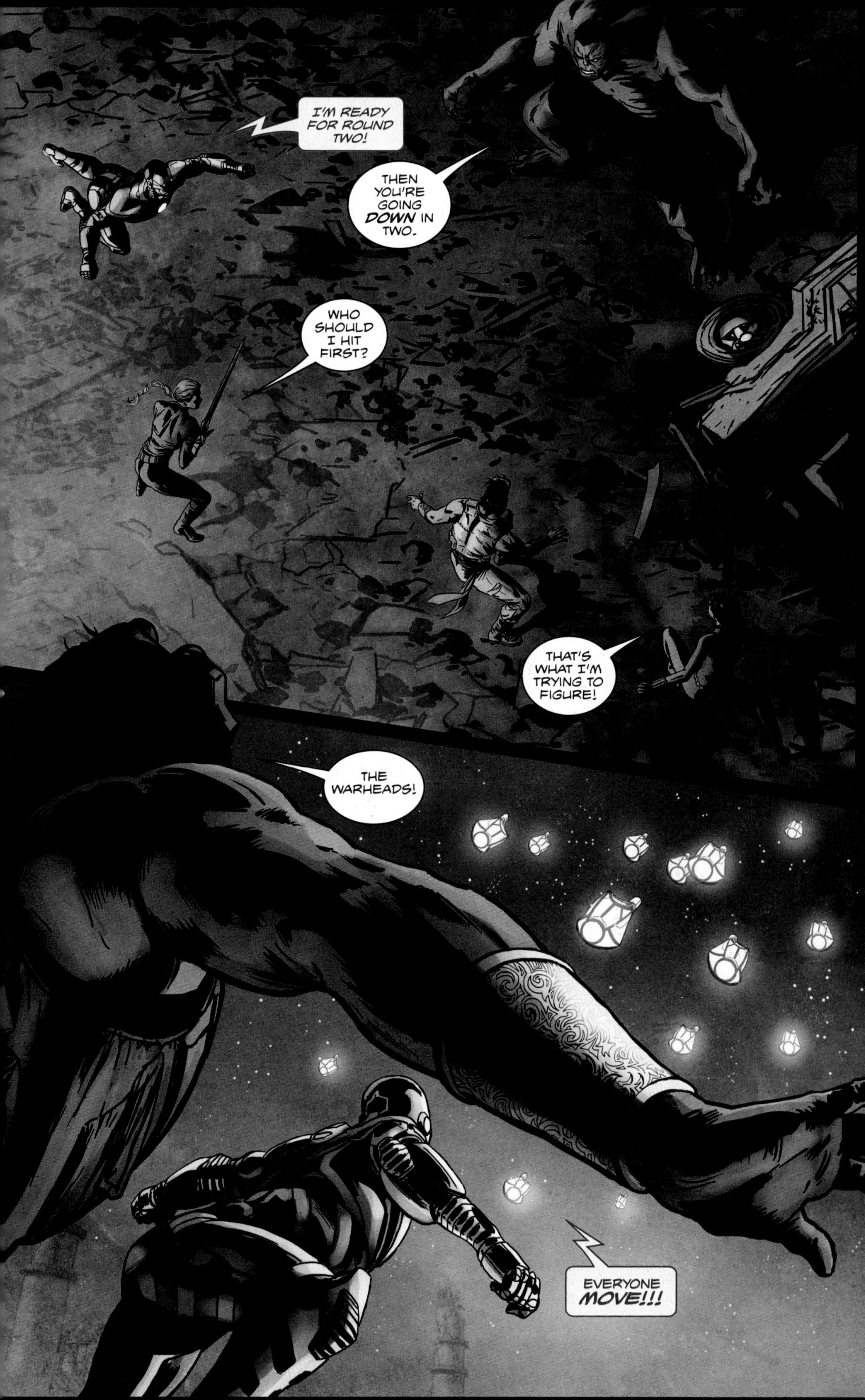
I'M READY FOR ROUND TWO!
THEN YOU'RE GOING DOWN IN TWO.
WHO SHOULD I HIT FIRST?
THAT'S WHAT I'M TRYING TO FIGURE!
THE WARHEADS!
EVERYONE MOVE!!!

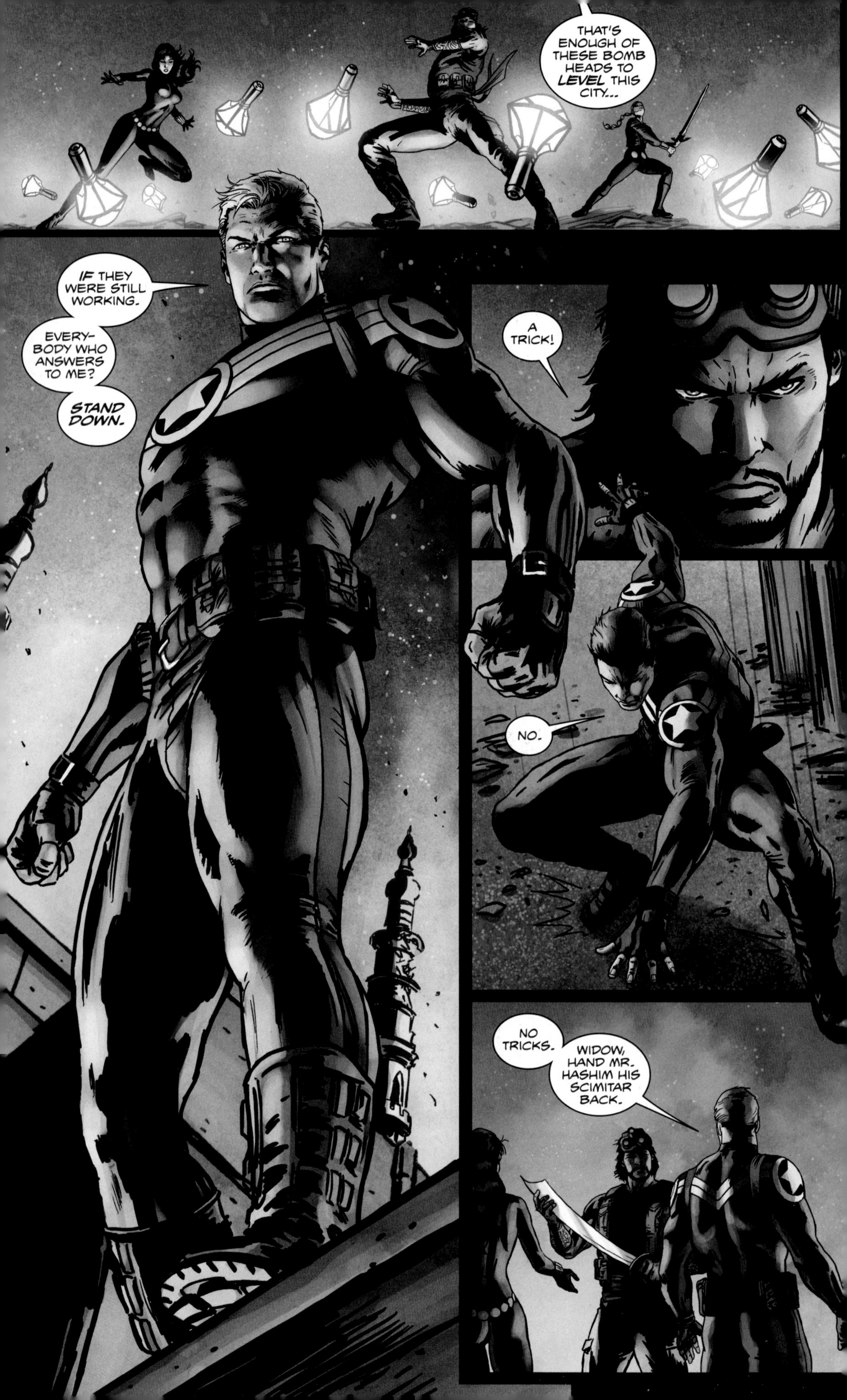
THAT'S ENOUGH OF THESE BOMB HEADS TO LEVEL THIS CITY...
IF THEY WERE STILL WORKING.
EVERY-BODY WHO ANSWERS TO ME?
STAND DOWN.
A TRICK!
NO.
NO TRICKS.
WIDOW, HAND MR. HASHIM HIS SCIMITAR BACK.

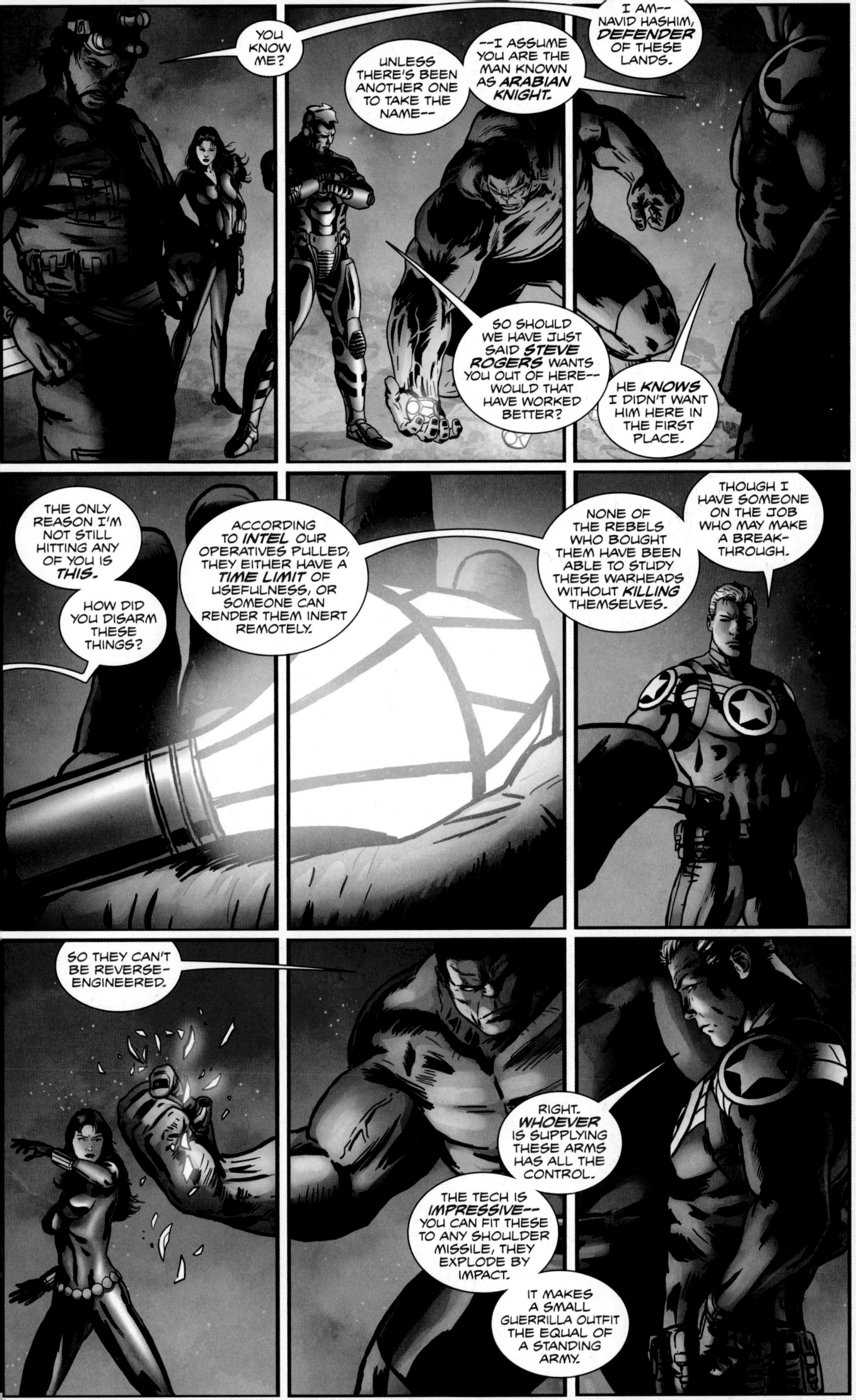
YOU KNOW ME?
UNLESS THERE'S BEEN ANOTHER ONE TO TAKE THE NAME--
--I ASSUME YOU ARE THE MAN KNOWN AS ARABIAN KNIGHT.
I AM-- NAVID HASHIM, DEFENDER OF THESE LANDS.
SO SHOULD WE HAVE JUST SAID STEVE ROGERS WANTS YOU OUT OF HERE-- WOULD THAT HAVE WORKED BETTER?
HE KNOWS I DIDN'T WANT HIM HERE IN THE FIRST PLACE.
THE ONLY REASON I'M NOT STILL HITTING ANY OF YOU IS THIS.
HOW DID YOU DISARM THESE THINGS?
ACCORDING TO INTEL OUR OPERATIVES PULLED, THEY EITHER HAVE A TIME LIMIT OF USEFULNESS, OR SOMEONE CAN RENDER THEM INERT REMOTELY.
NONE OF THE REBELS WHO BOUGHT THEM HAVE BEEN ABLE TO STUDY THESE WARHEADS WITHOUT KILLING THEMSELVES.
THOUGH I HAVE SOMEONE ON THE JOB WHO MAY MAKE A BREAK-THROUGH.
SO THEY CAN'T BE REVERSE-ENGINEERED.
RIGHT. WHOEVER IS SUPPLYING THESE ARMS HAS ALL THE CONTROL.
THE TECH IS IMPRESSIVE-- YOU CAN FIT THESE TO ANY SHOULDER MISSILE, THEY EXPLODE BY IMPACT.
IT MAKES A SMALL GUERRILLA OUTFIT THE EQUAL OF A STANDING ARMY.

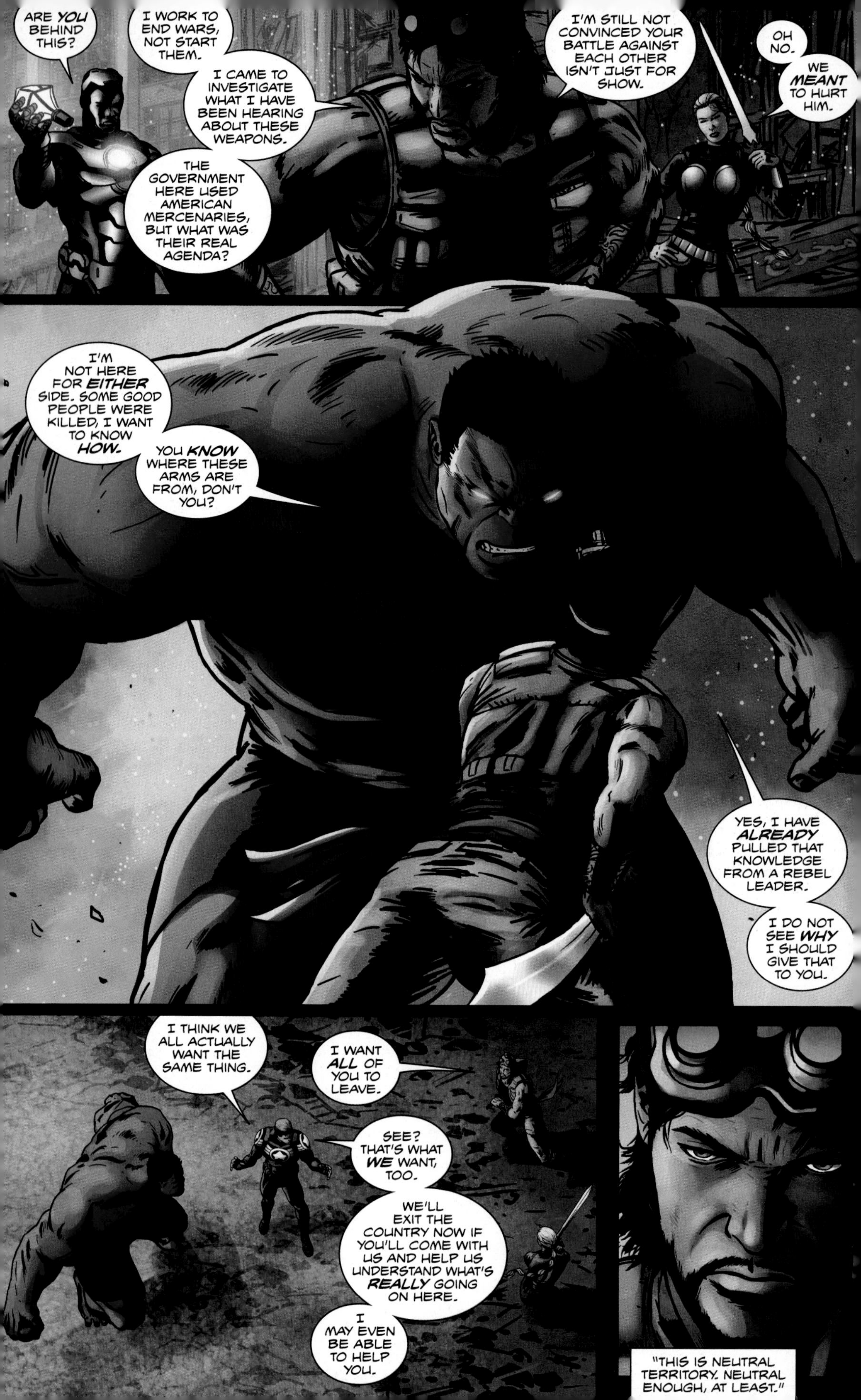

ARE YOU BEHIND THIS?
I WORK TO END WARS, NOT START THEM.
I CAME TO INVESTIGATE WHAT I HAVE BEEN HEARING ABOUT THESE WEAPONS.
THE GOVERNMENT HERE USED AMERICAN MERCENARIES, BUT WHAT WAS THEIR REAL AGENDA?
I'M STILL NOT CONVINCED YOUR BATTLE AGAINST EACH OTHER ISN'T JUST FOR SHOW.
OH NO.
WE MEANT TO HURT HIM.
I'M NOT HERE FOR EITHER SIDE. SOME GOOD PEOPLE WERE KILLED, I WANT TO KNOW HOW.
YOU KNOW WHERE THESE ARMS ARE FROM, DON'T YOU?
YES, I HAVE ALREADY PULLED THAT KNOWLEDGE FROM A REBEL LEADER.
I DO NOT SEE WHY I SHOULD GIVE THAT TO YOU.
I THINK WE ALL ACTUALLY WANT THE SAME THING.
I WANT ALL OF YOU TO LEAVE.
SEE? THAT'S WHAT WE WANT, TOO.
WE'LL EXIT THE COUNTRY NOW IF YOU'LL COME WITH US AND HELP US UNDERSTAND WHAT'S REALLY GOING ON HERE.
I MAY EVEN BE ABLE TO HELP YOU.
"THIS IS NEUTRAL TERRITORY. NEUTRAL ENOUGH, AT LEAST."

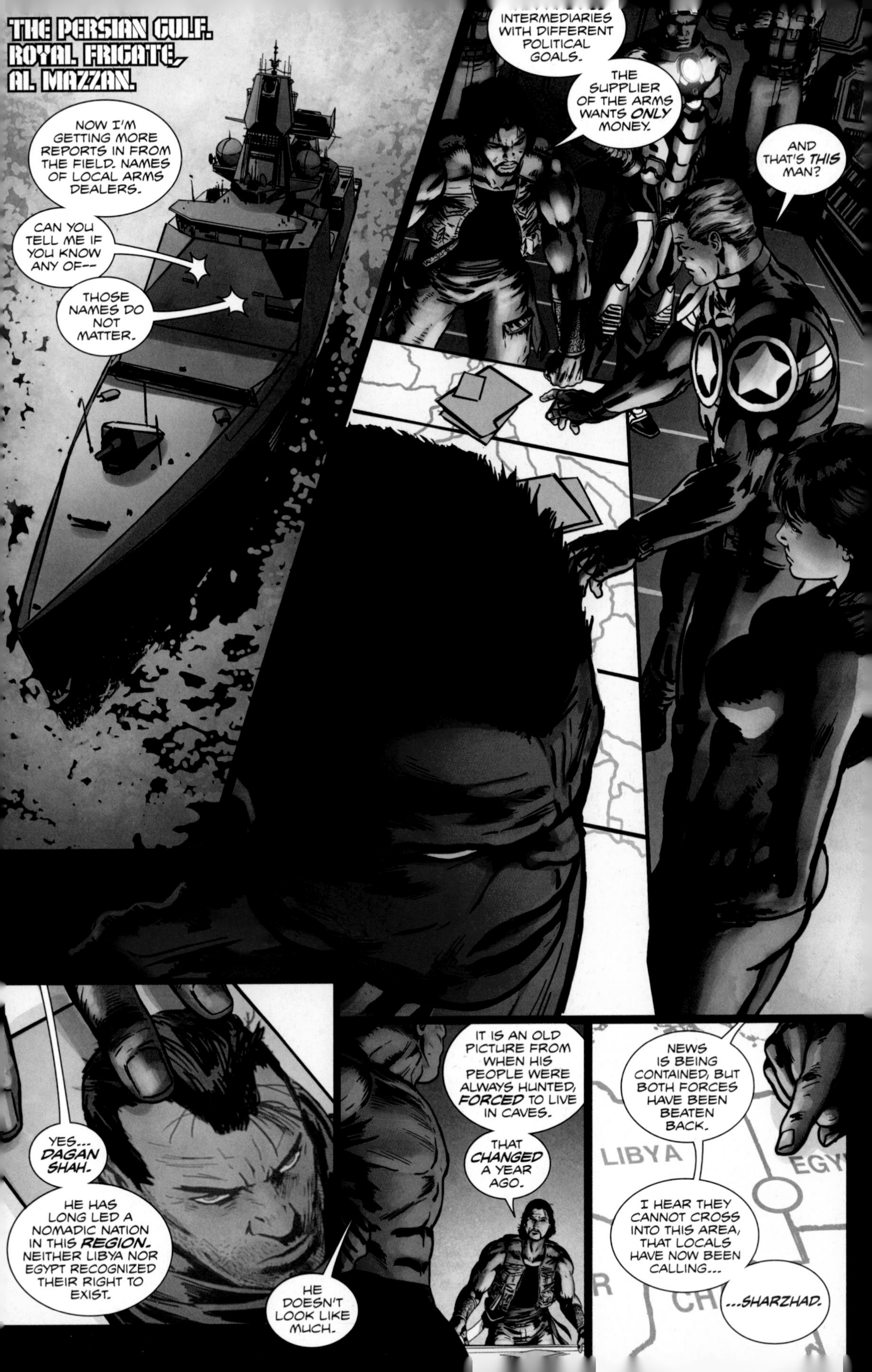
THE PERSIAN GULF. ROYAL FRIGATE, AL MAZZAN.
NOW I'M GETTING MORE REPORTS IN FROM THE FIELD. NAMES OF LOCAL ARMS DEALERS.
CAN YOU TELL ME IF YOU KNOW ANY OF--
THOSE NAMES DO NOT MATTER.
INTERMEDIARIES WITH DIFFERENT POLITICAL GOALS.
THE SUPPLIER OF THE ARMS WANTS ONLY MONEY.
AND THAT'S THIS MAN?
YES... DAGAN SHAH.
HE HAS LONG LED A NOMADIC NATION IN THIS REGION. NEITHER LIBYA NOR EGYPT RECOGNIZED THEIR RIGHT TO EXIST.
HE DOESN'T LOOK LIKE MUCH.
IT IS AN OLD PICTURE FROM WHEN HIS PEOPLE WERE ALWAYS HUNTED, FORCED TO LIVE IN CAVES.
THAT CHANGED A YEAR AGO.
NEWS IS BEING CONTAINED, BUT BOTH FORCES HAVE BEEN BEATEN BACK.
LIBYA
I HEAR THEY CANNOT CROSS INTO THIS AREA, THAT LOCALS HAVE NOW BEEN CALLING...
...SHARZHAD.

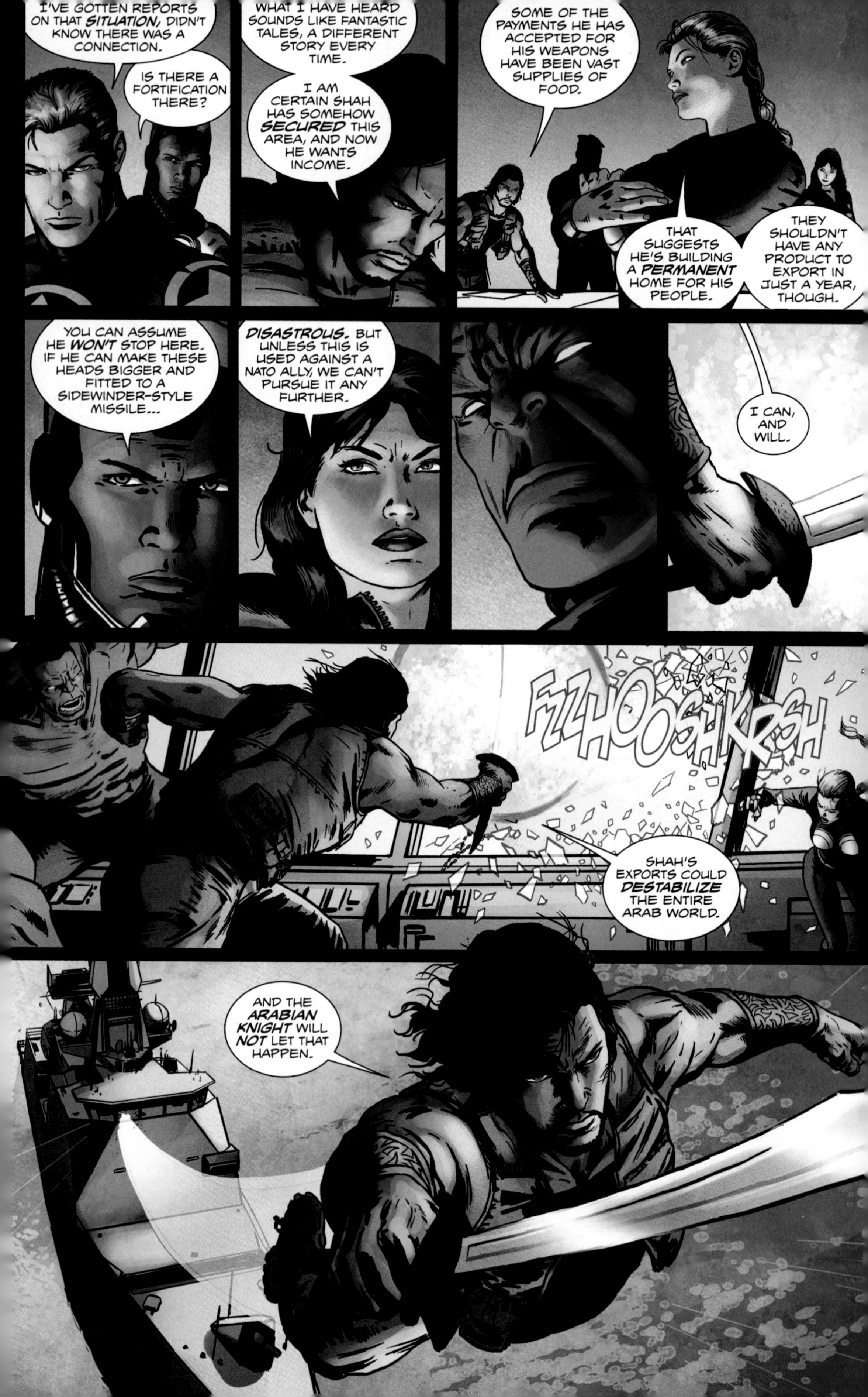
I'VE GOTTEN REPORTS ON THAT SITUATION, DIDN'T KNOW THERE WAS A CONNECTION.
IS THERE A FORTIFICATION THERE?
WHAT I HAVE HEARD SOUNDS LIKE FANTASTIC TALES, A DIFFERENT STORY EVERY TIME.
I AM CERTAIN SHAH HAS SOMEHOW SECURED THIS AREA, AND NOW HE WANTS INCOME.
SOME OF THE PAYMENTS HE HAS ACCEPTED FOR HIS WEAPONS HAVE BEEN VAST SUPPLIES OF FOOD.
THAT SUGGESTS HE'S BUILDING A PERMANENT HOME FOR HIS PEOPLE.
THEY SHOULDN'T HAVE ANY PRODUCT TO EXPORT IN JUST A YEAR, THOUGH.
YOU CAN ASSUME HE WON'T STOP HERE. IF HE CAN MAKE THESE HEADS BIGGER AND FITTED TO A SIDEWINDER-STYLE MISSILE...
DISASTROUS. BUT UNLESS THIS IS USED AGAINST A NATO ALLY, WE CAN'T PURSUE IT ANY FURTHER.
I CAN, AND WILL.
FZZHOOSHKRSH
SHAH'S EXPORTS COULD DESTABILIZE THE ENTIRE ARAB WORLD.
AND THE ARABIAN KNIGHT WILL NOT LET THAT HAPPEN.

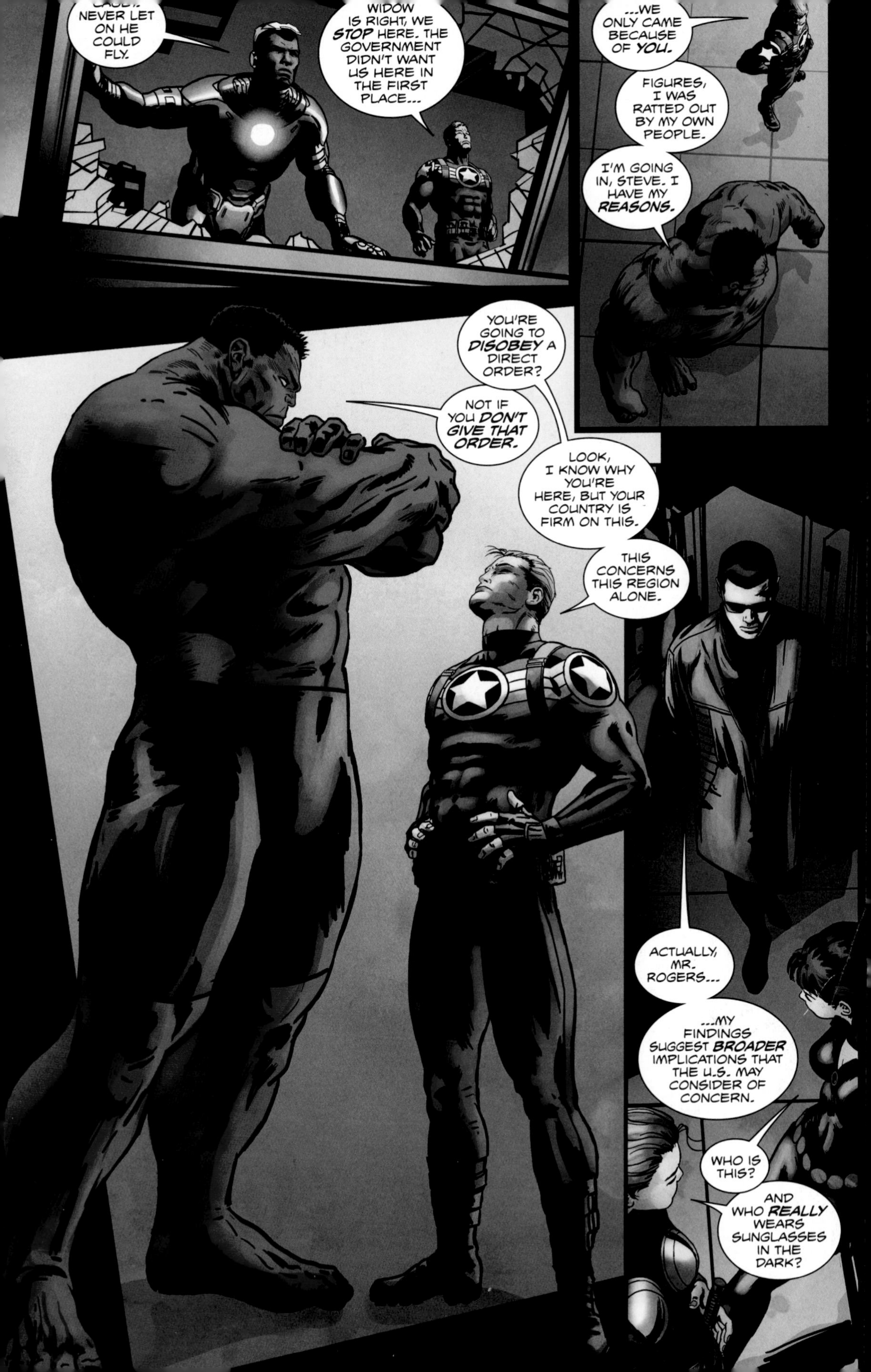
NEVER LET ON HE COULD FLY.
WIDOW IS RIGHT, WE STOP HERE. THE GOVERNMENT DIDN'T WANT US HERE IN THE FIRST PLACE...
...WE ONLY CAME BECAUSE OF YOU.
FIGURES, I WAS RATTED OUT BY MY OWN PEOPLE.
I'M GOING IN, STEVE. I HAVE MY REASONS.
YOU'RE GOING TO DISOBEY A DIRECT ORDER?
NOT IF YOU DON'T GIVE THAT ORDER.
LOOK, I KNOW WHY YOU'RE HERE, BUT YOUR COUNTRY IS FIRM ON THIS.
THIS CONCERNS THIS REGION ALONE.
ACTUALLY, MR. ROGERS...
...MY FINDINGS SUGGEST BROADER IMPLICATIONS THAT THE U.S. MAY CONSIDER OF CONCERN.
WHO IS THIS?
AND WHO REALLY WEARS SUNGLASSES IN THE DARK?

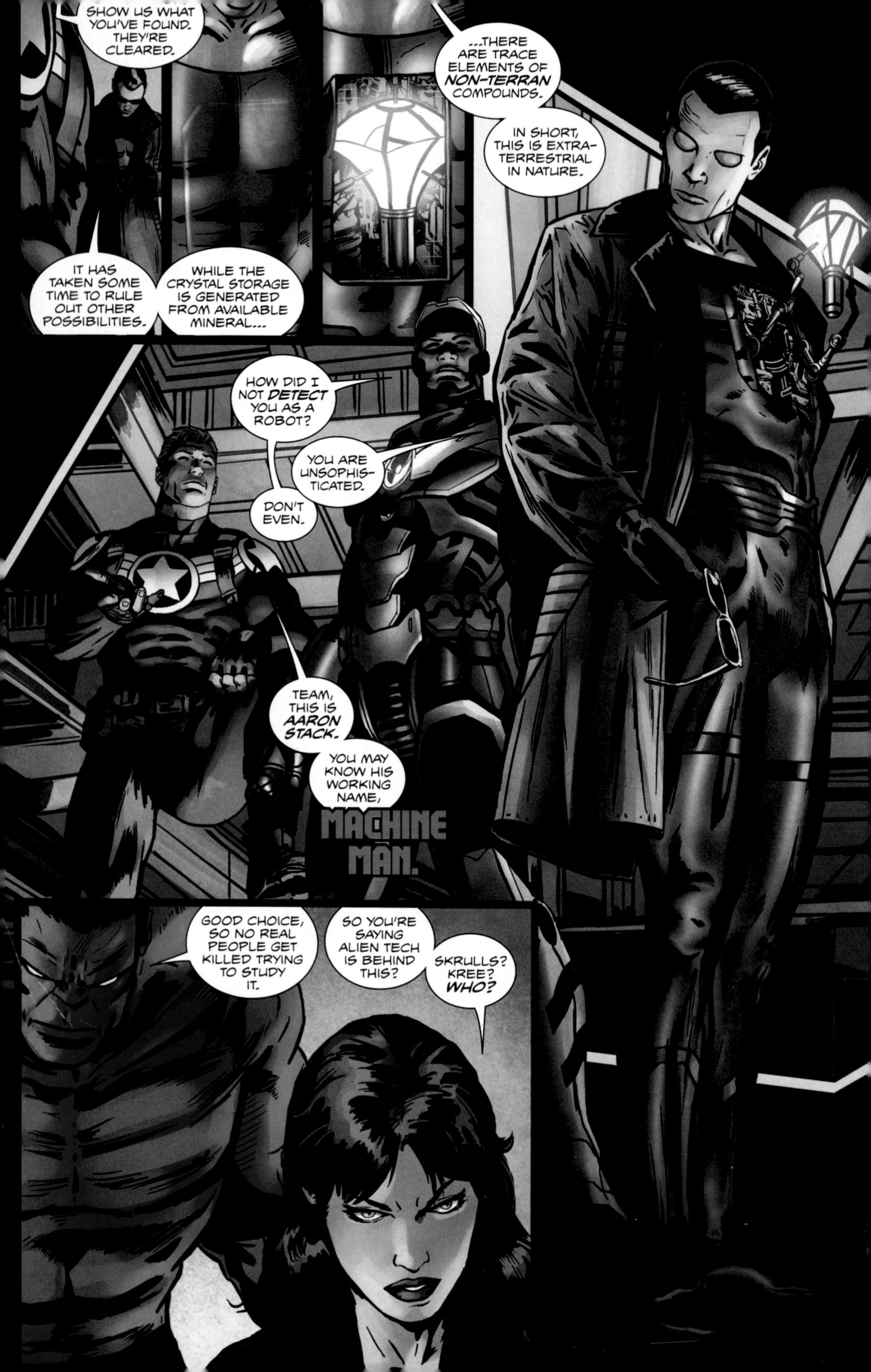
SHOW US WHAT YOU'VE FOUND. THEY'RE CLEARED.
IT HAS TAKEN SOME TIME TO RULE OUT OTHER POSSIBILITIES.
WHILE THE CRYSTAL STORAGE IS GENERATED FROM AVAILABLE MINERAL...
...THERE ARE TRACE ELEMENTS OF NON-TERRAN COMPOUNDS.
IN SHORT, THIS IS EXTRA-TERRESTRIAL IN NATURE.
HOW DID I NOT DETECT YOU AS A ROBOT?
YOU ARE UNSOPHIS-TICATED.
DON'T EVEN.
TEAM, THIS IS AARON STACK.
YOU MAY KNOW HIS WORKING NAME,
MACHINE MAN.
GOOD CHOICE, SO NO REAL PEOPLE GET KILLED TRYING TO STUDY IT.
SO YOU'RE SAYING ALIEN TECH IS BEHIND THIS?
SKRULLS? KREE? WHO?

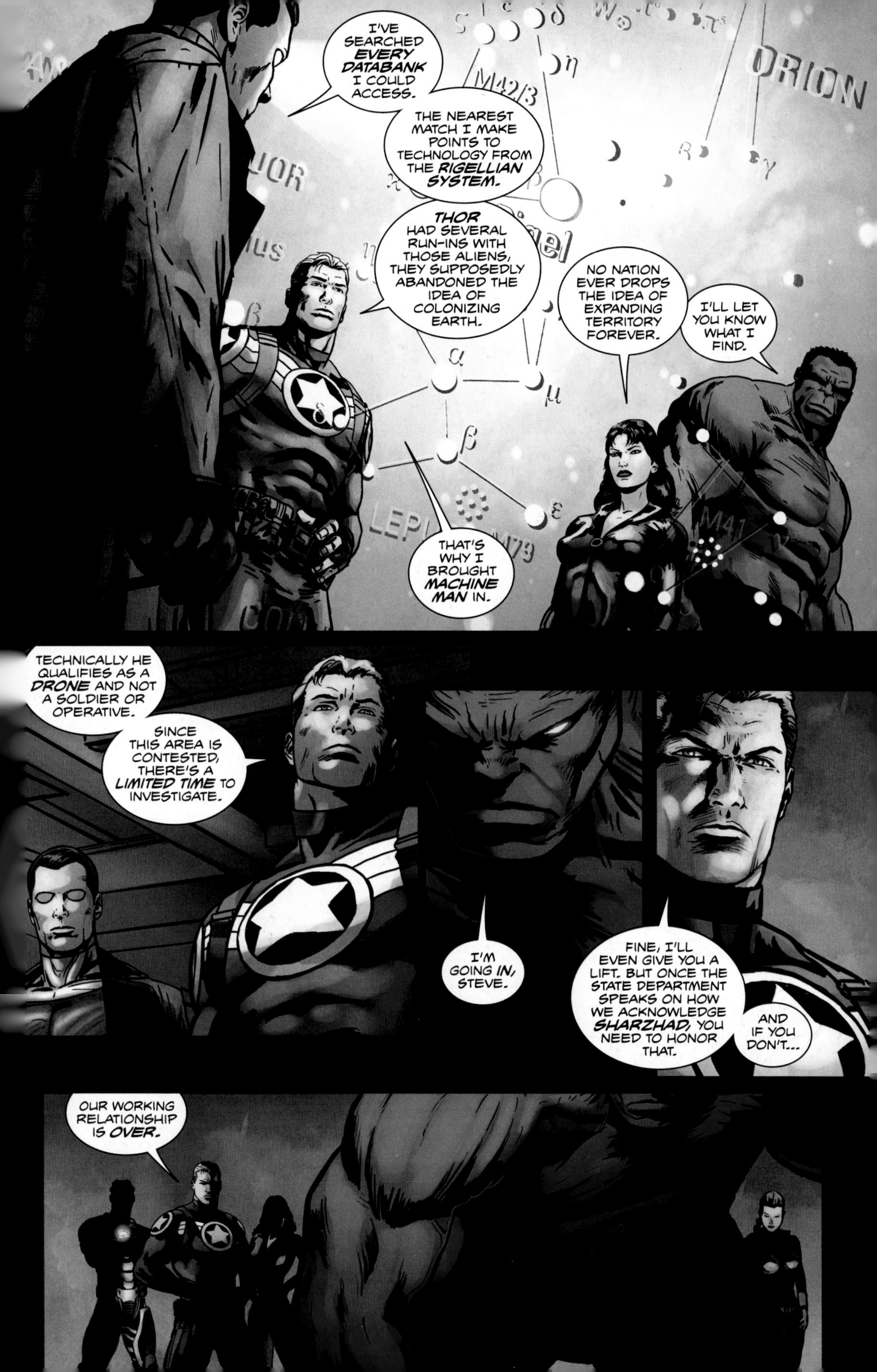
I'VE SEARCHED EVERY DATABANK I COULD ACCESS.
THE NEAREST MATCH I MAKE POINTS TO TECHNOLOGY FROM THE RIGELLIAN SYSTEM.
THOR HAD SEVERAL RUN-INS WITH THOSE ALIENS, THEY SUPPOSEDLY ABANDONED THE IDEA OF COLONIZING EARTH.
NO NATION EVER DROPS THE IDEA OF EXPANDING TERRITORY FOREVER.
I'LL LET YOU KNOW WHAT I FIND.
THAT'S WHY I BROUGHT MACHINE MAN IN.
ORION
TECHNICALLY HE QUALIFIES AS A DRONE AND NOT A SOLDIER OR OPERATIVE.
SINCE THIS AREA IS CONTESTED, THERE'S A LIMITED TIME TO INVESTIGATE.
I'M GOING IN, STEVE.
FINE, I'LL EVEN GIVE YOU A LIFT. BUT ONCE THE STATE DEPARTMENT SPEAKS ON HOW WE ACKNOWLEDGE SHARZHAD, YOU NEED TO HONOR THAT.
AND IF YOU DON'T...
OUR WORKING RELATIONSHIP IS OVER.

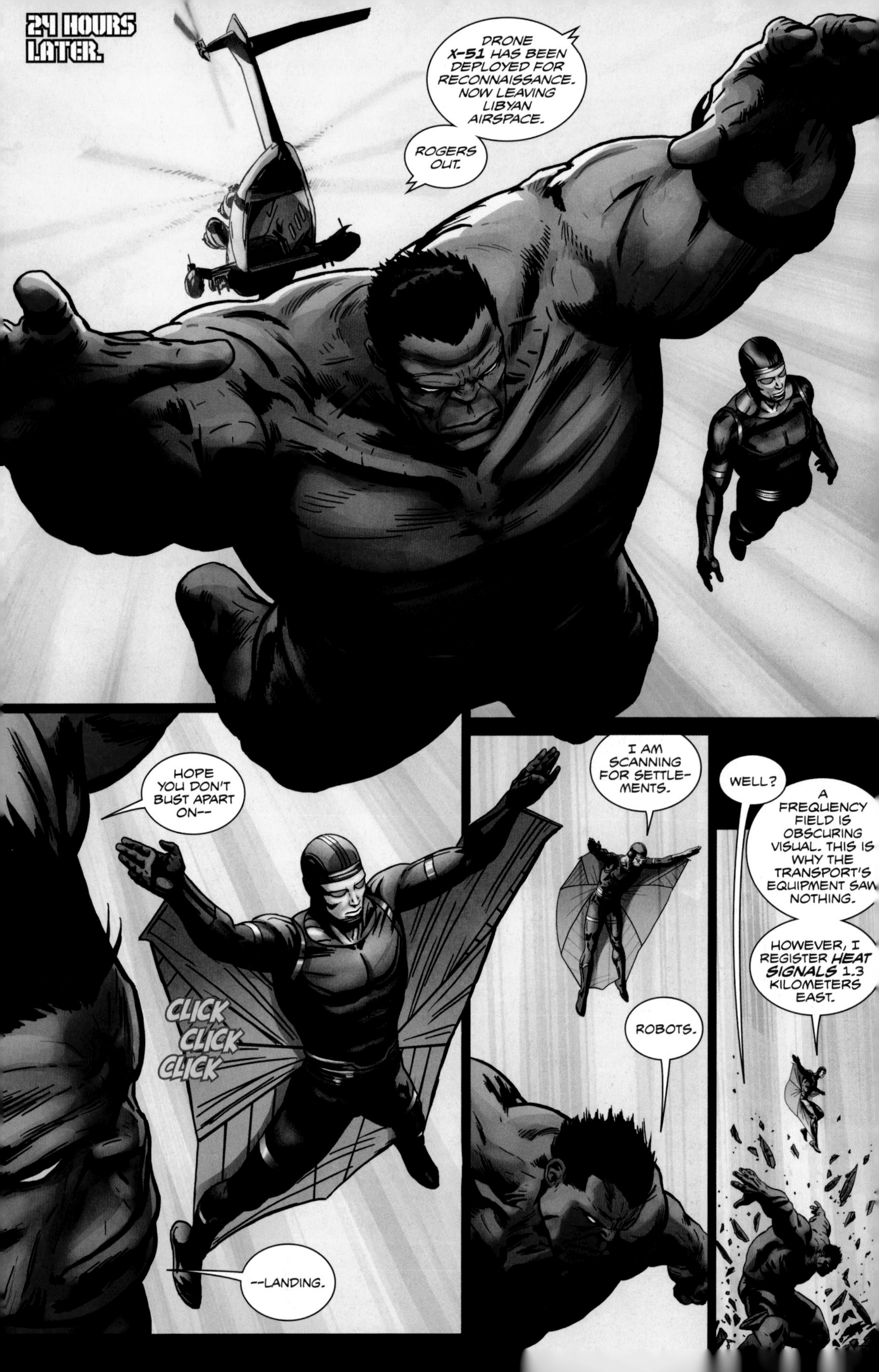
24 HOURS LATER.
DRONE X-51 HAS BEEN DEPLOYED FOR RECONNAISSANCE. NOW LEAVING LIBYAN AIRSPACE.
ROGERS OUT.
HOPE YOU DON'T BUST APART ON--
CLICK CLICK CLICK
--LANDING.
I AM SCANNING FOR SETTLE-MENTS.
ROBOTS.
WELL?
A FREQUENCY FIELD IS OBSCURING VISUAL. THIS IS WHY THE TRANSPORT'S EQUIPMENT SAW NOTHING.
HOWEVER, I REGISTER HEAT SIGNALS 1.3 KILOMETERS EAST.

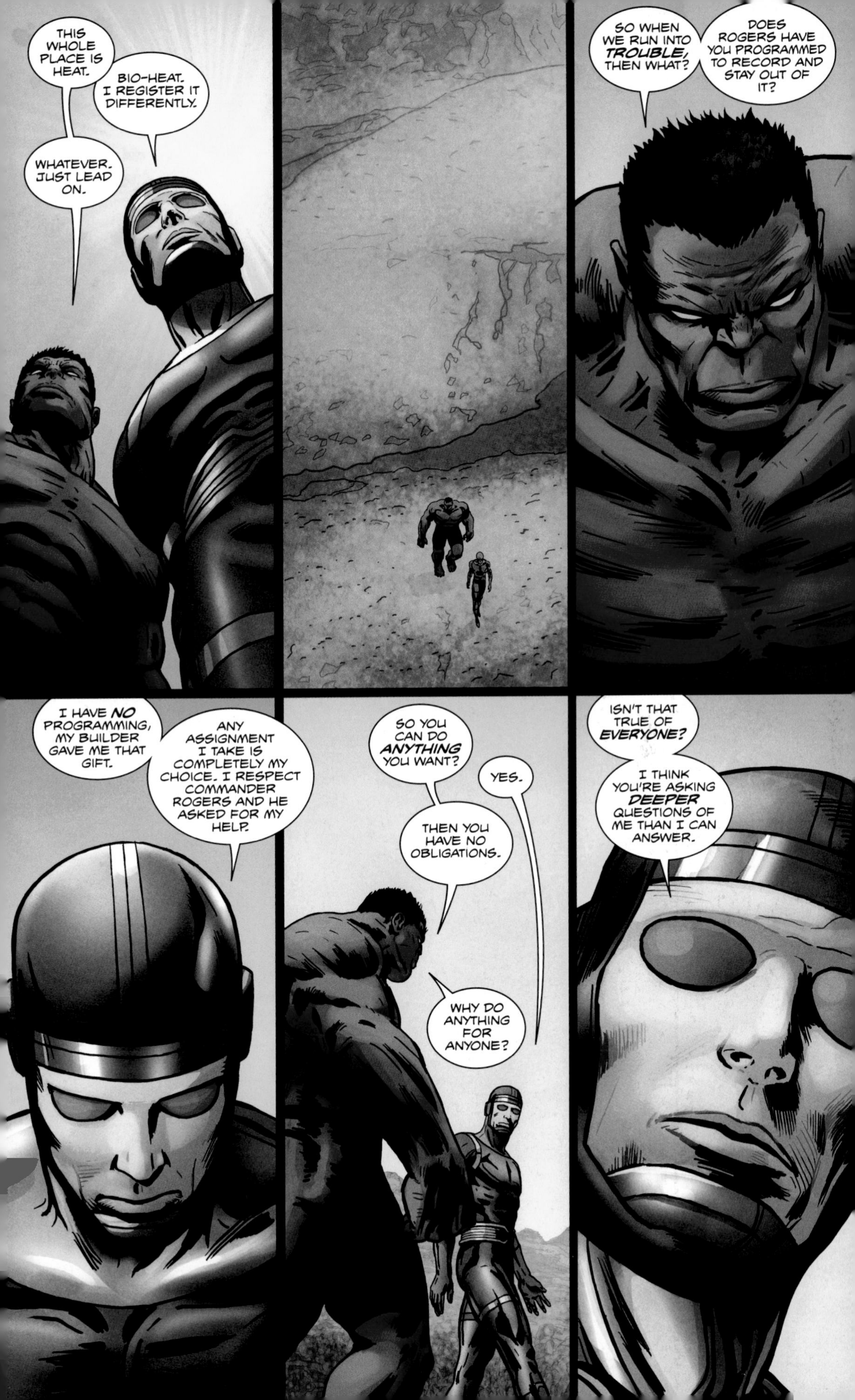
THIS WHOLE PLACE IS HEAT.
BIO-HEAT. I REGISTER IT DIFFERENTLY.
WHATEVER. JUST LEAD ON.
SO WHEN WE RUN INTO TROUBLE, THEN WHAT?
DOES ROGERS HAVE YOU PROGRAMMED TO RECORD AND STAY OUT OF IT?
I HAVE NO PROGRAMMING, MY BUILDER GAVE ME THAT GIFT.
ANY ASSIGNMENT I TAKE IS COMPLETELY MY CHOICE. I RESPECT COMMANDER ROGERS AND HE ASKED FOR MY HELP.
SO YOU CAN DO ANYTHING YOU WANT?
YES.
THEN YOU HAVE NO OBLIGATIONS.
WHY DO ANYTHING FOR ANYONE?
ISN'T THAT TRUE OF EVERYONE?
I THINK YOU'RE ASKING DEEPER QUESTIONS OF ME THAN I CAN ANSWER.

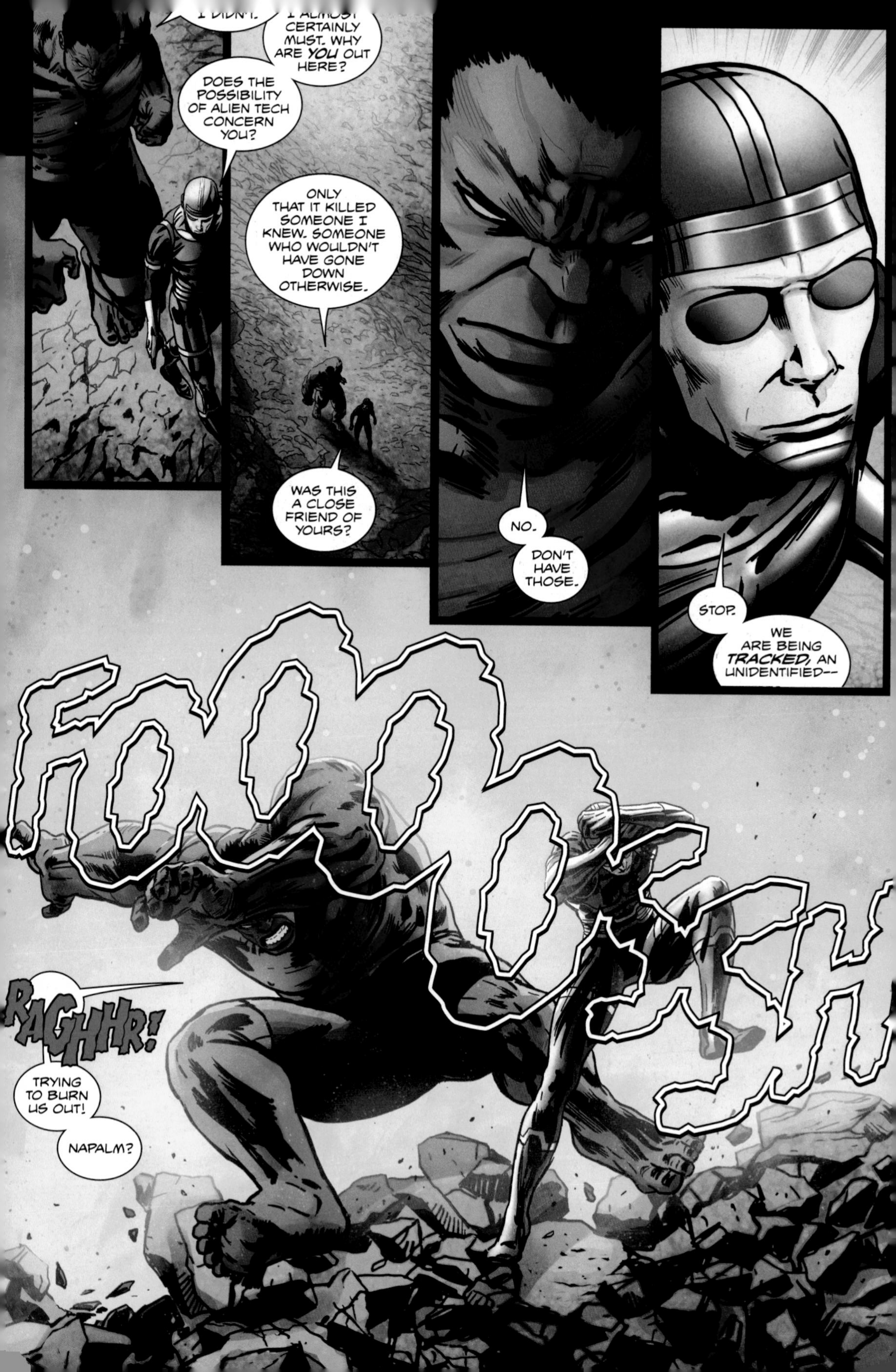
I DIDN'T.
I ALMOST CERTAINLY MUST. WHY ARE YOU OUT HERE?
DOES THE POSSIBILITY OF ALIEN TECH CONCERN YOU?
ONLY THAT IT KILLED SOMEONE I KNEW. SOMEONE WHO WOULDN'T HAVE GONE DOWN OTHERWISE.
WAS THIS A CLOSE FRIEND OF YOURS?
NO.
DON'T HAVE THOSE.
STOP.
WE ARE BEING TRACKED, AN UNIDENTIFIED--
RAGHHR!
TRYING TO BURN US OUT!
NAPALM?

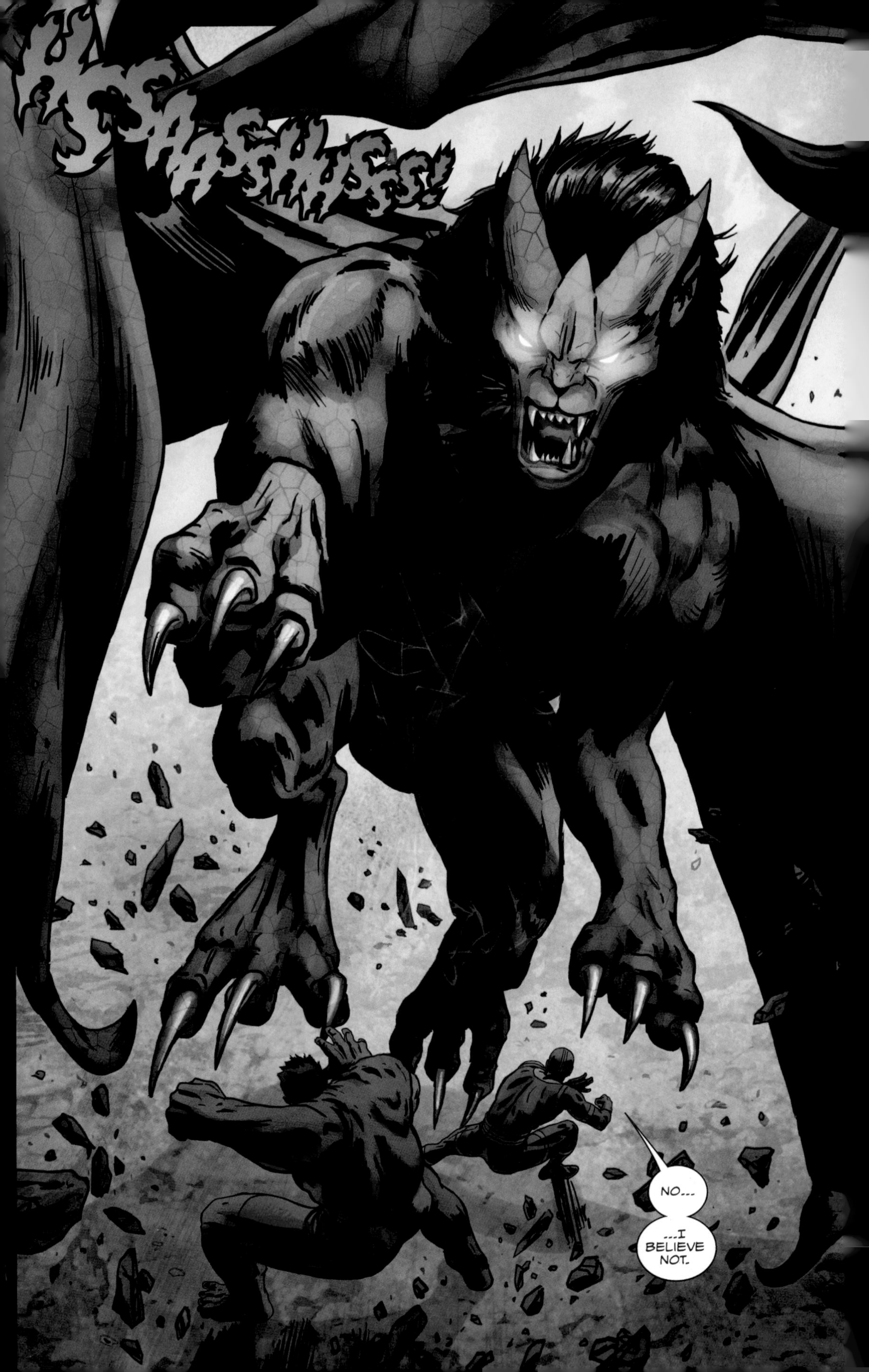
NO...
...I BELIEVE NOT.

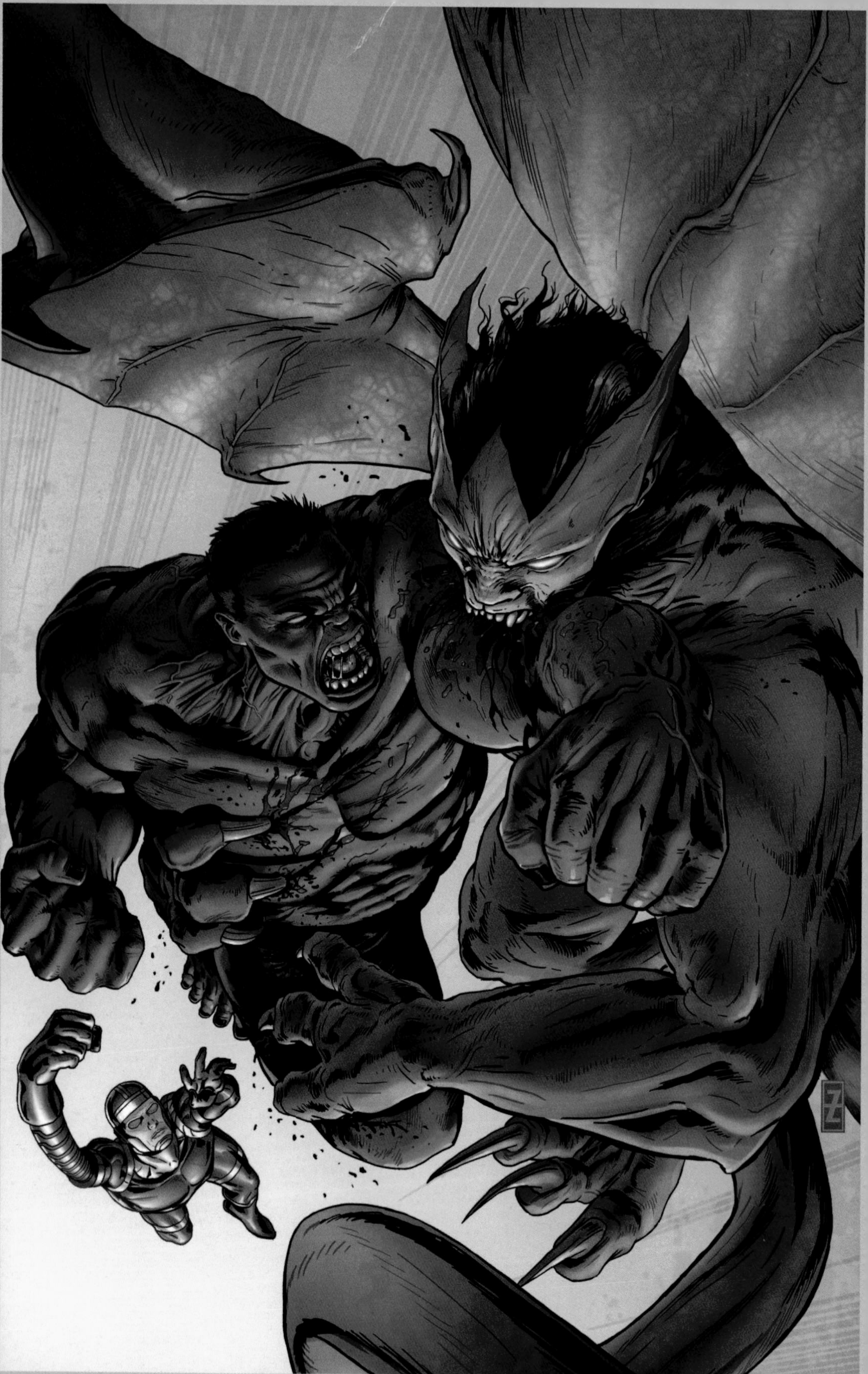

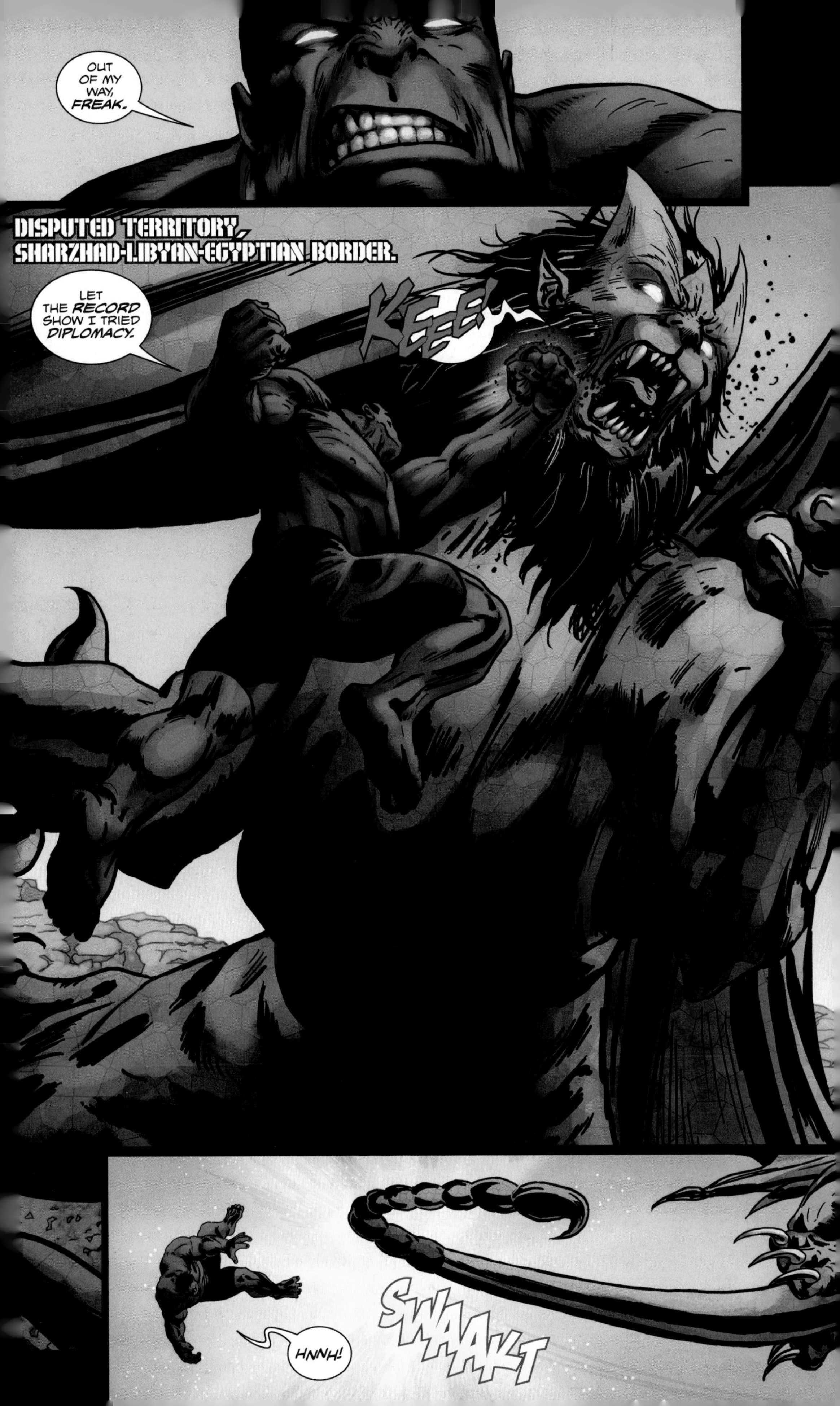
OUT OF MY WAY, FREAK.
DISPUTED TERRITORY, SHARZHAD-LIBYAN-EGYPTIAN BORDER.
LET THE RECORD SHOW I TRIED DIPLOMACY.
KEEEE!
HNNH!
SWAAKT

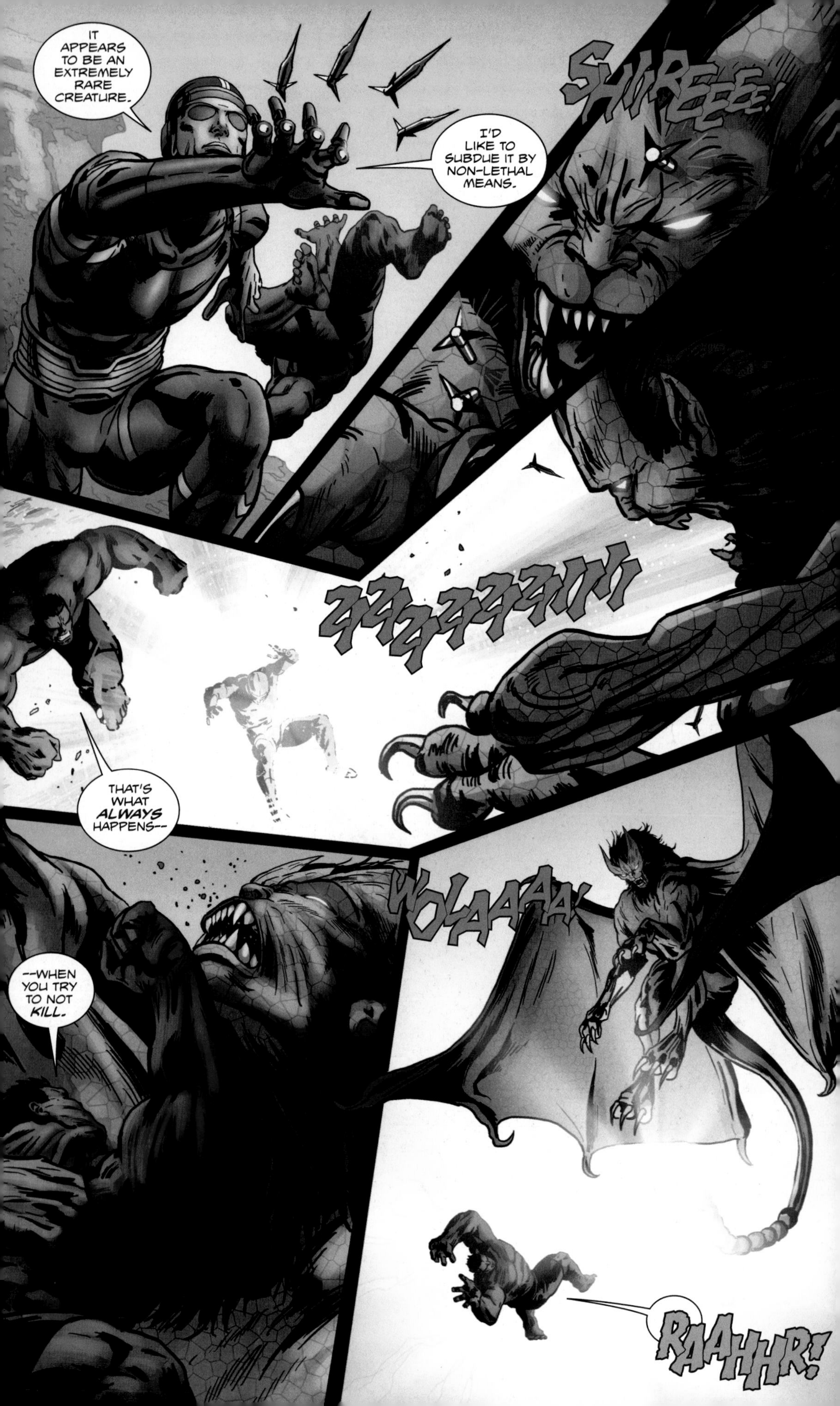
IT APPEARS TO BE AN EXTREMELY RARE CREATURE.
I'D LIKE TO SUBDUE IT BY NON-LETHAL MEANS.
SHREEEE!
ZZZZZZZZZM
THAT'S WHAT ALWAYS HAPPENS--
WOLAAAA!
--WHEN YOU TRY TO NOT KILL.
RAAHHR!

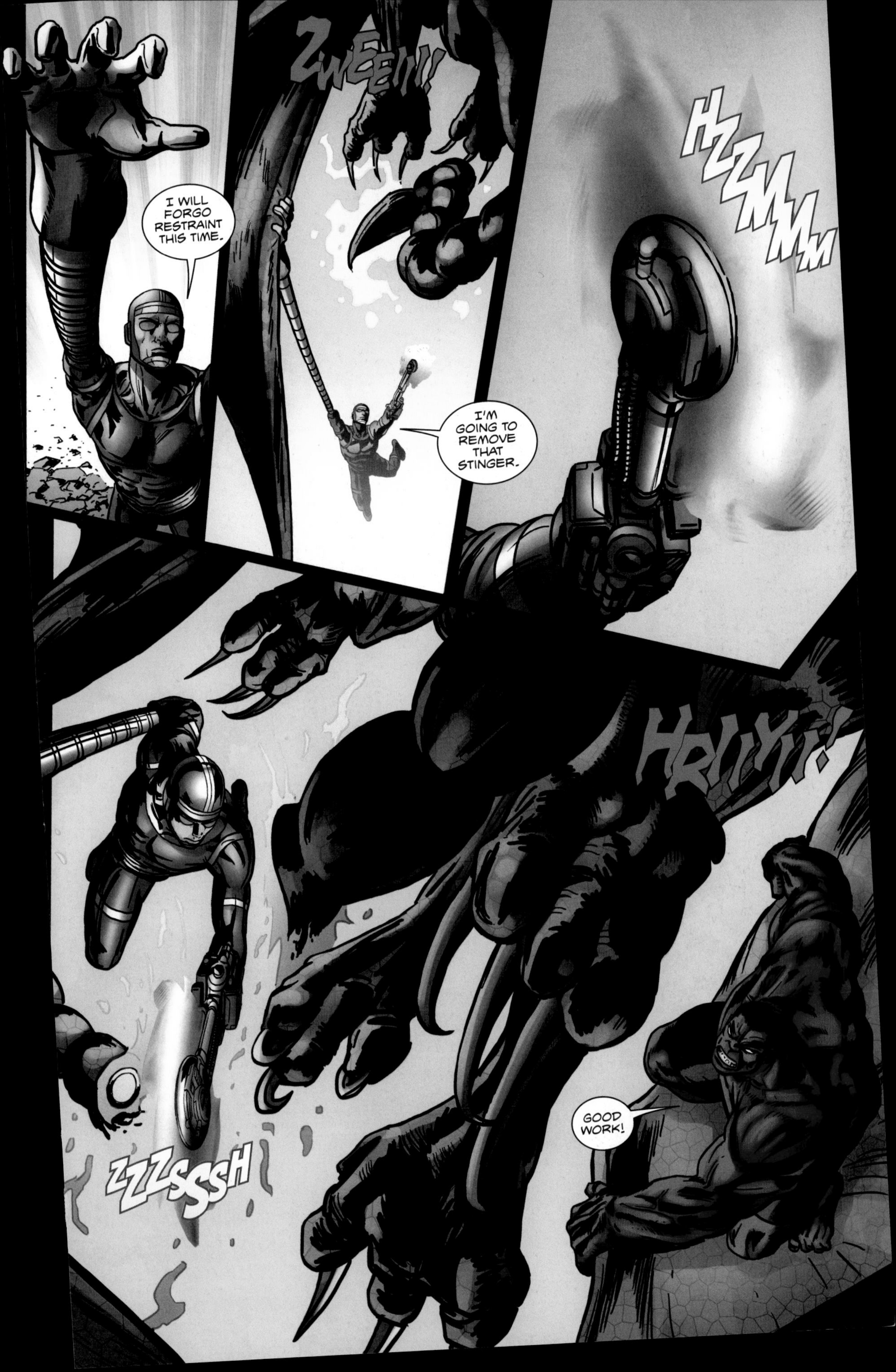
ZWEEN!!
I WILL FORGO RESTRAINT THIS TIME.
I'M GOING TO REMOVE THAT STINGER.
HZZMMMM
HRIIYII!
GOOD WORK!
ZZZSSSH

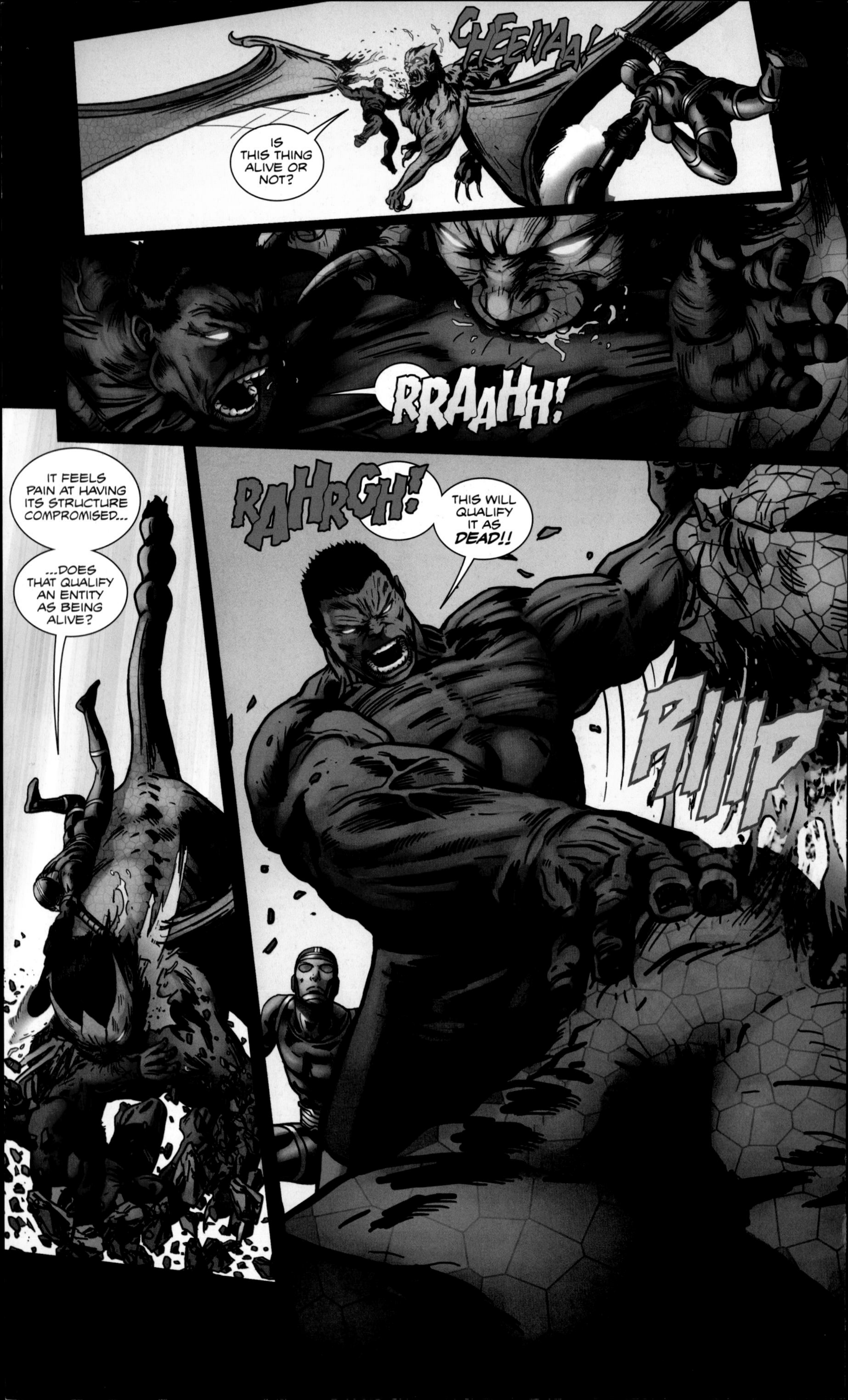
CHEEIIAA!
IS THIS THING ALIVE OR NOT?
RRAAHH!
IT FEELS PAIN AT HAVING ITS STRUCTURE COMPROMISED...
...DOES THAT QUALIFY AN ENTITY AS BEING ALIVE?
RAHRGH!
THIS WILL QUALIFY IT AS DEAD!!
RIIIP

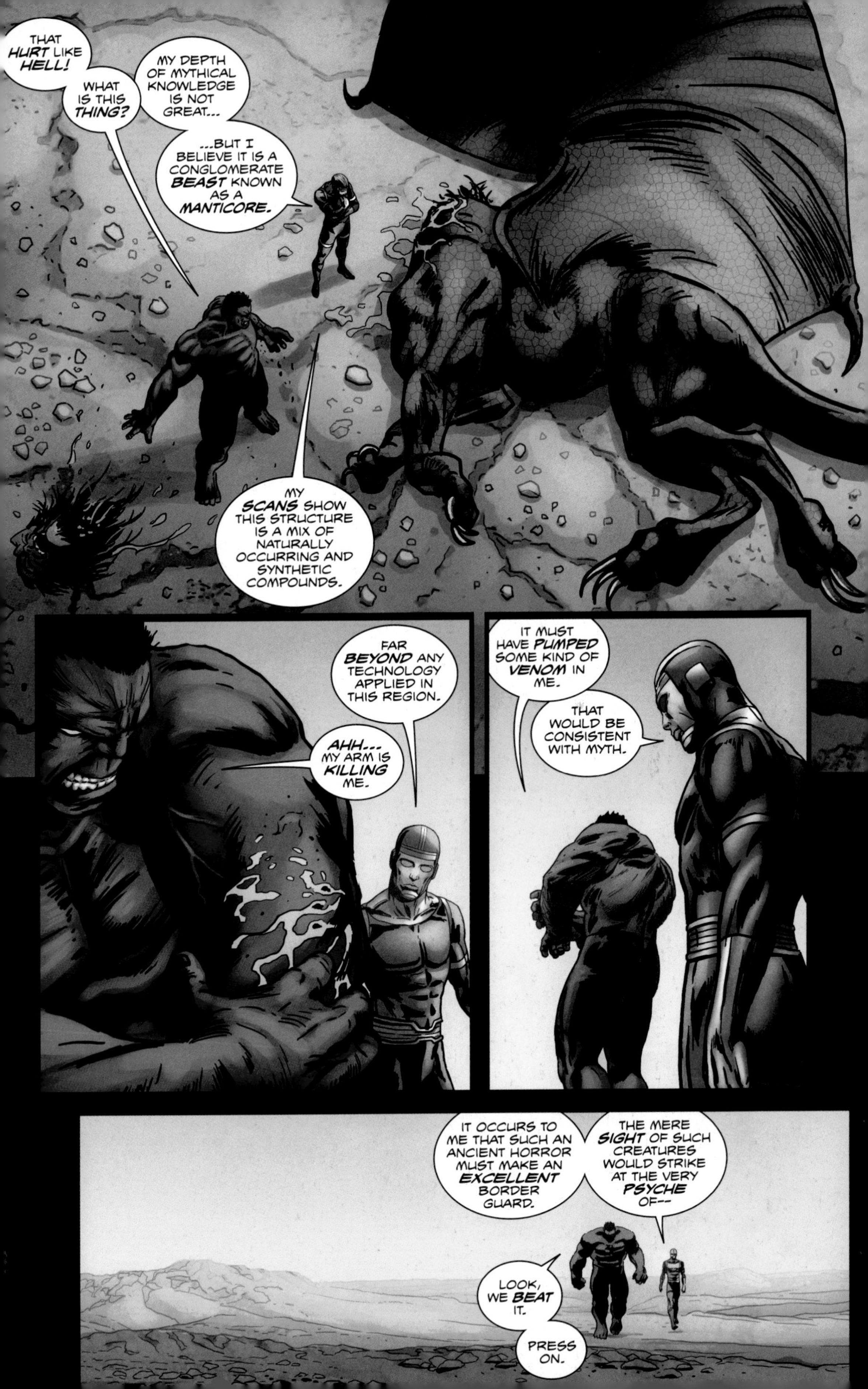

THAT HURT LIKE HELL!
WHAT IS THIS THING?
MY DEPTH OF MYTHICAL KNOWLEDGE IS NOT GREAT...
...BUT I BELIEVE IT IS A CONGLOMERATE BEAST KNOWN AS A MANTICORE.
MY SCANS SHOW THIS STRUCTURE IS A MIX OF NATURALLY OCCURRING AND SYNTHETIC COMPOUNDS.
FAR BEYOND ANY TECHNOLOGY APPLIED IN THIS REGION.
AHH... MY ARM IS KILLING ME.
IT MUST HAVE PUMPED SOME KIND OF VENOM IN ME.
THAT WOULD BE CONSISTENT WITH MYTH.
IT OCCURS TO ME THAT SUCH AN ANCIENT HORROR MUST MAKE AN EXCELLENT BORDER GUARD.
THE MERE SIGHT OF SUCH CREATURES WOULD STRIKE AT THE VERY PSYCHE OF--
LOOK, WE BEAT IT.
PRESS ON.

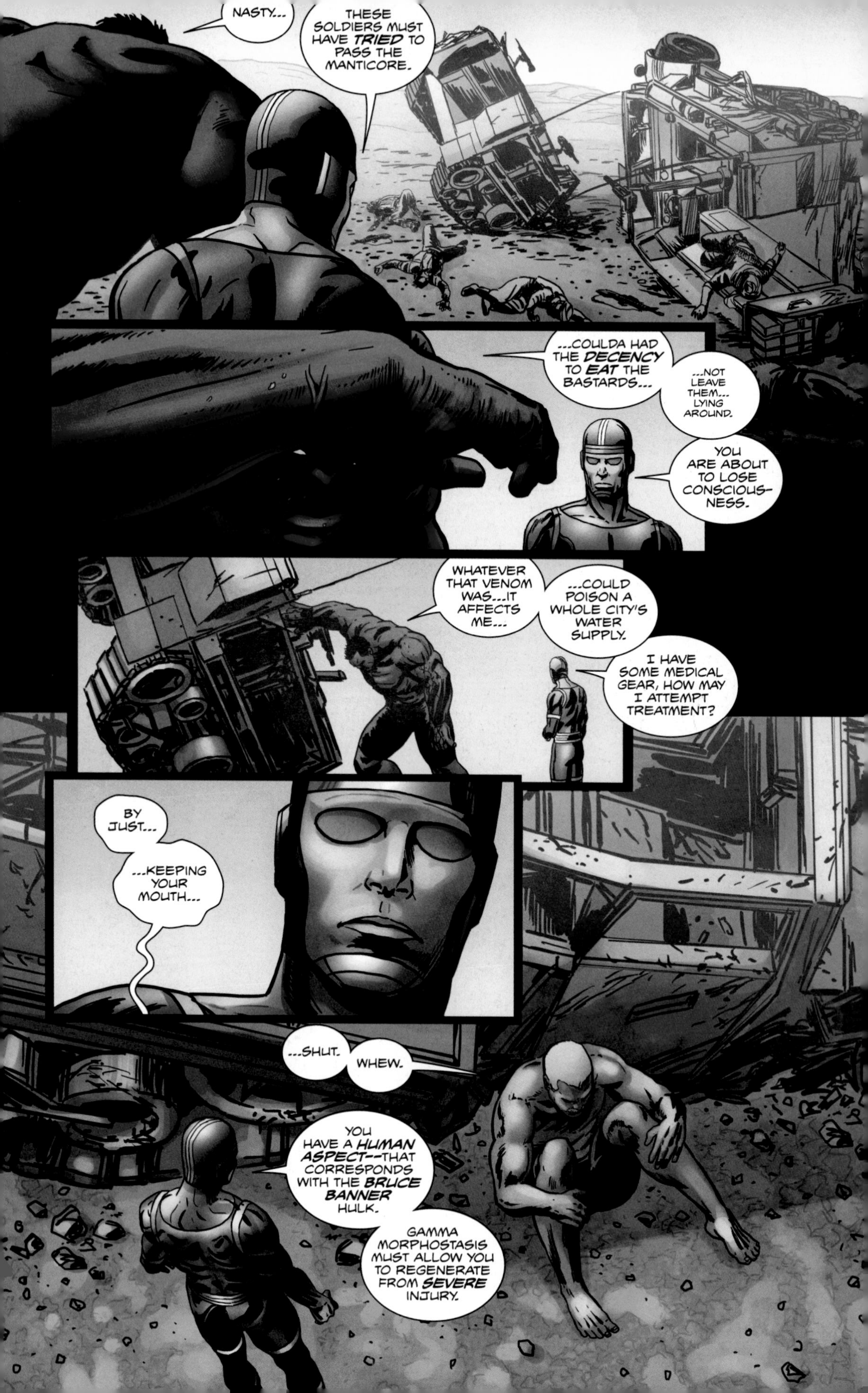
NASTY...
THESE SOLDIERS MUST HAVE TRIED TO PASS THE MANTICORE.
...COULDA HAD THE DECENCY TO EAT THE BASTARDS...
...NOT LEAVE THEM... LYING AROUND.
YOU ARE ABOUT TO LOSE CONSCIOUS-NESS.
WHATEVER THAT VENOM WAS...IT AFFECTS ME...
...COULD POISON A WHOLE CITY'S WATER SUPPLY.
I HAVE SOME MEDICAL GEAR, HOW MAY I ATTEMPT TREATMENT?
BY JUST...
...KEEPING YOUR MOUTH...
...SHUT.
WHEW.
YOU HAVE A HUMAN ASPECT--THAT CORRESPONDS WITH THE BRUCE BANNER HULK.
GAMMA MORPHOSTASIS MUST ALLOW YOU TO REGENERATE FROM SEVERE INJURY.

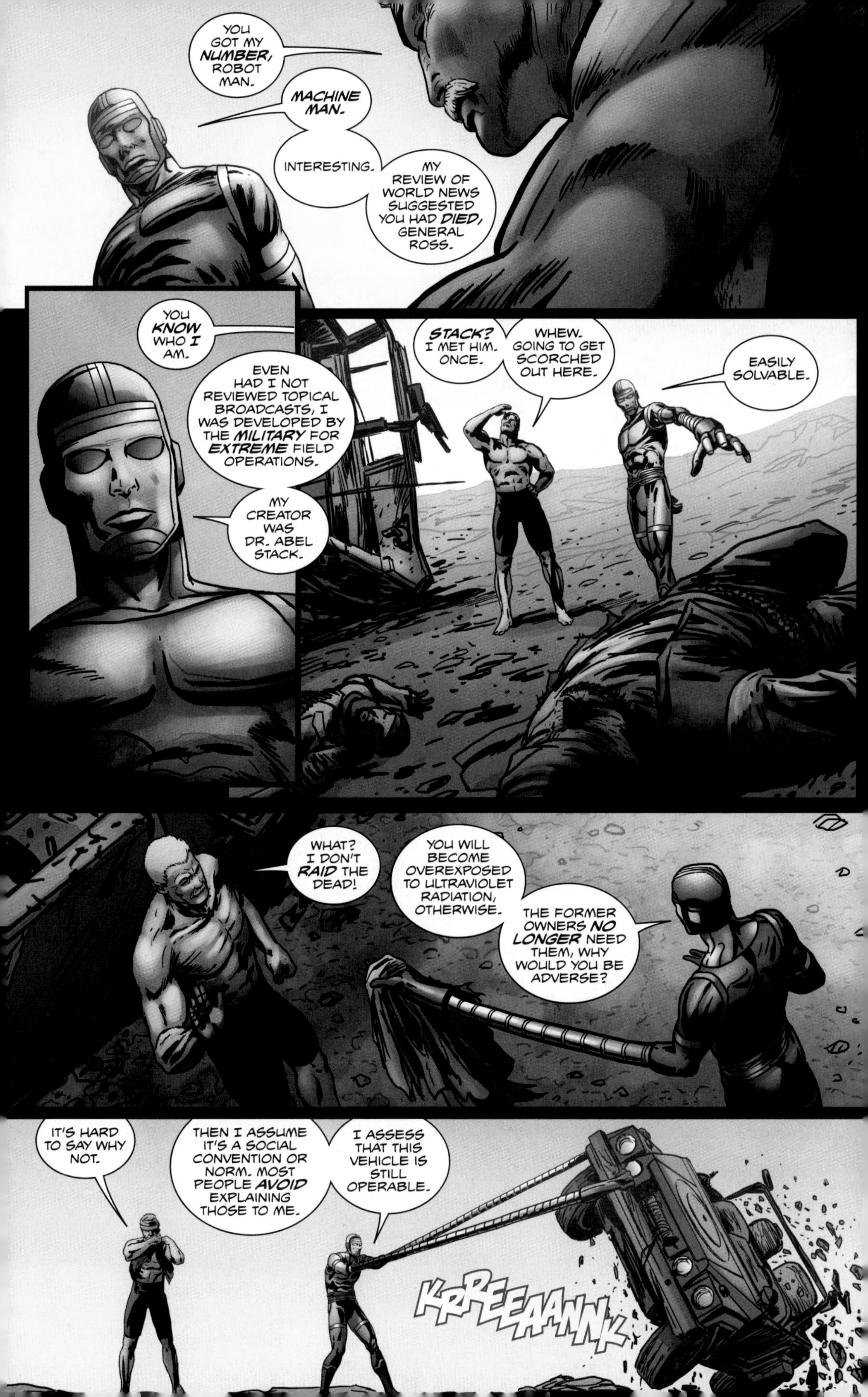
YOU GOT MY NUMBER, ROBOT MAN.
MACHINE MAN.
INTERESTING.
MY REVIEW OF WORLD NEWS SUGGESTED YOU HAD DIED, GENERAL ROSS.
YOU KNOW WHO I AM.
EVEN HAD I NOT REVIEWED TOPICAL BROADCASTS, I WAS DEVELOPED BY THE MILITARY FOR EXTREME FIELD OPERATIONS.
MY CREATOR WAS DR. ABEL STACK.
STACK? I MET HIM. ONCE.
WHEW. GOING TO GET SCORCHED OUT HERE.
EASILY SOLVABLE.
WHAT? I DON'T RAID THE DEAD!
YOU WILL BECOME OVEREXPOSED TO ULTRAVIOLET RADIATION, OTHERWISE.
THE FORMER OWNERS NO LONGER NEED THEM, WHY WOULD YOU BE ADVERSE?
IT'S HARD TO SAY WHY NOT.
THEN I ASSUME IT'S A SOCIAL CONVENTION OR NORM. MOST PEOPLE AVOID EXPLAINING THOSE TO ME.
I ASSESS THAT THIS VEHICLE IS STILL OPERABLE.
KRREEAANNK

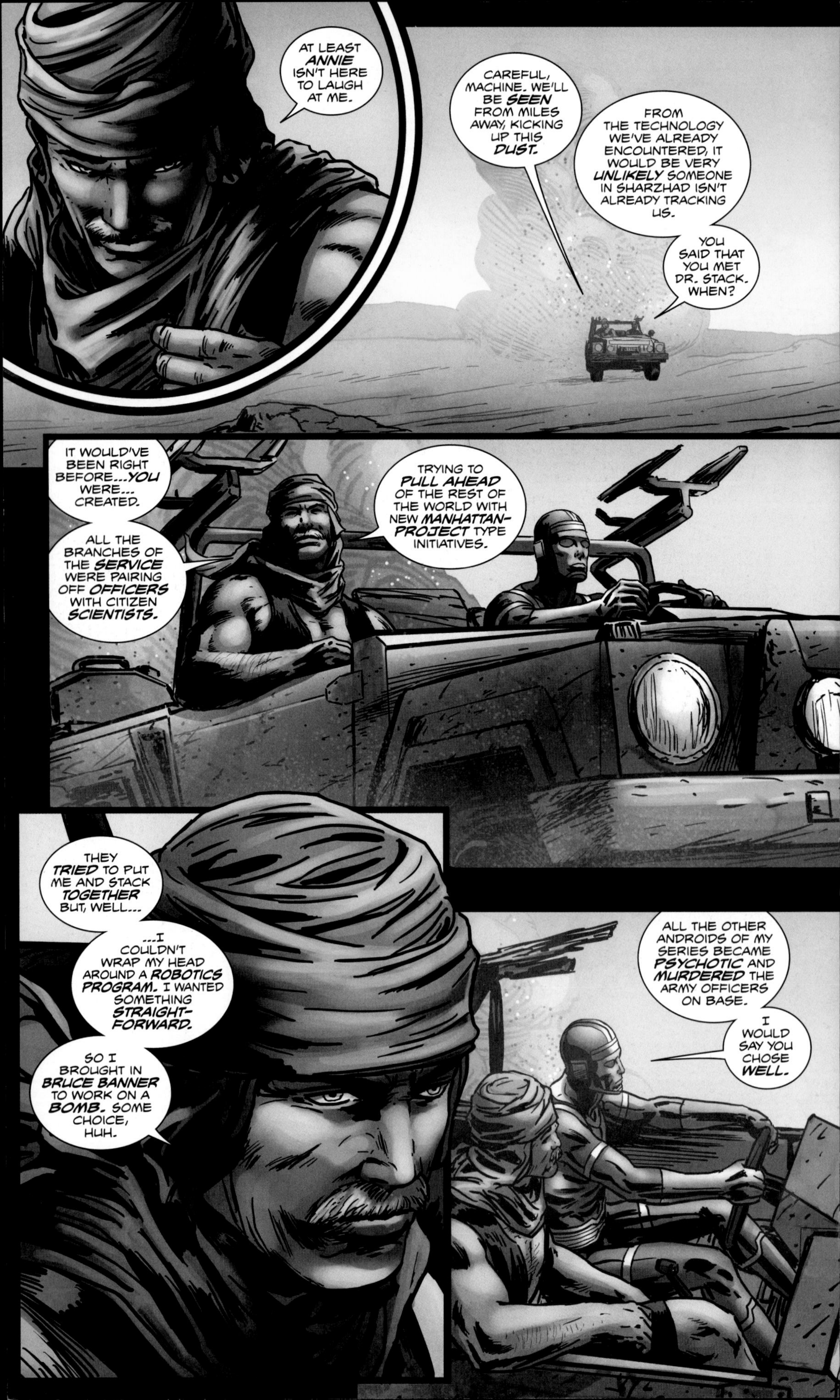

AT LEAST ANNIE ISN'T HERE TO LAUGH AT ME.
CAREFUL, MACHINE. WE'LL BE SEEN FROM MILES AWAY, KICKING UP THIS DUST.
FROM THE TECHNOLOGY WE'VE ALREADY ENCOUNTERED, IT WOULD BE VERY UNLIKELY SOMEONE IN SHARZHAD ISN'T ALREADY TRACKING US.
YOU SAID THAT YOU MET DR. STACK. WHEN?
IT WOULD'VE BEEN RIGHT BEFORE...YOU WERE... CREATED.
ALL THE BRANCHES OF THE SERVICE WERE PAIRING OFF OFFICERS WITH CITIZEN SCIENTISTS.
TRYING TO PULL AHEAD OF THE REST OF THE WORLD WITH NEW MANHATTAN-PROJECT TYPE INITIATIVES.
THEY TRIED TO PUT ME AND STACK TOGETHER BUT, WELL...
...I COULDN'T WRAP MY HEAD AROUND A ROBOTICS PROGRAM. I WANTED SOMETHING STRAIGHT-FORWARD.
SO I BROUGHT IN BRUCE BANNER TO WORK ON A BOMB. SOME CHOICE, HUH.
ALL THE OTHER ANDROIDS OF MY SERIES BECAME PSYCHOTIC AND MURDERED THE ARMY OFFICERS ON BASE.
I WOULD SAY YOU CHOSE WELL.

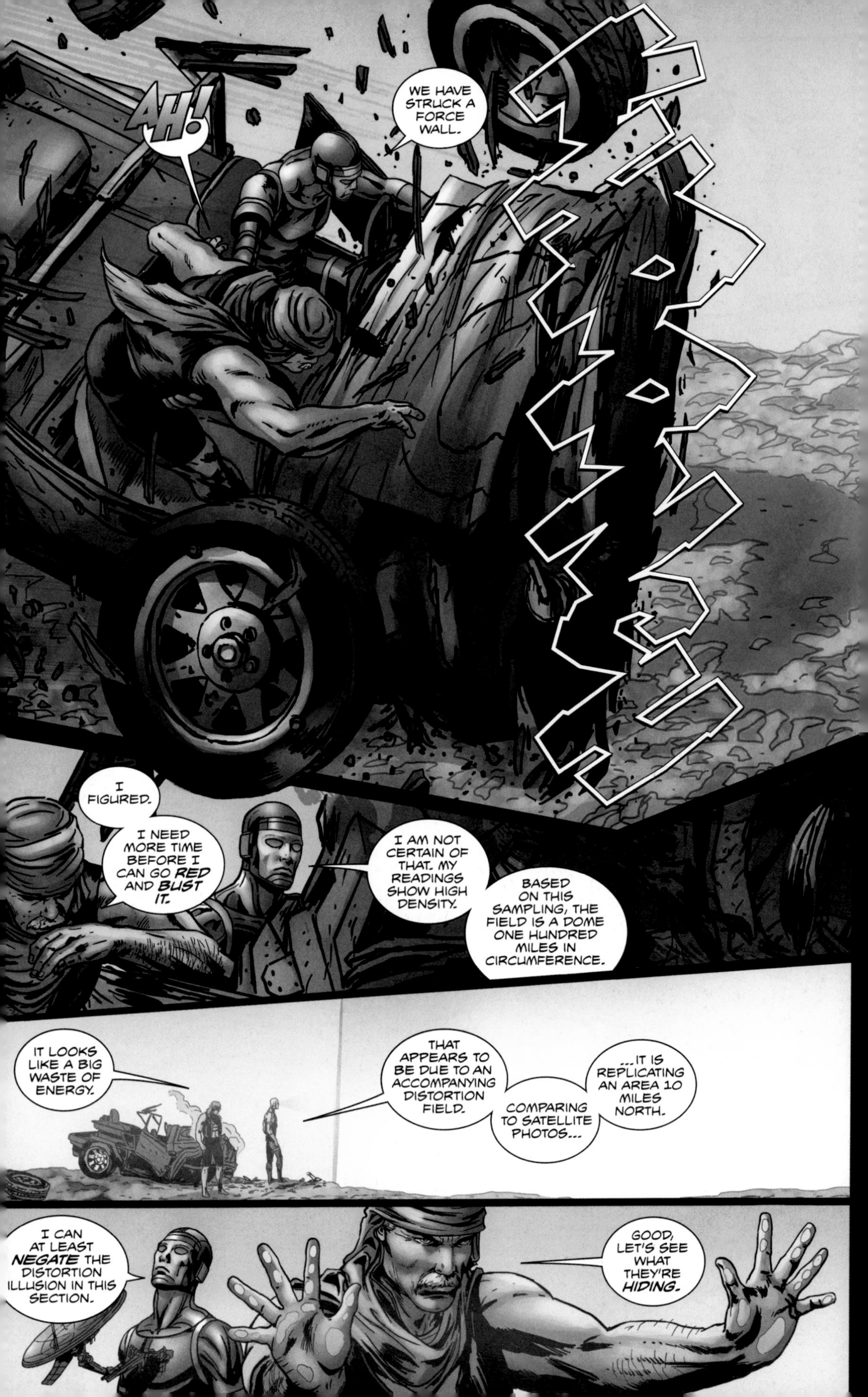
AH!
WE HAVE STRUCK A FORCE WALL.
I FIGURED.
I NEED MORE TIME BEFORE I CAN GO RED AND BUST IT.
I AM NOT CERTAIN OF THAT. MY READINGS SHOW HIGH DENSITY.
BASED ON THIS SAMPLING, THE FIELD IS A DOME ONE HUNDRED MILES IN CIRCUMFERENCE.
IT LOOKS LIKE A BIG WASTE OF ENERGY.
THAT APPEARS TO BE DUE TO AN ACCOMPANYING DISTORTION FIELD.
COMPARING TO SATELLITE PHOTOS...
...IT IS REPLICATING AN AREA 10 MILES NORTH.
I CAN AT LEAST NEGATE THE DISTORTION ILLUSION IN THIS SECTION.
GOOD, LET'S SEE WHAT THEY'RE HIDING.

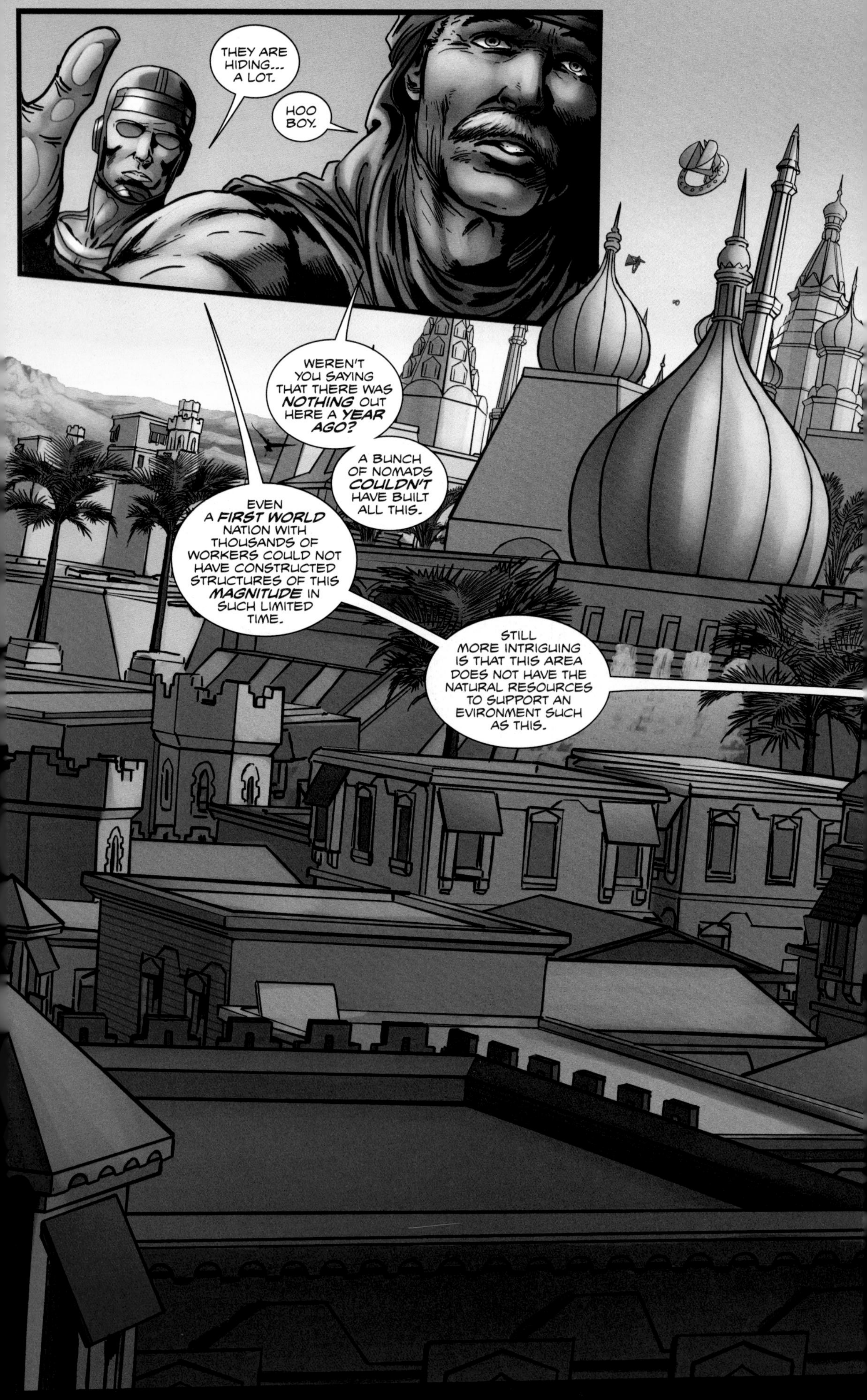
THEY ARE HIDING... A LOT.
HOO BOY.
WEREN'T YOU SAYING THAT THERE WAS NOTHING OUT HERE A YEAR AGO?
A BUNCH OF NOMADS COULDN'T HAVE BUILT ALL THIS.
EVEN A FIRST WORLD NATION WITH THOUSANDS OF WORKERS COULD NOT HAVE CONSTRUCTED STRUCTURES OF THIS MAGNITUDE IN SUCH LIMITED TIME.
STILL MORE INTRIGUING IS THAT THIS AREA DOES NOT HAVE THE NATURAL RESOURCES TO SUPPORT AN EVIRONMENT SUCH AS THIS.

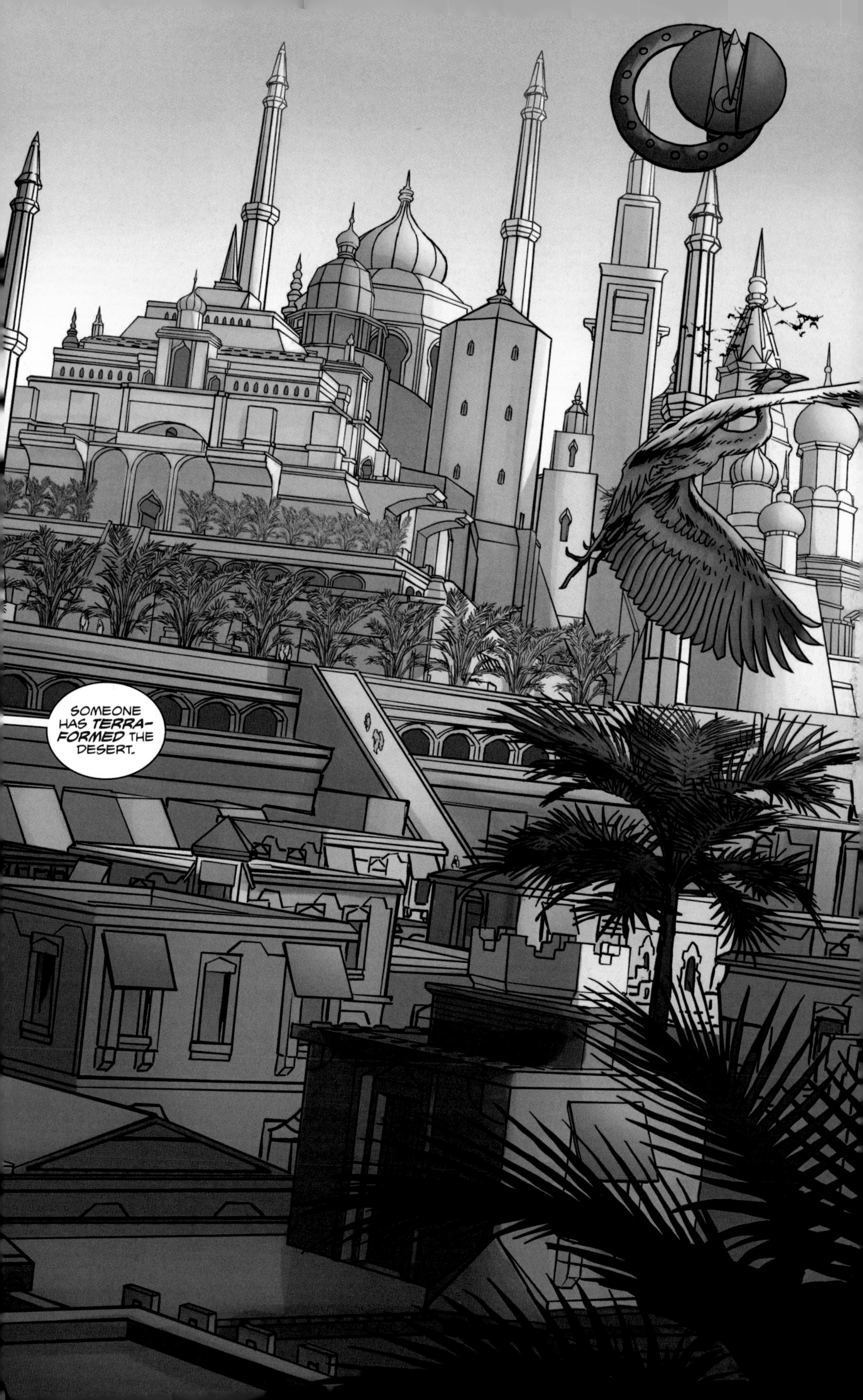
SOMEONE HAS *TERRA-FORMED* THE DESERT.

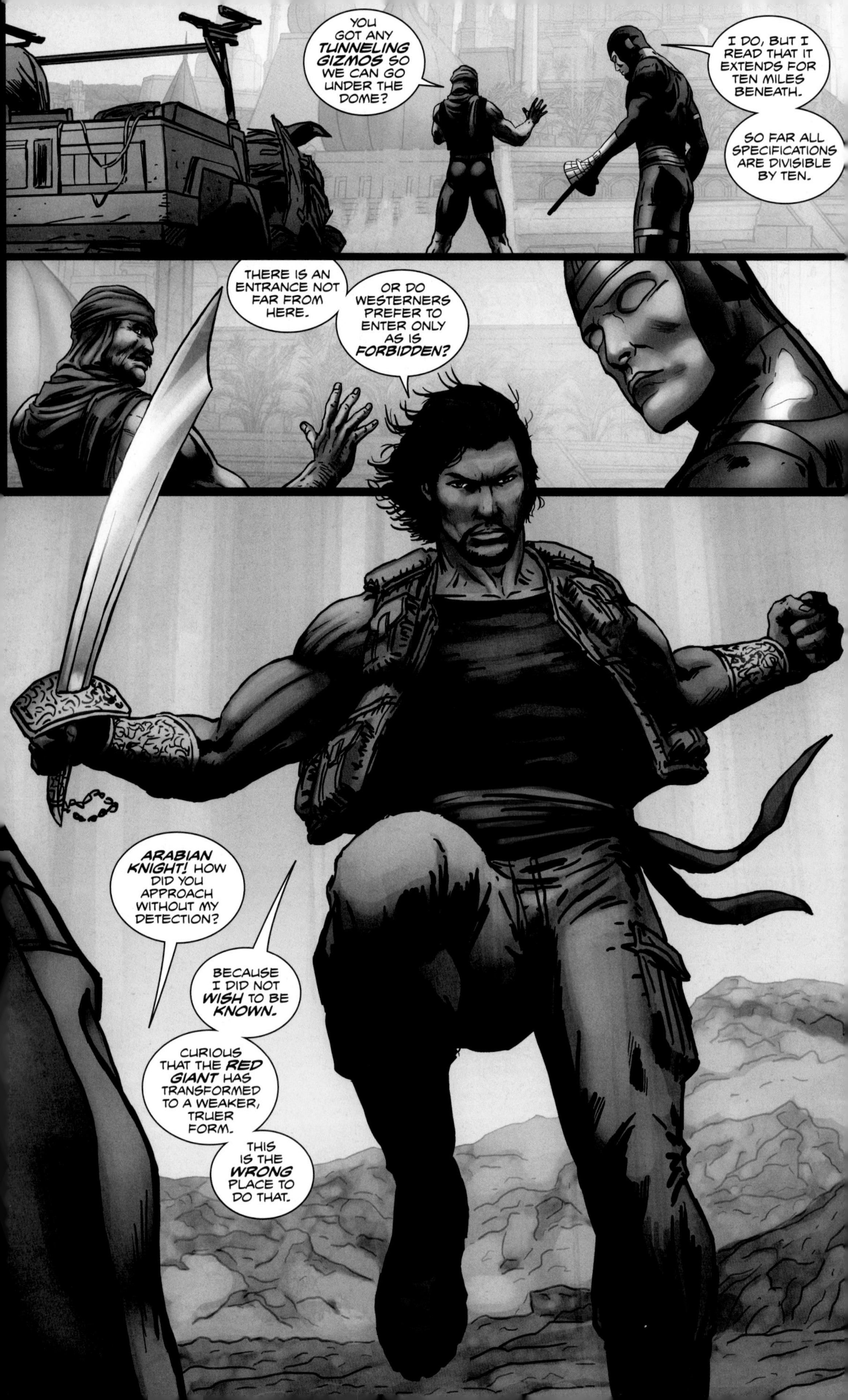

YOU GOT ANY TUNNELING GIZMOS SO WE CAN GO UNDER THE DOME?
I DO, BUT I READ THAT IT EXTENDS FOR TEN MILES BENEATH.
SO FAR ALL SPECIFICATIONS ARE DIVISIBLE BY TEN.
THERE IS AN ENTRANCE NOT FAR FROM HERE.
OR DO WESTERNERS PREFER TO ENTER ONLY AS IS FORBIDDEN?
ARABIAN KNIGHT! HOW DID YOU APPROACH WITHOUT MY DETECTION?
BECAUSE I DID NOT WISH TO BE KNOWN.
CURIOUS THAT THE RED GIANT HAS TRANSFORMED TO A WEAKER, TRUER FORM.
THIS IS THE WRONG PLACE TO DO THAT.

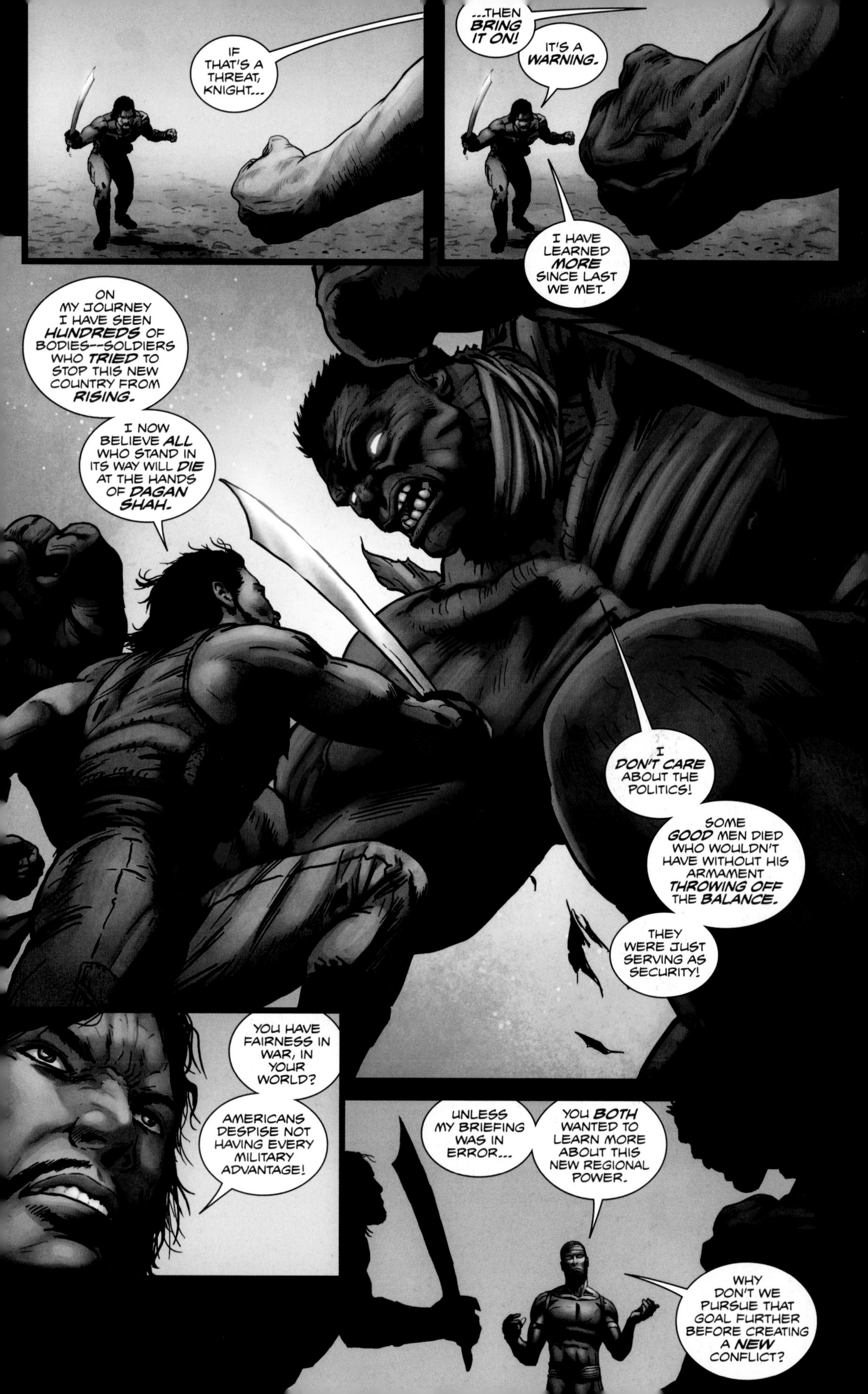
IF THAT'S A THREAT, KNIGHT...
...THEN BRING IT ON!
IT'S A WARNING.
I HAVE LEARNED MORE SINCE LAST WE MET.
ON MY JOURNEY I HAVE SEEN HUNDREDS OF BODIES--SOLDIERS WHO TRIED TO STOP THIS NEW COUNTRY FROM RISING.
I NOW BELIEVE ALL WHO STAND IN ITS WAY WILL DIE AT THE HANDS OF DAGAN SHAH.
I DON'T CARE ABOUT THE POLITICS!
SOME GOOD MEN DIED WHO WOULDN'T HAVE WITHOUT HIS ARMAMENT THROWING OFF THE BALANCE.
THEY WERE JUST SERVING AS SECURITY!
YOU HAVE FAIRNESS IN WAR, IN YOUR WORLD?
AMERICANS DESPISE NOT HAVING EVERY MILITARY ADVANTAGE!
UNLESS MY BRIEFING WAS IN ERROR...
YOU BOTH WANTED TO LEARN MORE ABOUT THIS NEW REGIONAL POWER.
WHY DON'T WE PURSUE THAT GOAL FURTHER BEFORE CREATING A NEW CONFLICT?

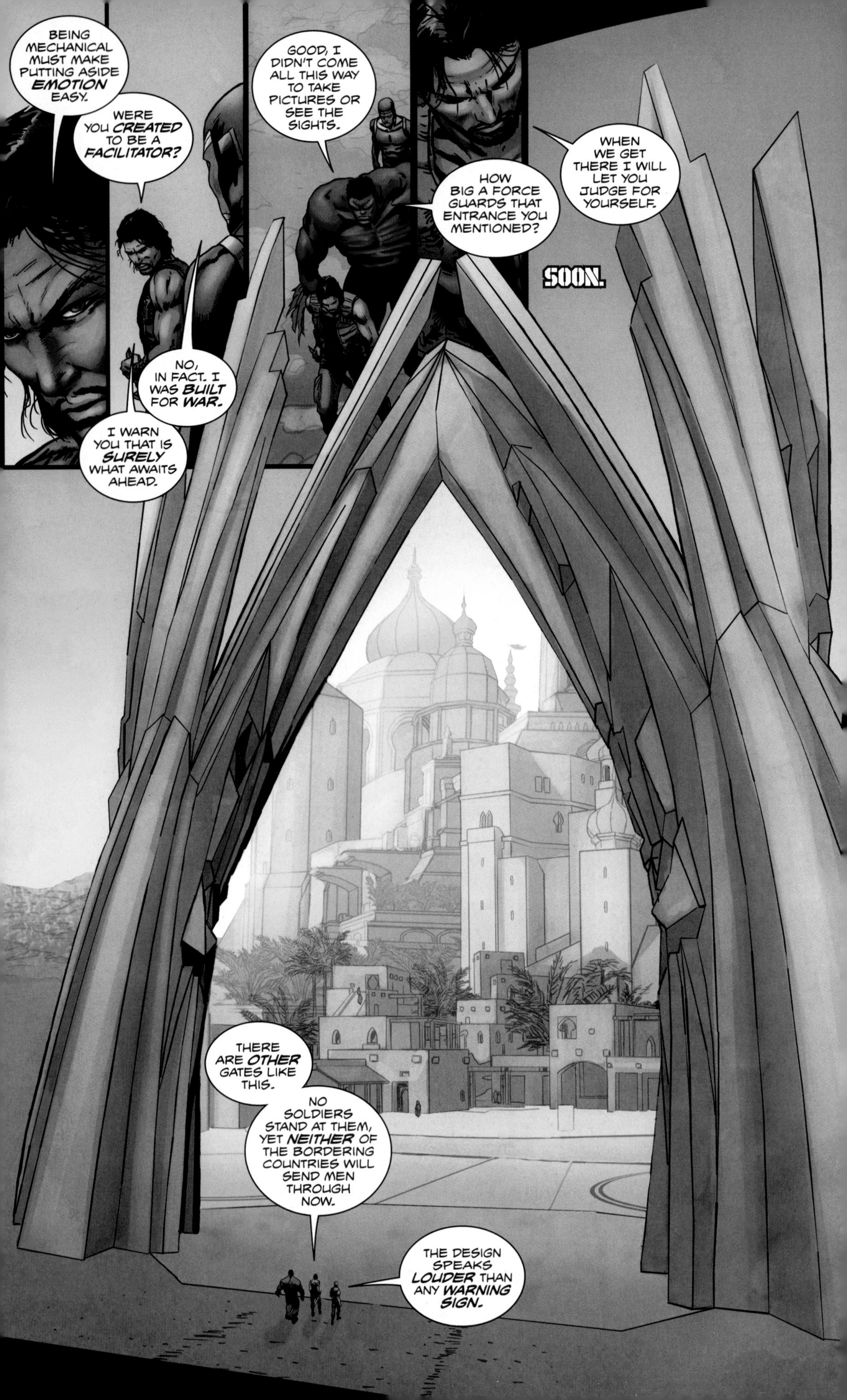
BEING MECHANICAL MUST MAKE PUTTING ASIDE EMOTION EASY.
WERE YOU CREATED TO BE A FACILITATOR?
NO, IN FACT. I WAS BUILT FOR WAR.
I WARN YOU THAT IS SURELY WHAT AWAITS AHEAD.
GOOD, I DIDN'T COME ALL THIS WAY TO TAKE PICTURES OR SEE THE SIGHTS.
HOW BIG A FORCE GUARDS THAT ENTRANCE YOU MENTIONED?
WHEN WE GET THERE I WILL LET YOU JUDGE FOR YOURSELF.
SOON.
THERE ARE OTHER GATES LIKE THIS.
NO SOLDIERS STAND AT THEM, YET NEITHER OF THE BORDERING COUNTRIES WILL SEND MEN THROUGH NOW.
THE DESIGN SPEAKS LOUDER THAN ANY WARNING SIGN.

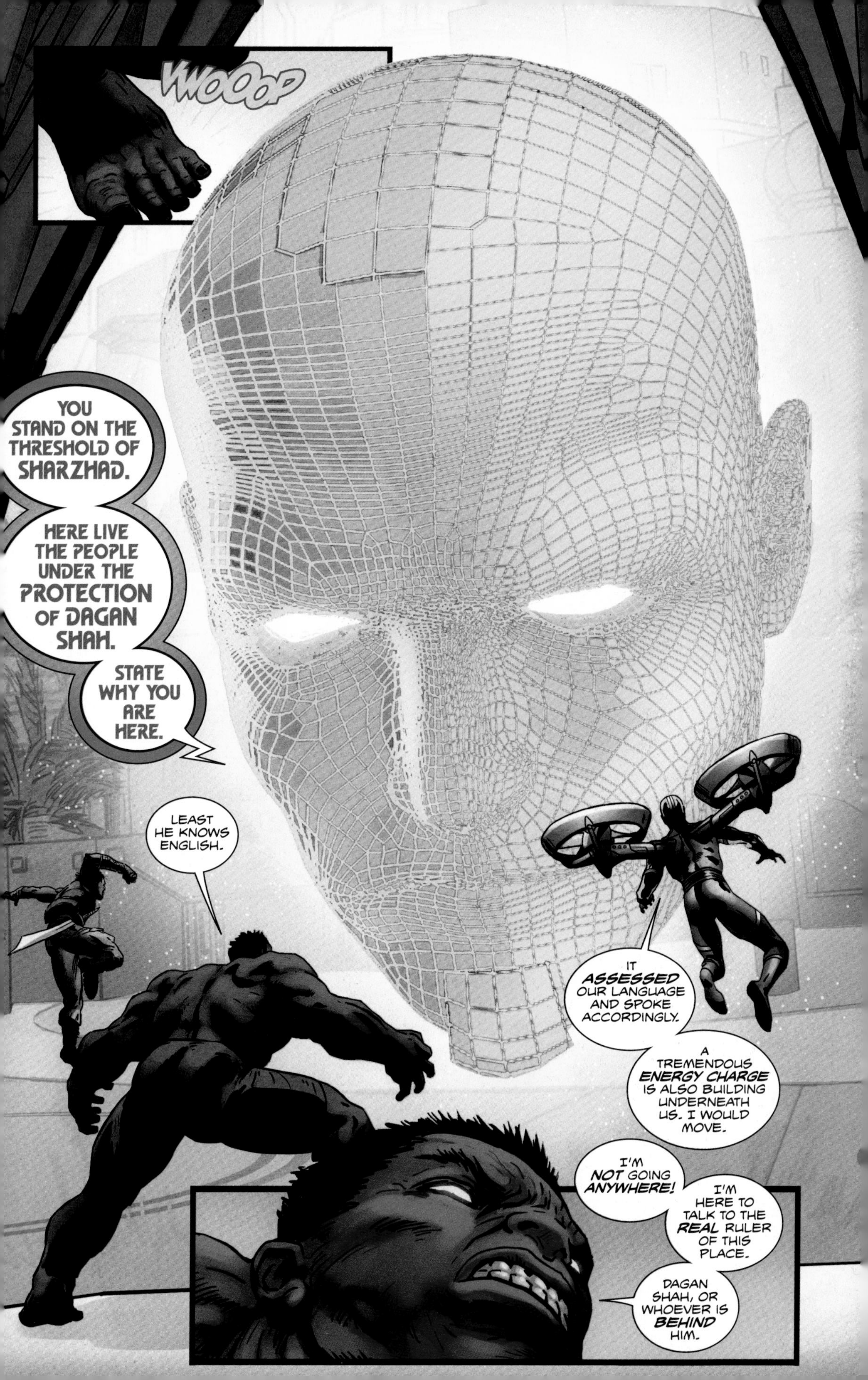
VWOOOP
YOU STAND ON THE THRESHOLD OF SHARZHAD.
HERE LIVE THE PEOPLE UNDER THE PROTECTION OF DAGAN SHAH.
STATE WHY YOU ARE HERE.
LEAST HE KNOWS ENGLISH.
IT ASSESSED OUR LANGUAGE AND SPOKE ACCORDINGLY.
A TREMENDOUS ENERGY CHARGE IS ALSO BUILDING UNDERNEATH US. I WOULD MOVE.
I'M NOT GOING ANYWHERE!
I'M HERE TO TALK TO THE REAL RULER OF THIS PLACE.
DAGAN SHAH, OR WHOEVER IS BEHIND HIM.

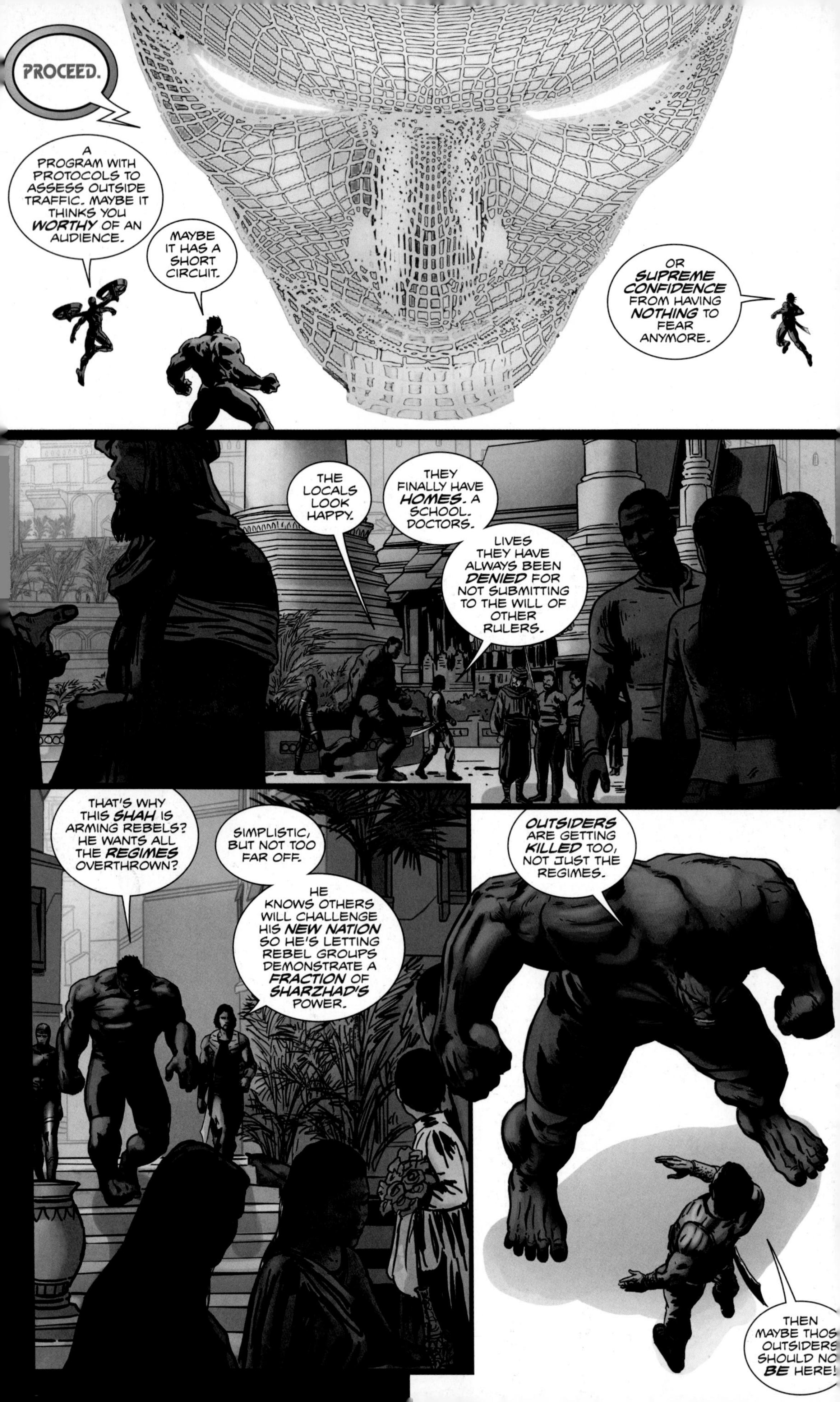
PROCEED.
A PROGRAM WITH PROTOCOLS TO ASSESS OUTSIDE TRAFFIC. MAYBE IT THINKS YOU WORTHY OF AN AUDIENCE.
MAYBE IT HAS A SHORT CIRCUIT.
OR SUPREME CONFIDENCE FROM HAVING NOTHING TO FEAR ANYMORE.
THE LOCALS LOOK HAPPY.
THEY FINALLY HAVE HOMES. A SCHOOL. DOCTORS.
LIVES THEY HAVE ALWAYS BEEN DENIED FOR NOT SUBMITTING TO THE WILL OF OTHER RULERS.
THAT'S WHY THIS SHAH IS ARMING REBELS? HE WANTS ALL THE REGIMES OVERTHROWN?
SIMPLISTIC, BUT NOT TOO FAR OFF.
HE KNOWS OTHERS WILL CHALLENGE HIS NEW NATION SO HE'S LETTING REBEL GROUPS DEMONSTRATE A FRACTION OF SHARZHAD'S POWER.
OUTSIDERS ARE GETTING KILLED TOO, NOT JUST THE REGIMES.
THEN MAYBE THOS OUTSIDERS SHOULD NO BE HERE!

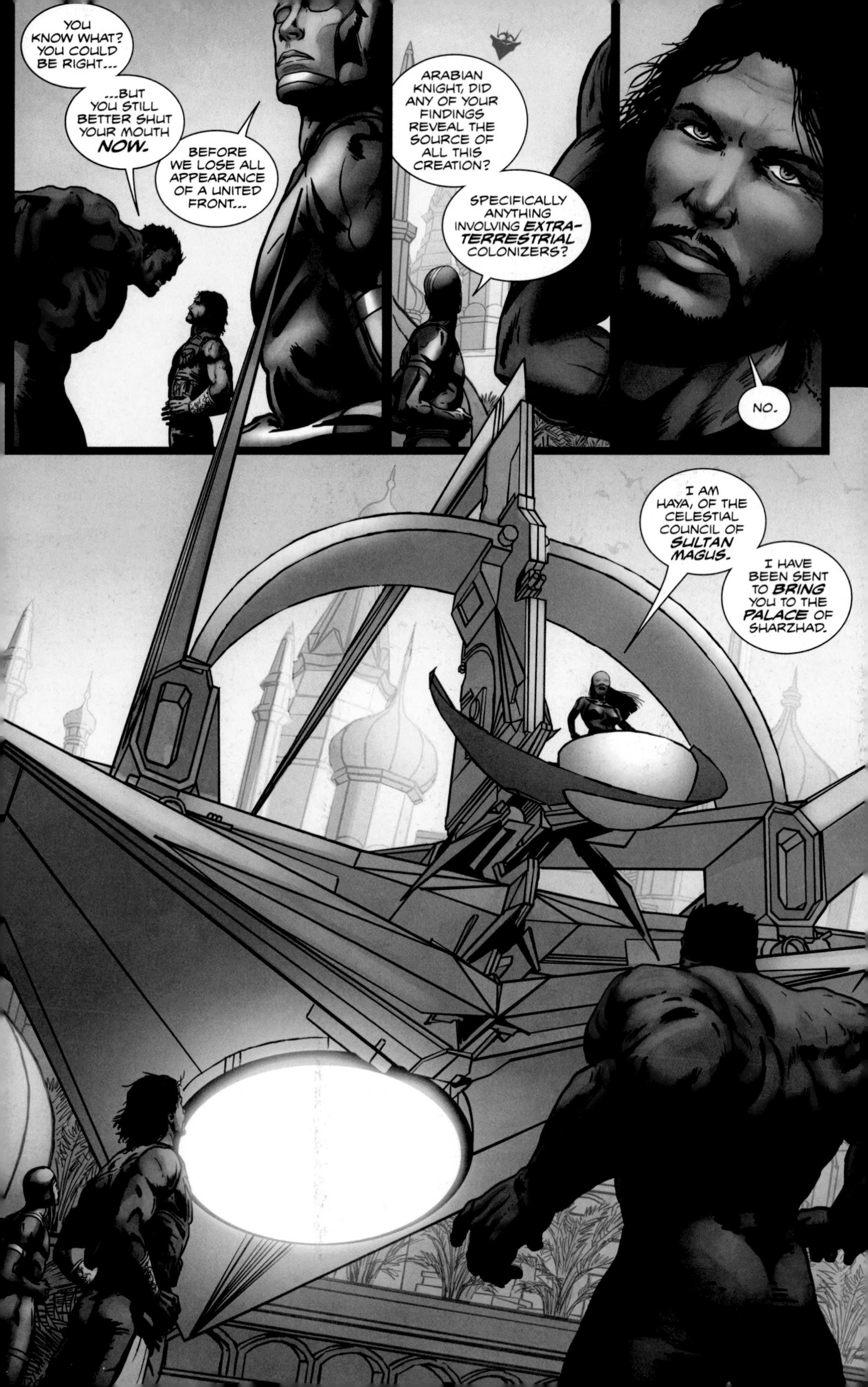
YOU KNOW WHAT? YOU COULD BE RIGHT...
...BUT YOU STILL BETTER SHUT YOUR MOUTH NOW.
BEFORE WE LOSE ALL APPEARANCE OF A UNITED FRONT...
ARABIAN KNIGHT, DID ANY OF YOUR FINDINGS REVEAL THE SOURCE OF ALL THIS CREATION?
SPECIFICALLY ANYTHING INVOLVING EXTRA-TERRESTRIAL COLONIZERS?
NO.
I AM HAYA, OF THE CELESTIAL COUNCIL OF SULTAN MAGUS.
I HAVE BEEN SENT TO BRING YOU TO THE PALACE OF SHARZHAD.

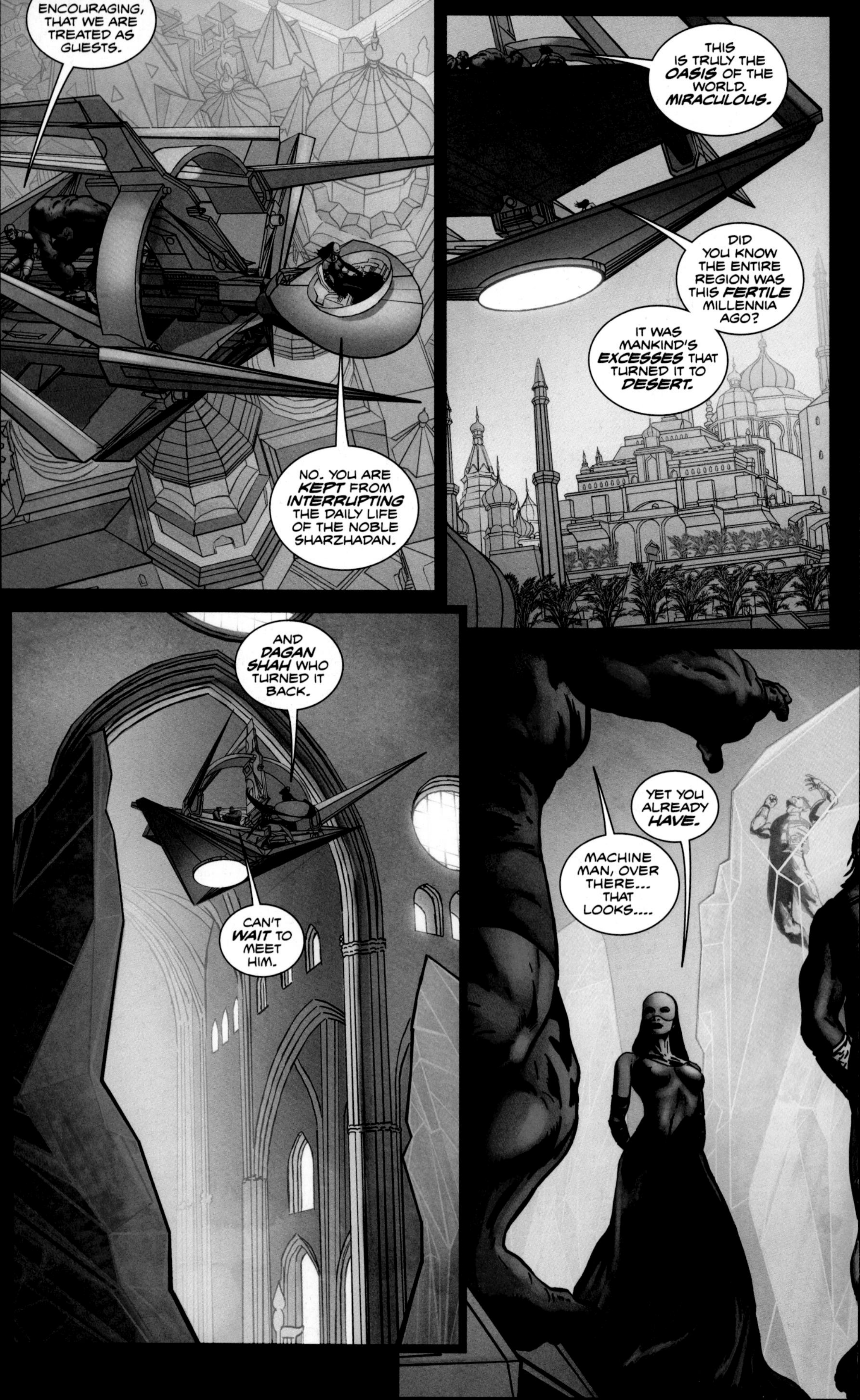
ENCOURAGING, THAT WE ARE TREATED AS GUESTS.
NO. YOU ARE KEPT FROM INTERRUPTING THE DAILY LIFE OF THE NOBLE SHARZHADAN.
THIS IS TRULY THE OASIS OF THE WORLD. MIRACULOUS.
DID YOU KNOW THE ENTIRE REGION WAS THIS FERTILE MILLENNIA AGO?
IT WAS MANKIND'S EXCESSES THAT TURNED IT TO DESERT.
AND DAGAN SHAH WHO TURNED IT BACK.
CAN'T WAIT TO MEET HIM.
YET YOU ALREADY HAVE.
MACHINE MAN, OVER THERE... THAT LOOKS....

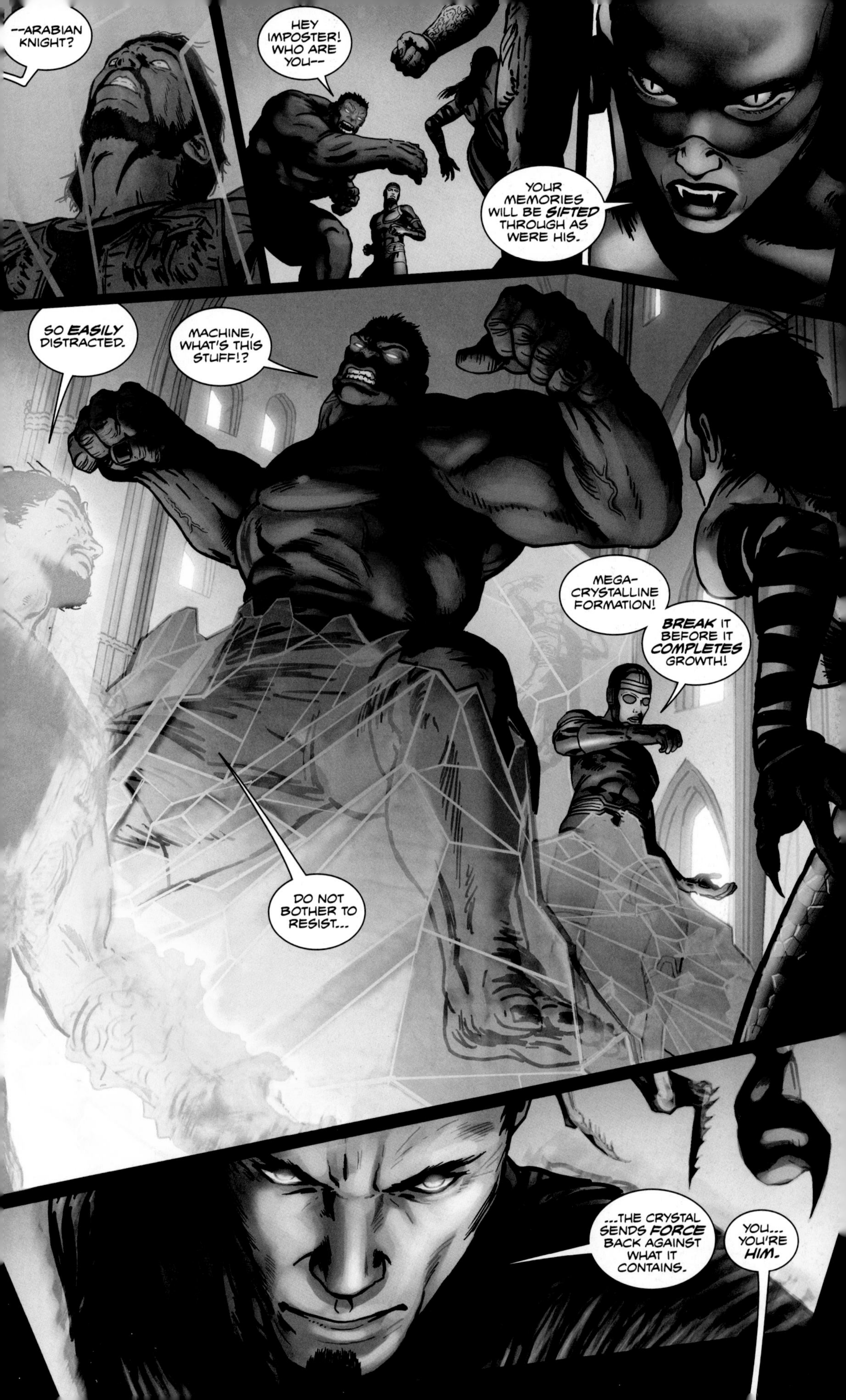
--ARABIAN KNIGHT?
HEY IMPOSTER! WHO ARE YOU--
YOUR MEMORIES WILL BE SIFTED THROUGH AS WERE HIS.
SO EASILY DISTRACTED.
MACHINE, WHAT'S THIS STUFF!?
MEGA-CRYSTALLINE FORMATION!
BREAK IT BEFORE IT COMPLETES GROWTH!
DO NOT BOTHER TO RESIST...
...THE CRYSTAL SENDS FORCE BACK AGAINST WHAT IT CONTAINS.
YOU... YOU'RE HIM.

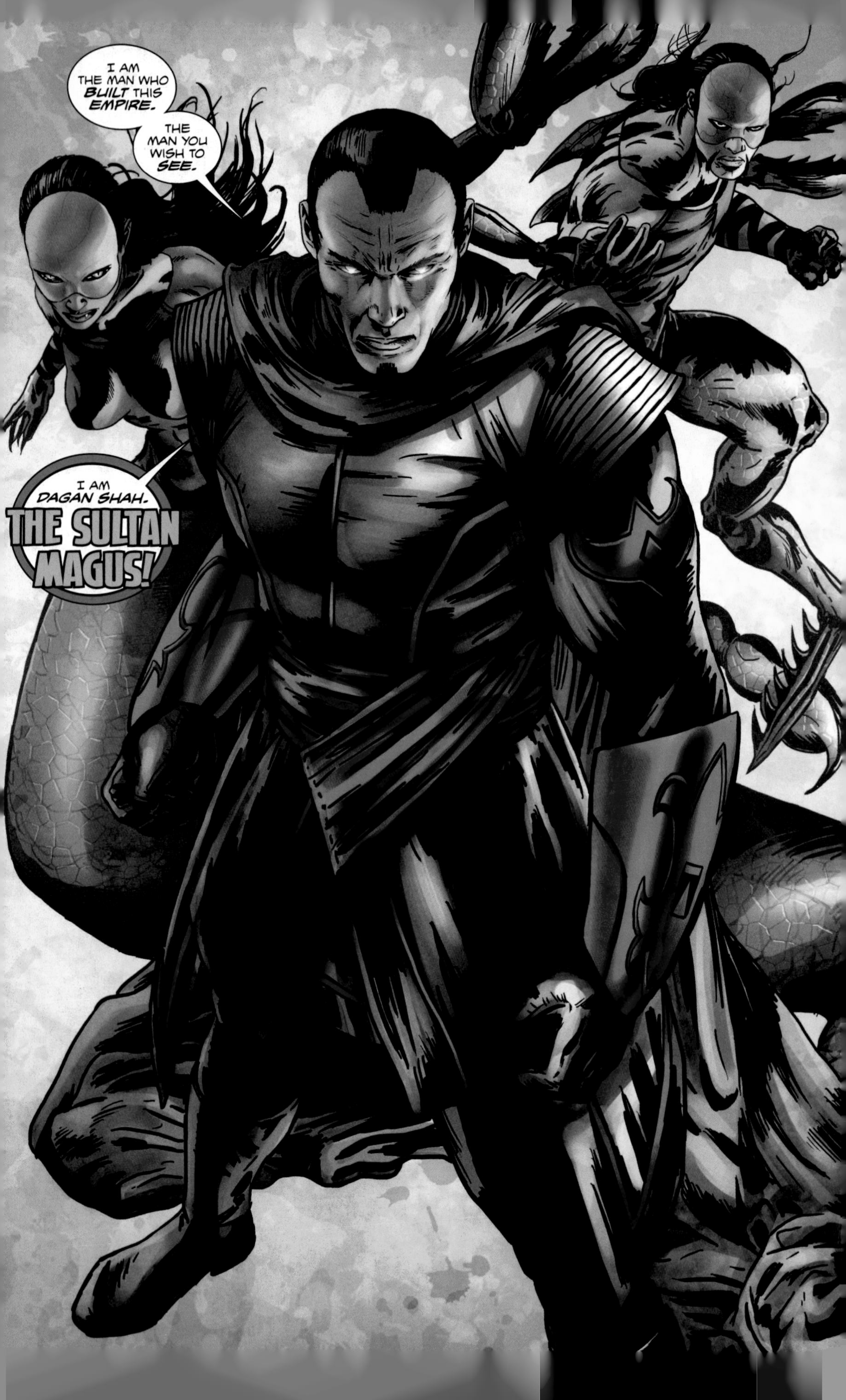
I AM THE MAN WHO BUILT THIS EMPIRE.
THE MAN YOU WISH TO SEE.
I AM DAGAN SHAH. THE SULTAN MAGUS!

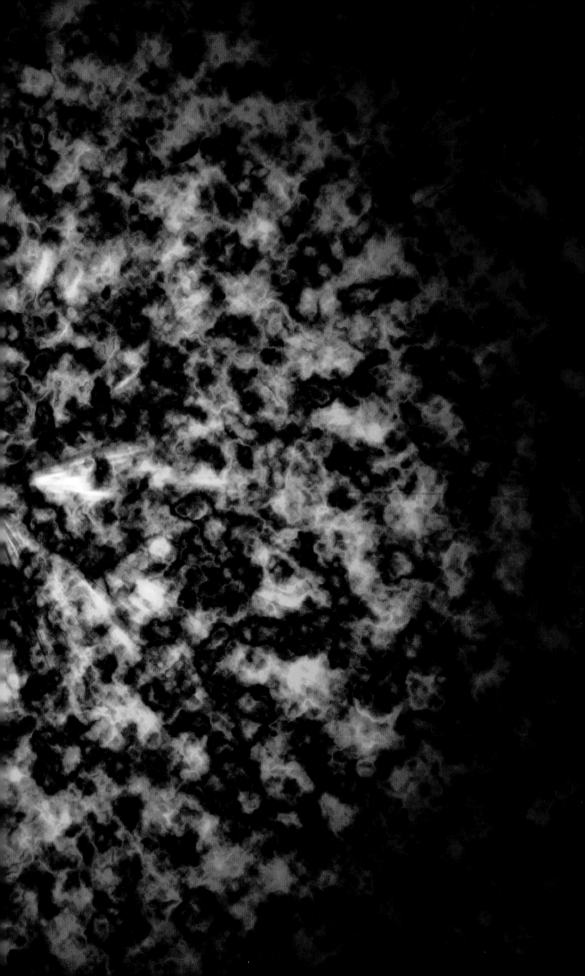

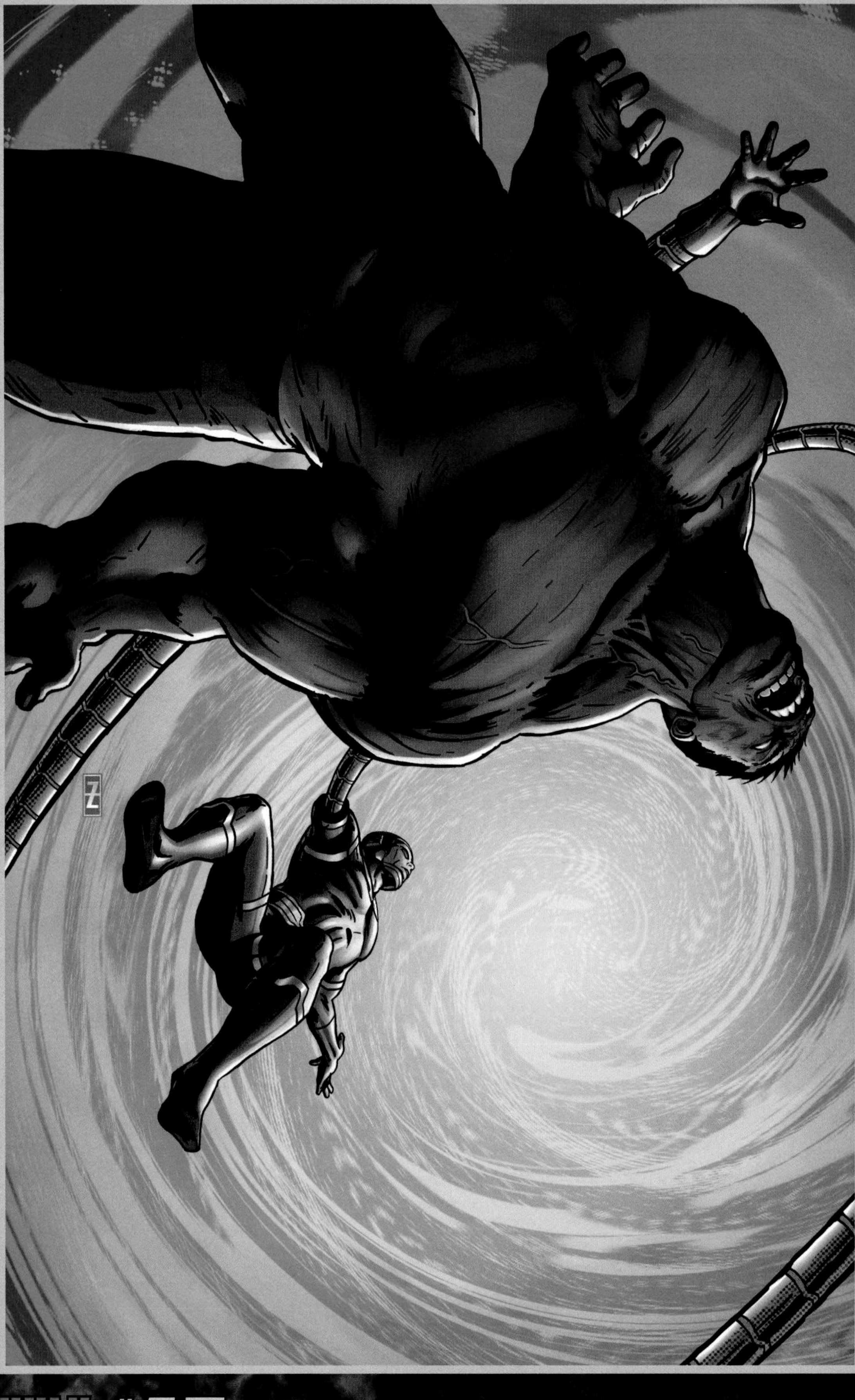

HULK #45

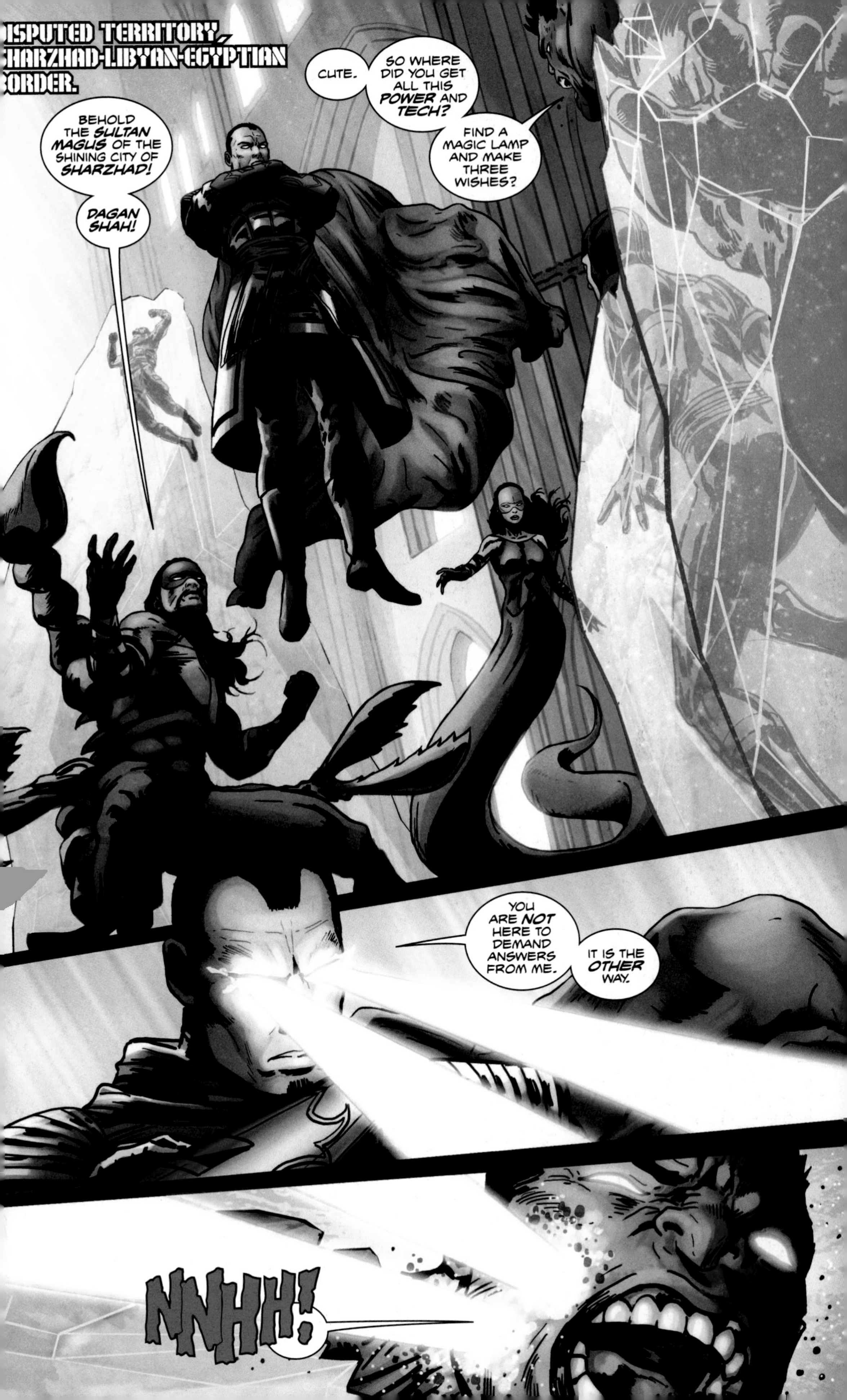

ISPUTED TERRITORY, HARZHAD-LIBYAN-EGYPTIAN ORDER.
CUTE.
SO WHERE DID YOU GET ALL THIS POWER AND TECH?
FIND A MAGIC LAMP AND MAKE THREE WISHES?
BEHOLD THE SULTAN MAGUS OF THE SHINING CITY OF SHARZHAD!
DAGAN SHAH!
YOU ARE NOT HERE TO DEMAND ANSWERS FROM ME.
IT IS THE OTHER WAY.
NNHH!

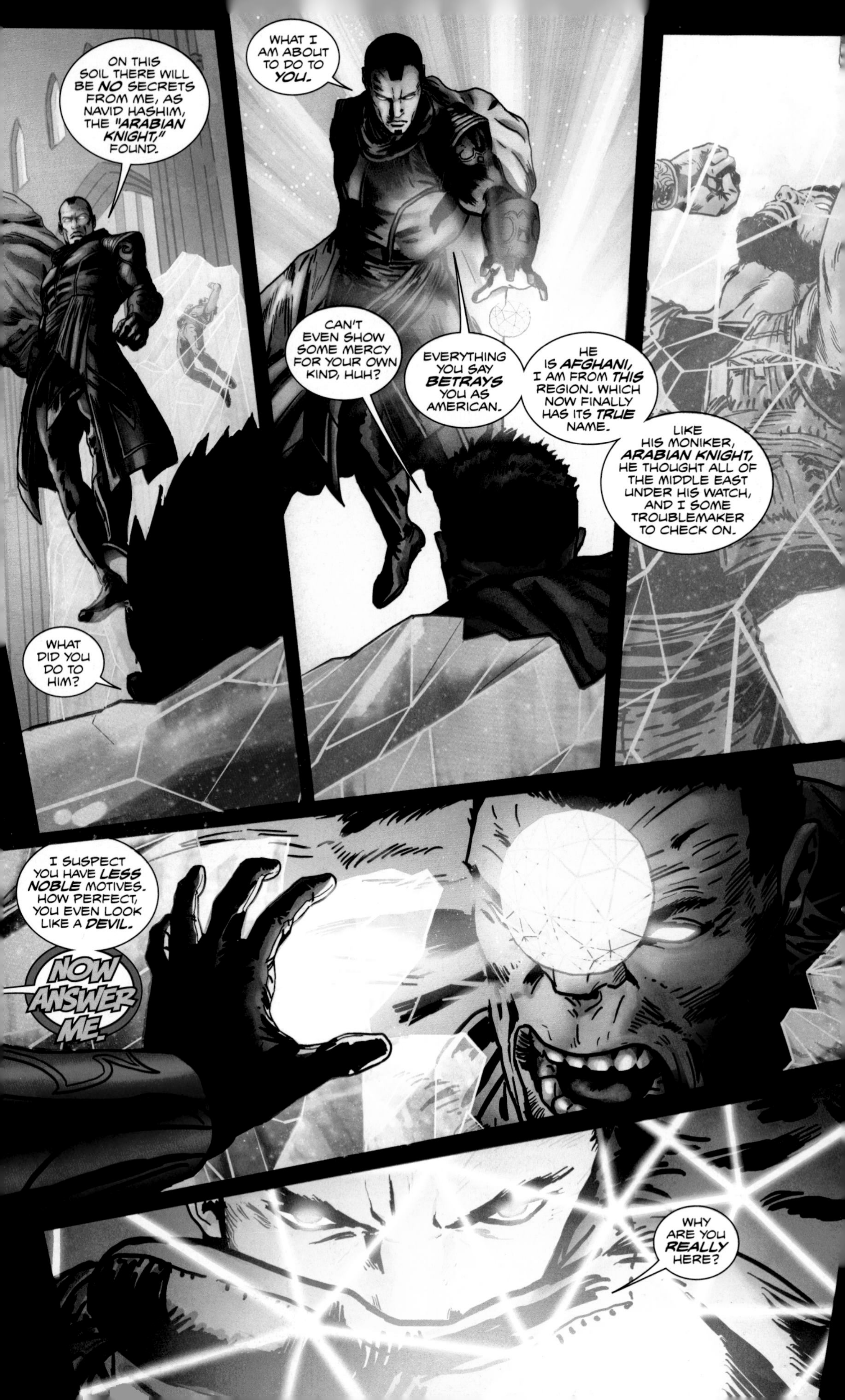
ON THIS SOIL THERE WILL BE NO SECRETS FROM ME, AS NAVID HASHIM, THE "ARABIAN KNIGHT," FOUND.
WHAT DID YOU DO TO HIM?
WHAT I AM ABOUT TO DO TO YOU.
CAN'T EVEN SHOW SOME MERCY FOR YOUR OWN KIND, HUH?
EVERYTHING YOU SAY BETRAYS YOU AS AMERICAN.
HE IS AFGHANI, I AM FROM THIS REGION. WHICH NOW FINALLY HAS ITS TRUE NAME.
LIKE HIS MONIKER, ARABIAN KNIGHT, HE THOUGHT ALL OF THE MIDDLE EAST UNDER HIS WATCH, AND I SOME TROUBLEMAKER TO CHECK ON.
I SUSPECT YOU HAVE LESS NOBLE MOTIVES. HOW PERFECT, YOU EVEN LOOK LIKE A DEVIL.
NOW ANSWER ME.
WHY ARE YOU REALLY HERE?

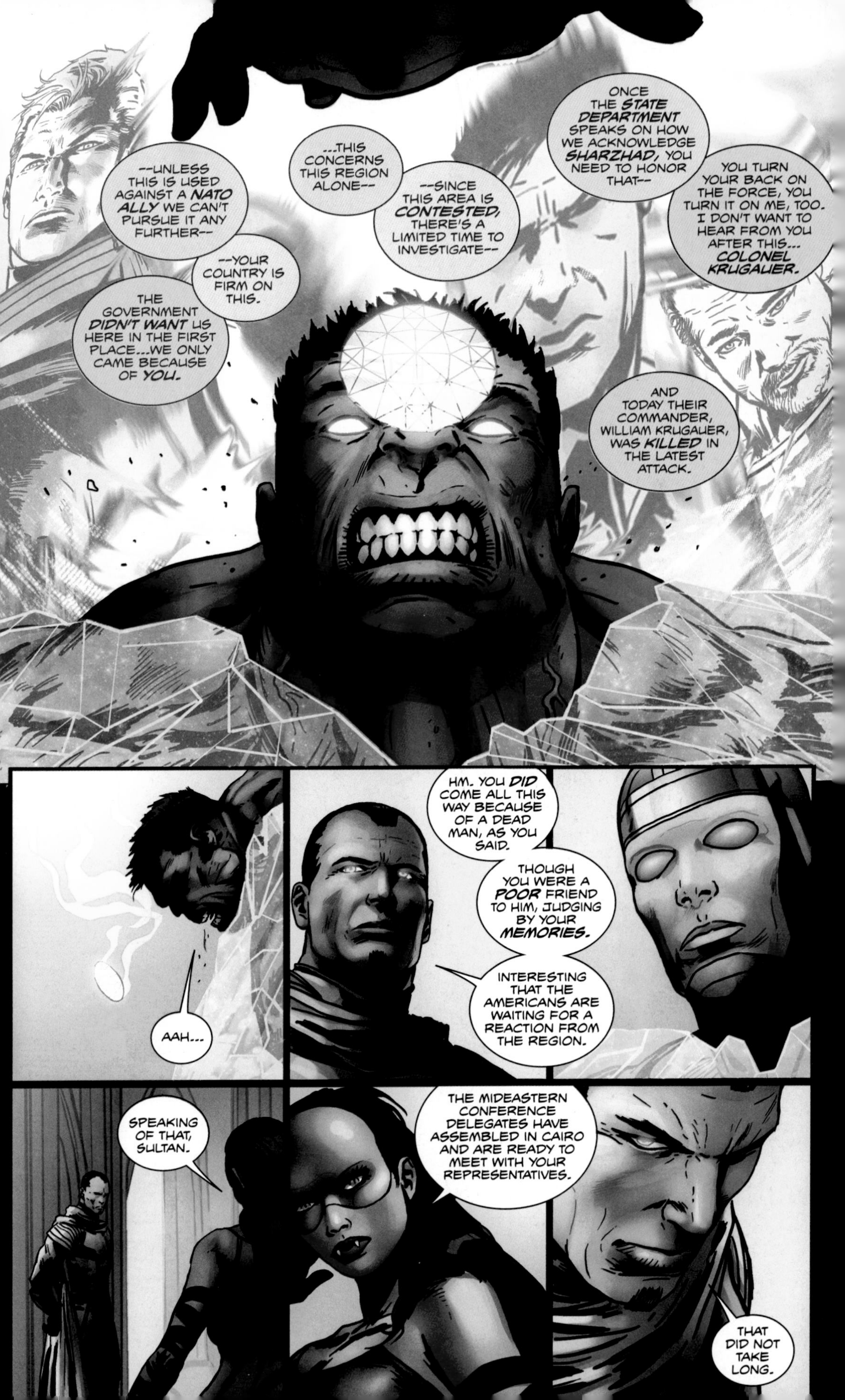
--UNLESS THIS IS USED AGAINST A NATO ALLY WE CAN'T PURSUE IT ANY FURTHER--
--YOUR COUNTRY IS FIRM ON THIS.
THE GOVERNMENT DIDN'T WANT US HERE IN THE FIRST PLACE...WE ONLY CAME BECAUSE OF YOU.
...THIS CONCERNS THIS REGION ALONE--
--SINCE THIS AREA IS CONTESTED, THERE'S A LIMITED TIME TO INVESTIGATE--
ONCE THE STATE DEPARTMENT SPEAKS ON HOW WE ACKNOWLEDGE SHARZHAD, YOU NEED TO HONOR THAT--
YOU TURN YOUR BACK ON THE FORCE, YOU TURN IT ON ME, TOO. I DON'T WANT TO HEAR FROM YOU AFTER THIS... COLONEL KRUGAUER.
AND TODAY THEIR COMMANDER, WILLIAM KRUGAUER, WAS KILLED IN THE LATEST ATTACK.
AAH...
HM. YOU DID COME ALL THIS WAY BECAUSE OF A DEAD MAN, AS YOU SAID.
THOUGH YOU WERE A POOR FRIEND TO HIM, JUDGING BY YOUR MEMORIES.
INTERESTING THAT THE AMERICANS ARE WAITING FOR A REACTION FROM THE REGION.
SPEAKING OF THAT, SULTAN.
THE MIDEASTERN CONFERENCE DELEGATES HAVE ASSEMBLED IN CAIRO AND ARE READY TO MEET WITH YOUR REPRESENTATIVES.
THAT DID NOT TAKE LONG.

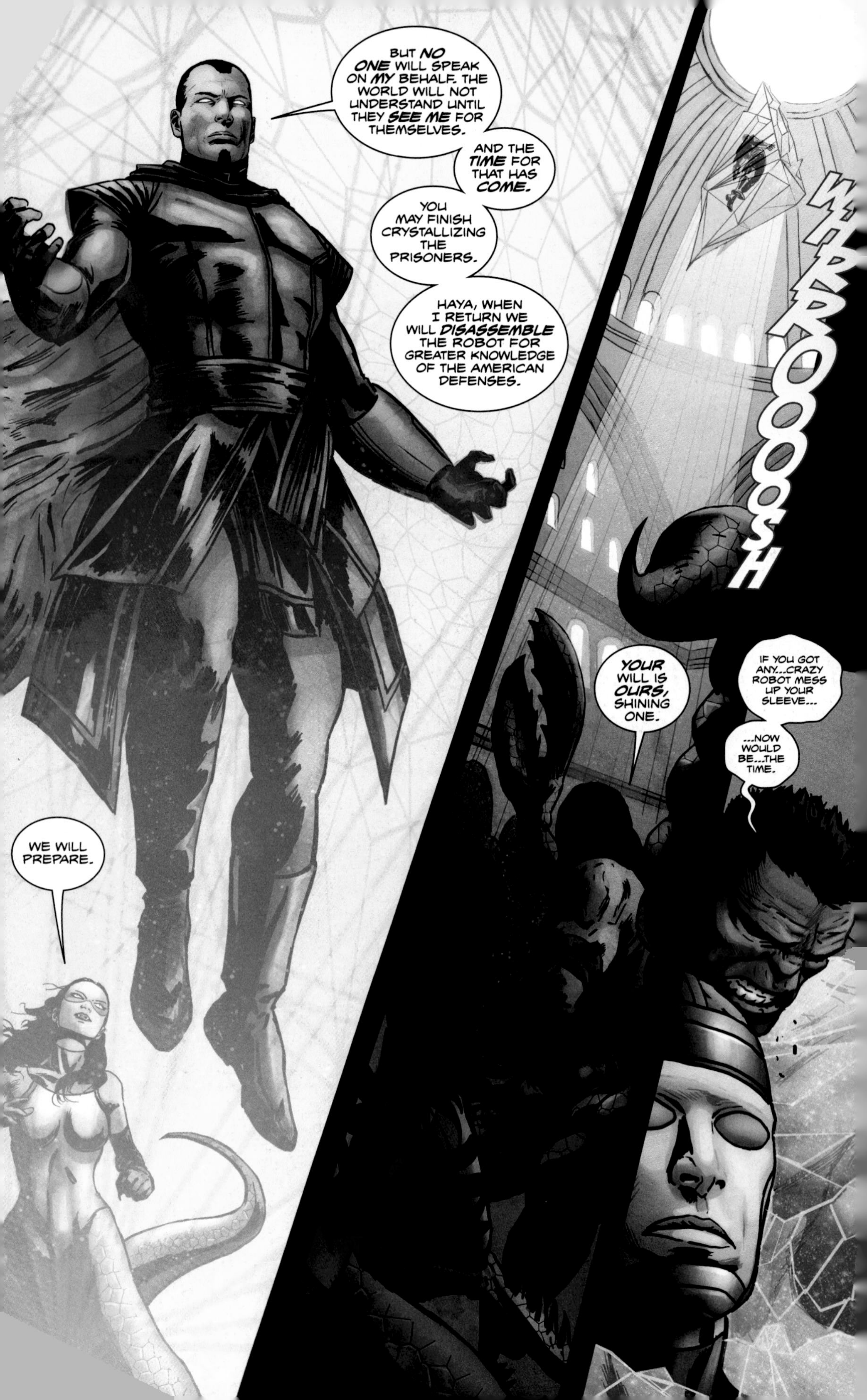
BUT NO ONE WILL SPEAK ON MY BEHALF. THE WORLD WILL NOT UNDERSTAND UNTIL THEY SEE ME FOR THEMSELVES.
AND THE TIME FOR THAT HAS COME.
YOU MAY FINISH CRYSTALLIZING THE PRISONERS.
HAYA, WHEN I RETURN WE WILL DISASSEMBLE THE ROBOT FOR GREATER KNOWLEDGE OF THE AMERICAN DEFENSES.
WE WILL PREPARE.
WHROOOOOSH
YOUR WILL IS OURS, SHINING ONE.
IF YOU GOT ANY...CRAZY ROBOT MESS UP YOUR SLEEVE...
...NOW WOULD BE...THE TIME.

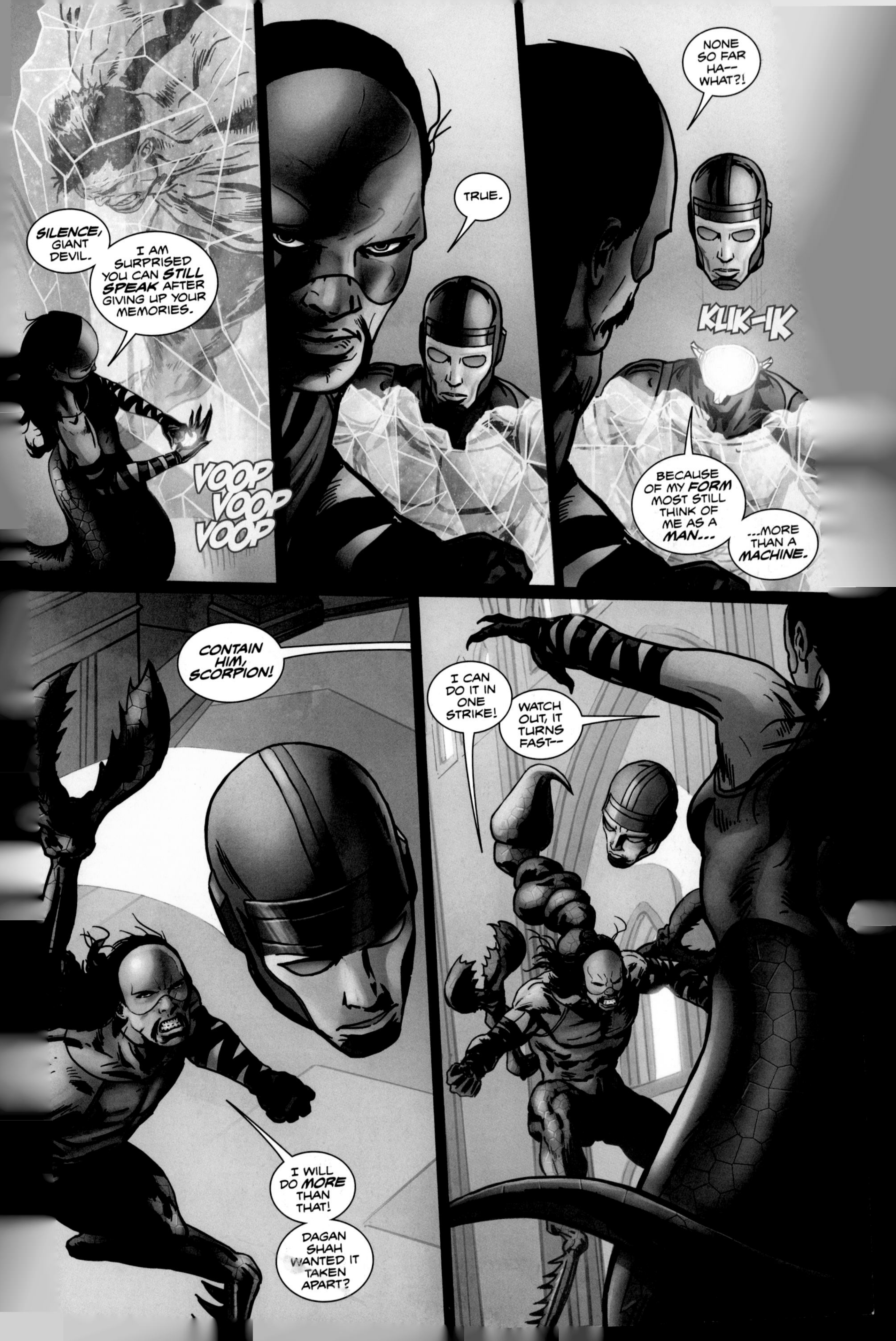
SILENCE, GIANT DEVIL.
I AM SURPRISED YOU CAN STILL SPEAK AFTER GIVING UP YOUR MEMORIES.
VOOP VOOP VOOP
TRUE.
NONE SO FAR HA-- WHAT?!
KLIK-IK
BECAUSE OF MY FORM MOST STILL THINK OF ME AS A MAN...
...MORE THAN A MACHINE.
CONTAIN HIM, SCORPION!
I WILL DO MORE THAN THAT!
DAGAN SHAH WANTED IT TAKEN APART?
I CAN DO IT IN ONE STRIKE!
WATCH OUT, IT TURNS FAST--

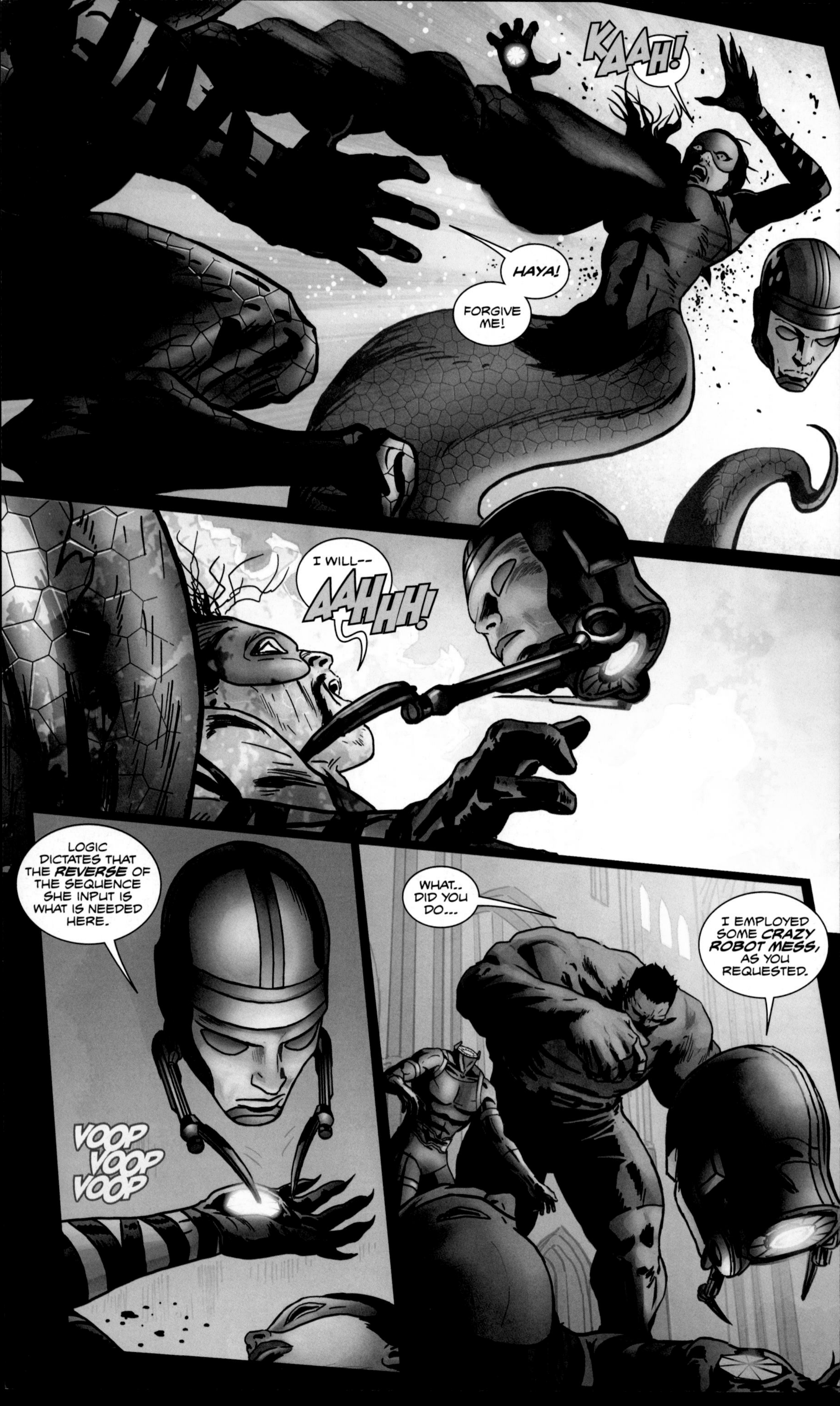

KAAH!
HAYA!
FORGIVE ME!
I WILL--
AAHHH!
LOGIC DICTATES THAT THE REVERSE OF THE SEQUENCE SHE INPUT IS WHAT IS NEEDED HERE.
VOOP VOOP VOOP
WHAT.. DID YOU DO...
I EMPLOYED SOME CRAZY ROBOT MESS, AS YOU REQUESTED.

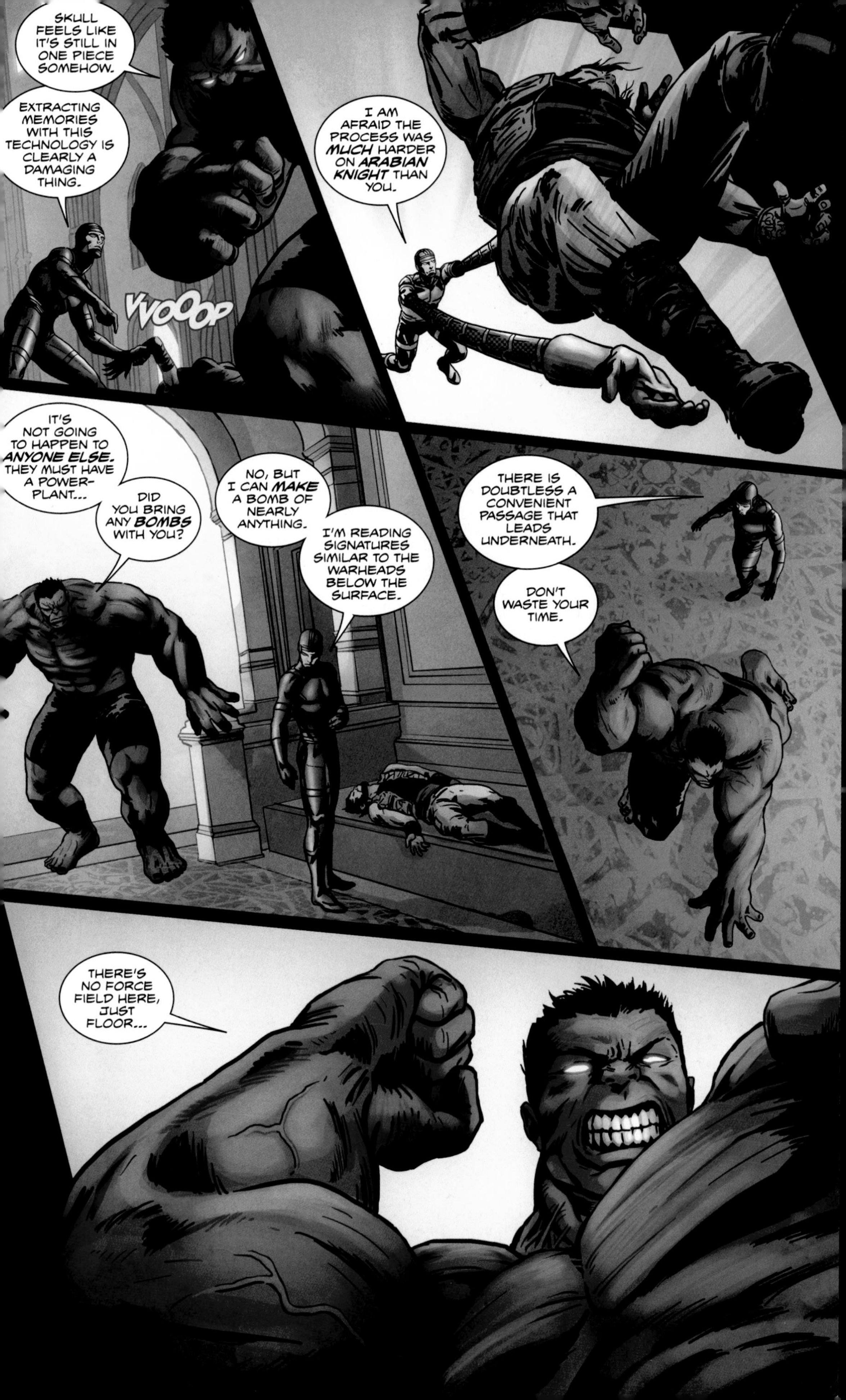
SKULL FEELS LIKE IT'S STILL IN ONE PIECE SOMEHOW.
EXTRACTING MEMORIES WITH THIS TECHNOLOGY IS CLEARLY A DAMAGING THING.
VVOOOP
I AM AFRAID THE PROCESS WAS MUCH HARDER ON ARABIAN KNIGHT THAN YOU.
IT'S NOT GOING TO HAPPEN TO ANYONE ELSE. THEY MUST HAVE A POWER-PLANT...
DID YOU BRING ANY BOMBS WITH YOU?
NO, BUT I CAN MAKE A BOMB OF NEARLY ANYTHING.
I'M READING SIGNATURES SIMILAR TO THE WARHEADS BELOW THE SURFACE.
THERE IS DOUBTLESS A CONVENIENT PASSAGE THAT LEADS UNDERNEATH.
DON'T WASTE YOUR TIME.
THERE'S NO FORCE FIELD HERE, JUST FLOOR...

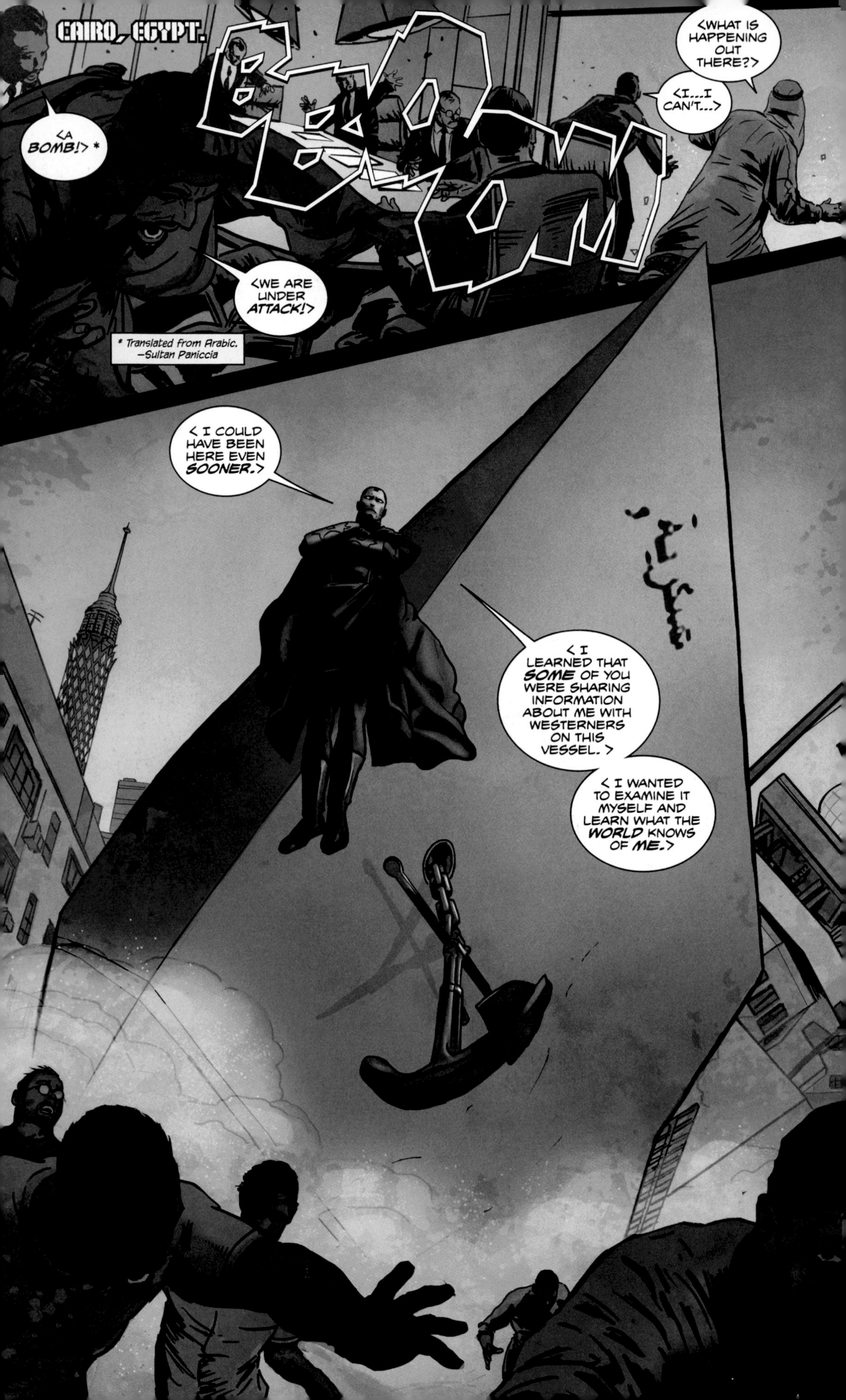
CAIRO, EGYPT.
<A BOMB!> *
<WE ARE UNDER ATTACK!>
<WHAT IS HAPPENING OUT THERE?>
<I...I CAN'T...>
* Translated from Arabic. —Sultan Paniccia
< I COULD HAVE BEEN HERE EVEN SOONER.>
< I LEARNED THAT SOME OF YOU WERE SHARING INFORMATION ABOUT ME WITH WESTERNERS ON THIS VESSEL. >
< I WANTED TO EXAMINE IT MYSELF AND LEARN WHAT THE WORLD KNOWS OF ME.>

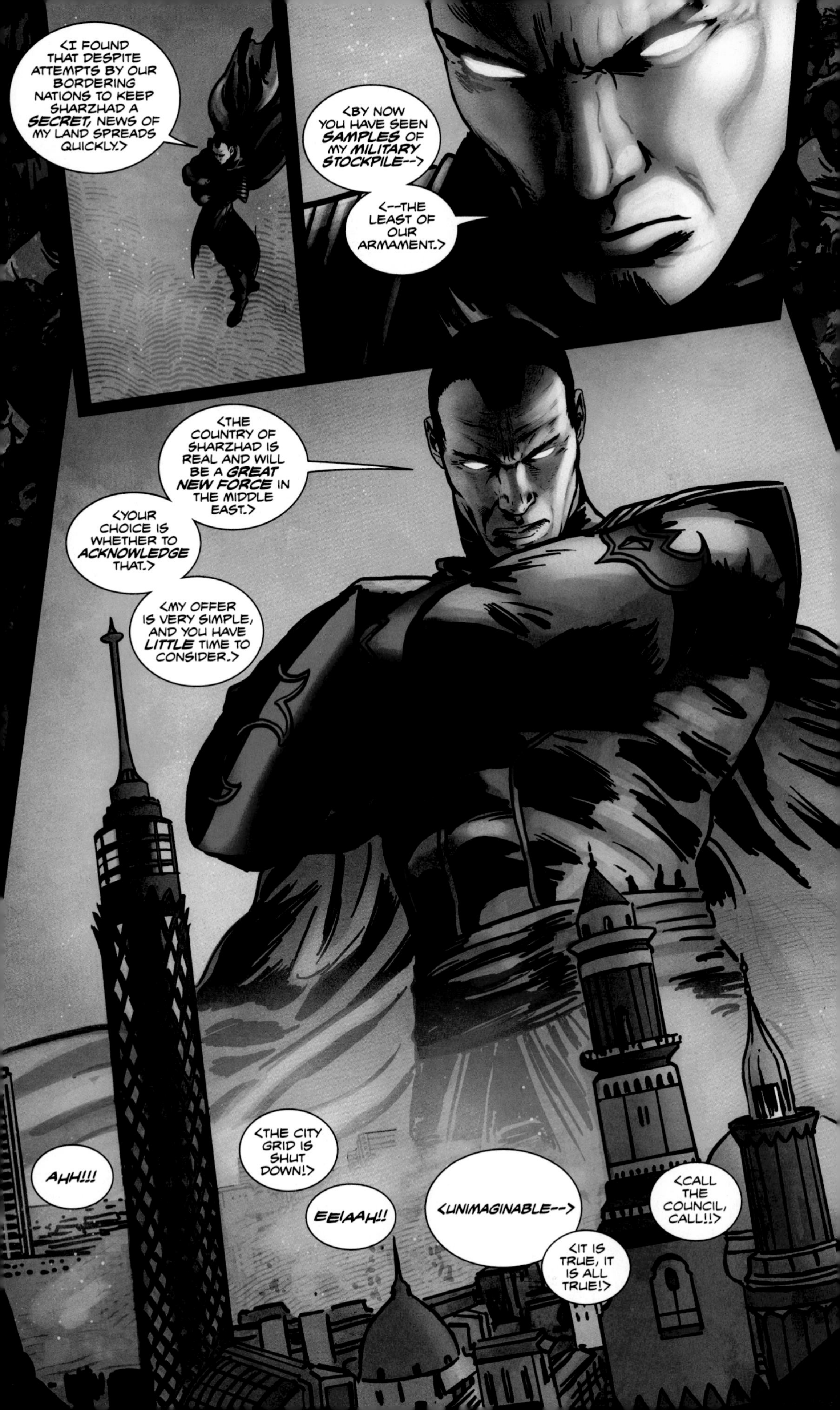
<I FOUND THAT DESPITE ATTEMPTS BY OUR BORDERING NATIONS TO KEEP SHARZHAD A *SECRET,* NEWS OF MY LAND SPREADS QUICKLY.>
<BY NOW YOU HAVE SEEN *SAMPLES* OF MY *MILITARY STOCKPILE*-->
<--THE LEAST OF OUR ARMAMENT.>
<THE COUNTRY OF SHARZHAD IS REAL AND WILL BE A *GREAT NEW FORCE* IN THE MIDDLE EAST.>
<YOUR CHOICE IS WHETHER TO *ACKNOWLEDGE* THAT.>
<MY OFFER IS VERY SIMPLE, AND YOU HAVE *LITTLE* TIME TO CONSIDER.>
AHH!!!
<THE CITY GRID IS SHUT DOWN!>
EEIAAH!!
<UNIMAGINABLE-->
<CALL THE COUNCIL, CALL!!>
<IT IS TRUE, IT IS ALL TRUE!>

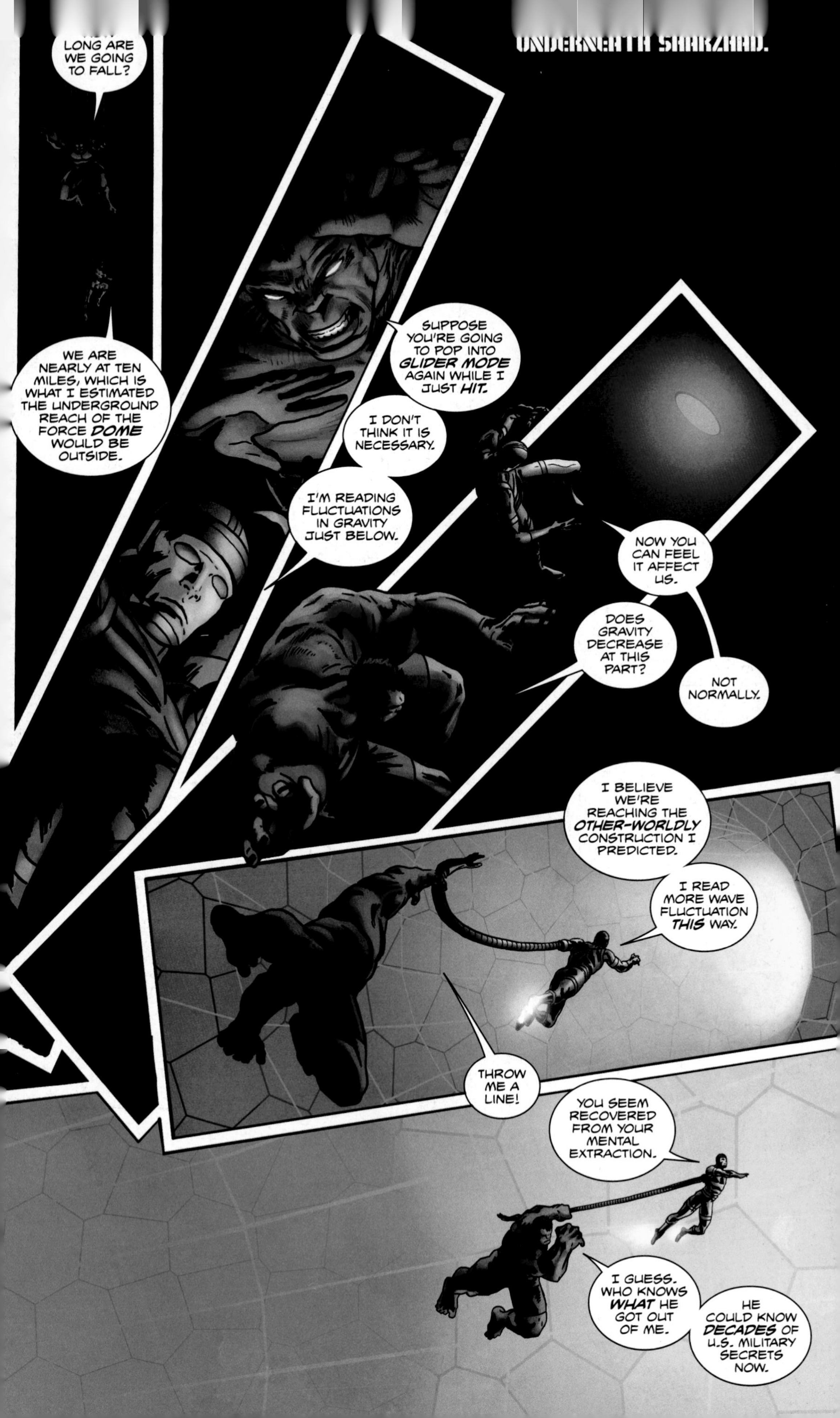
UNDERNEATH SHARZHAD.
LONG ARE WE GOING TO FALL?
WE ARE NEARLY AT TEN MILES, WHICH IS WHAT I ESTIMATED THE UNDERGROUND REACH OF THE FORCE DOME WOULD BE OUTSIDE.
SUPPOSE YOU'RE GOING TO POP INTO GLIDER MODE AGAIN WHILE I JUST HIT.
I DON'T THINK IT IS NECESSARY.
I'M READING FLUCTUATIONS IN GRAVITY JUST BELOW.
NOW YOU CAN FEEL IT AFFECT US.
DOES GRAVITY DECREASE AT THIS PART?
NOT NORMALLY.
I BELIEVE WE'RE REACHING THE OTHER-WORLDLY CONSTRUCTION I PREDICTED.
I READ MORE WAVE FLUCTUATION THIS WAY.
THROW ME A LINE!
YOU SEEM RECOVERED FROM YOUR MENTAL EXTRACTION.
I GUESS. WHO KNOWS WHAT HE GOT OUT OF ME.
HE COULD KNOW DECADES OF U.S. MILITARY SECRETS NOW.

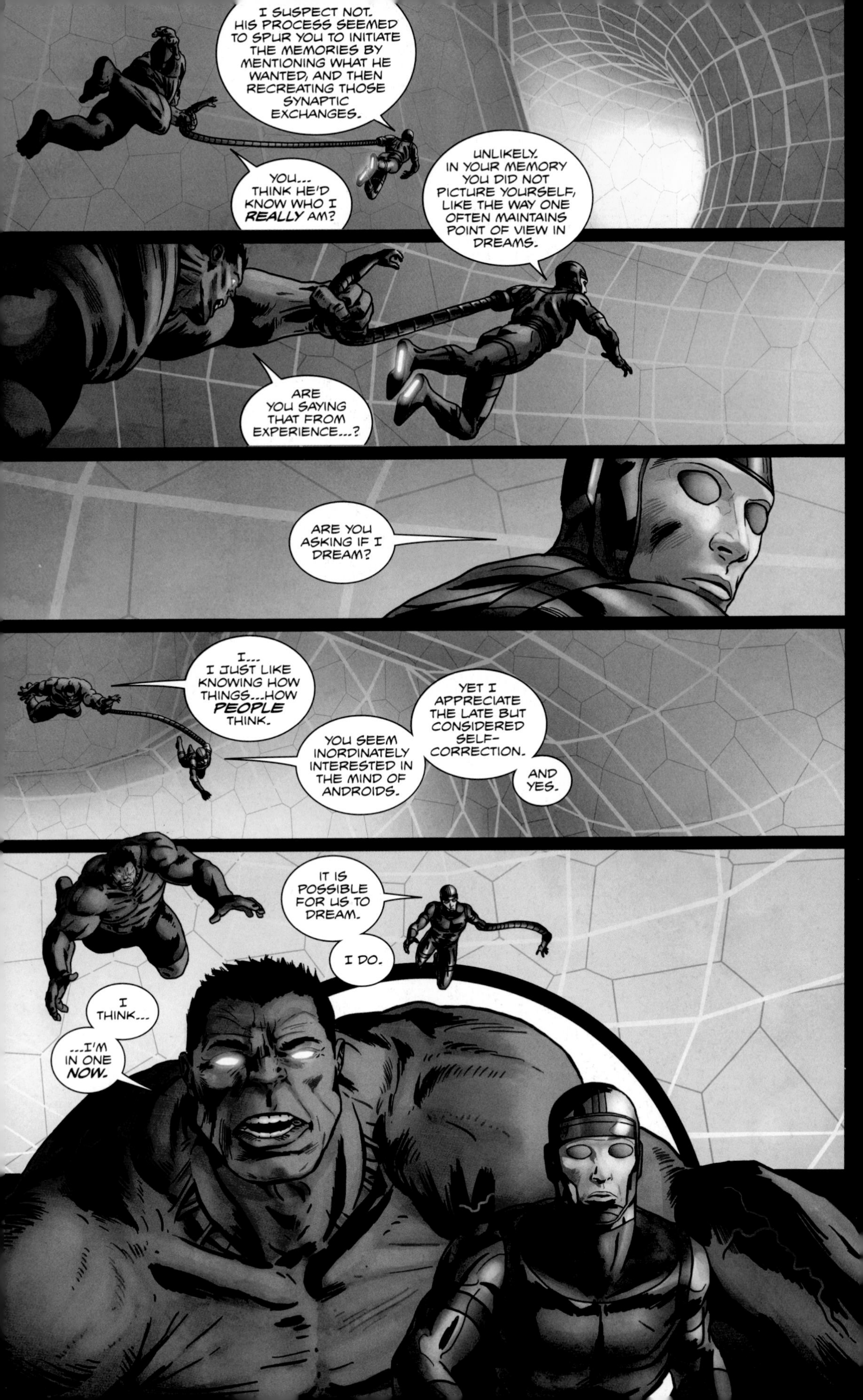
I SUSPECT NOT. HIS PROCESS SEEMED TO SPUR YOU TO INITIATE THE MEMORIES BY MENTIONING WHAT HE WANTED, AND THEN RECREATING THOSE SYNAPTIC EXCHANGES.
YOU... THINK HE'D KNOW WHO I *REALLY* AM?
UNLIKELY. IN YOUR MEMORY YOU DID NOT PICTURE YOURSELF, LIKE THE WAY ONE OFTEN MAINTAINS POINT OF VIEW IN DREAMS.
ARE YOU SAYING THAT FROM EXPERIENCE...?
ARE YOU ASKING IF I DREAM?
I... I JUST LIKE KNOWING HOW THINGS...HOW *PEOPLE* THINK.
YOU SEEM INORDINATELY INTERESTED IN THE MIND OF ANDROIDS.
YET I APPRECIATE THE LATE BUT CONSIDERED SELF-CORRECTION.
AND YES.
IT IS POSSIBLE FOR US TO DREAM.
I DO.
I THINK...
...I'M IN ONE *NOW*.

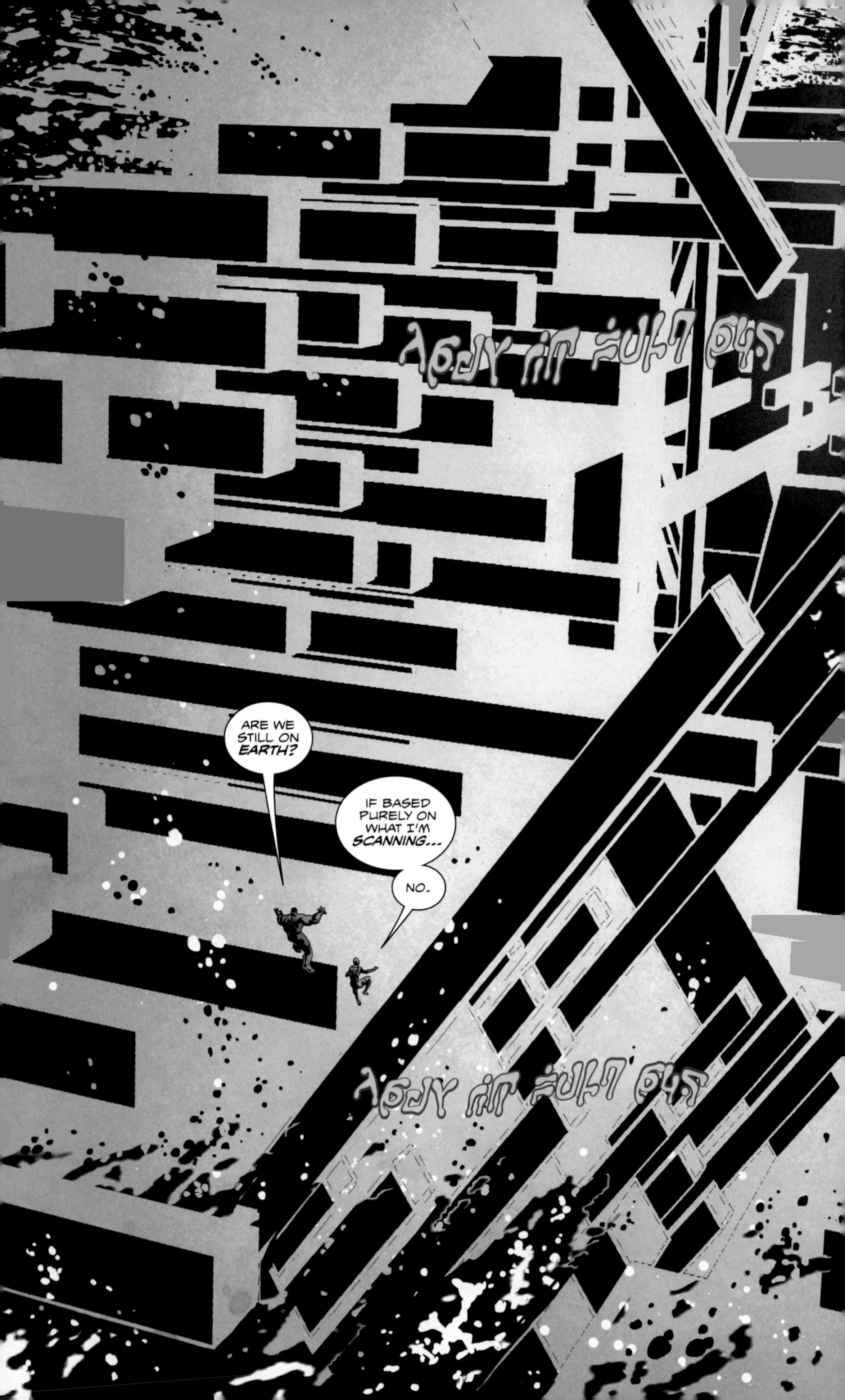
ARE WE STILL ON EARTH?
IF BASED PURELY ON WHAT I'M SCANNING...
NO.

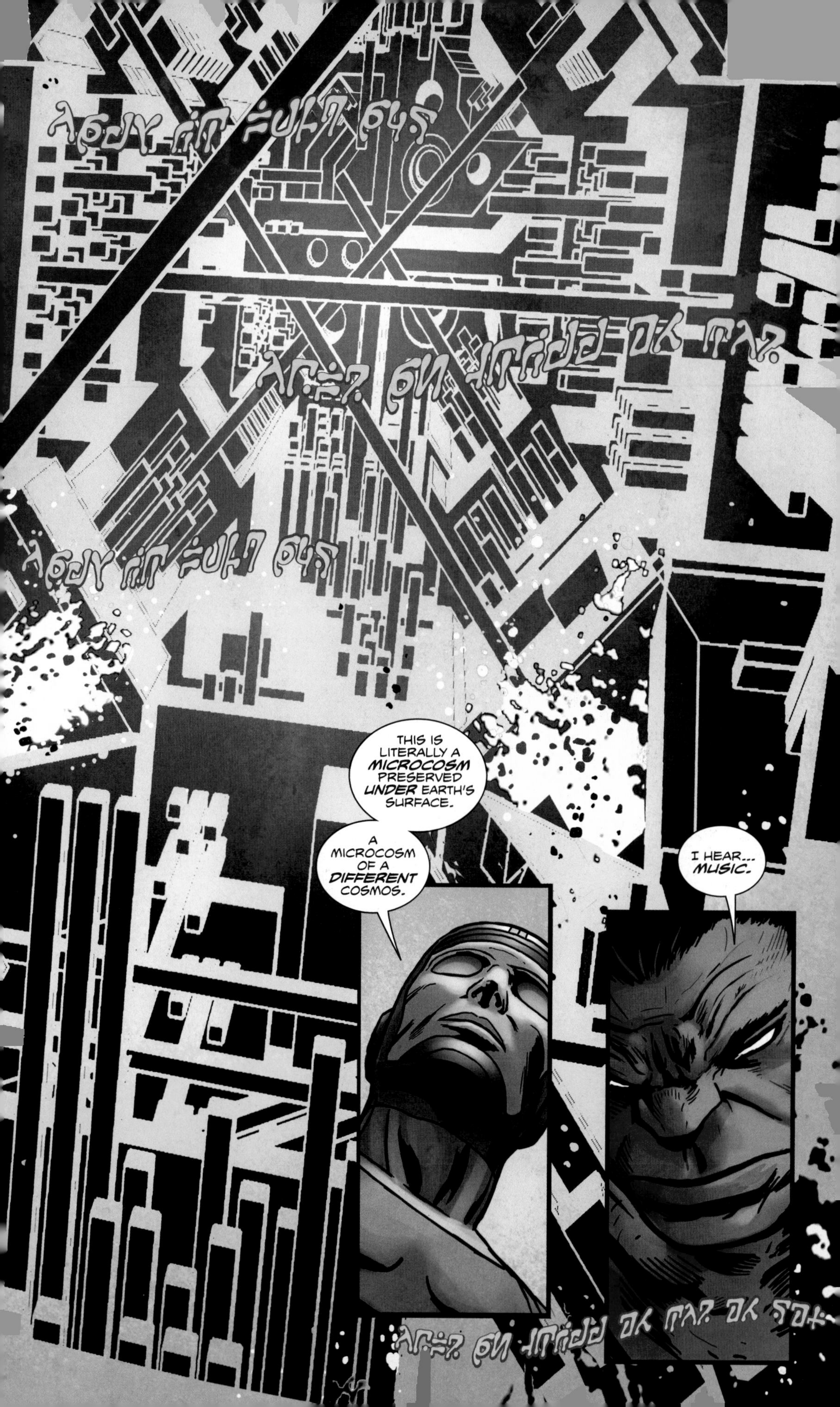
THIS IS LITERALLY A MICROCOSM PRESERVED UNDER EARTH'S SURFACE.
A MICROCOSM OF A DIFFERENT COSMOS.
I HEAR... MUSIC.

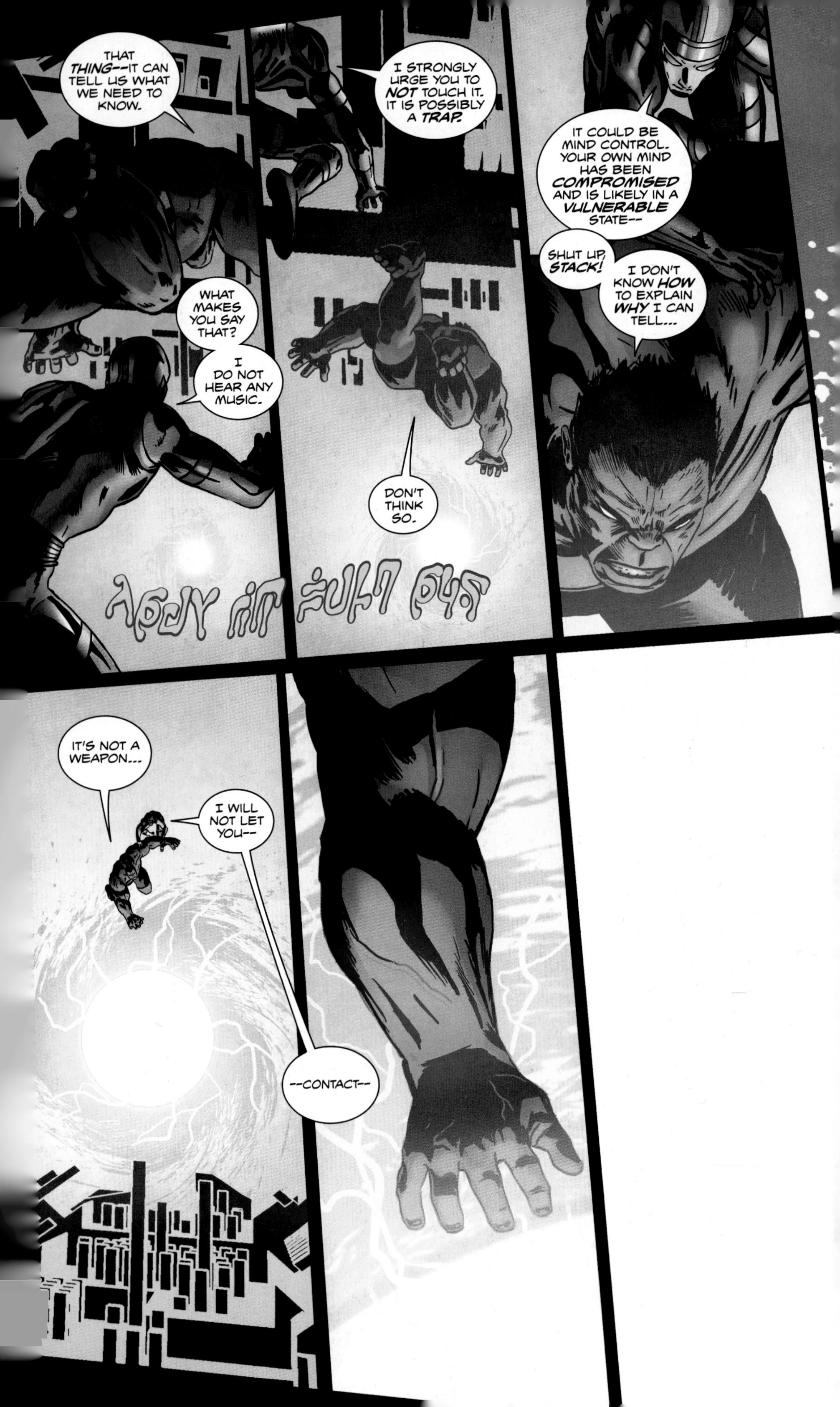
THAT THING--IT CAN TELL US WHAT WE NEED TO KNOW.
WHAT MAKES YOU SAY THAT?
I DO NOT HEAR ANY MUSIC.
I STRONGLY URGE YOU TO NOT TOUCH IT. IT IS POSSIBLY A TRAP.
DON'T THINK SO.
IT COULD BE MIND CONTROL. YOUR OWN MIND HAS BEEN COMPROMISED AND IS LIKELY IN A VULNERABLE STATE--
SHUT UP, STACK!
I DON'T KNOW HOW TO EXPLAIN WHY I CAN TELL...
IT'S NOT A WEAPON...
I WILL NOT LET YOU--
--CONTACT--

ΛΛΖΙ ΨͰ... IS THE COSMORECEPTOR OF THE RIGELLIAN SPECIES CONGLOMERATE. THIS POD CONTAINS THE COMPRESSED KNOWLEDGE OF RIGEL AND POWER CELLS TO BEGIN AND MAINTAIN GENERATION.

WHERE **ARE** WE?

WE'VE GONE NOWHERE. I THINK YOU'RE RECEIVING AN INFINITE BROADCAST.

IT IS FOR BIO-ORGANISMS. I CAN ONLY UNDERSTAND IT TRANSMITTED THROUGH YOU.

THIS POD REACHED THIS WORLD 50,000 SOLAR REVOLUTIONS AGO TO PREPARE THIS CHAMBER FOR THE ARRIVAL OF THE STAGE TWO COSMO-LIGAND.

THAT'S IT?

IT SEEMS INFORMATIONAL IN NATURE. TRY ASKING IT A QUESTION.

WHAT WAS STAGE TWO?

THE STAGE TWO COSMO-LIGAND CONTAINED 10 MILLION BLASTOCYSTS CHOSEN FOR COLONIZATION.

THIS PROCESS HAS BEEN INITIATED FOR 100 COMPATIBLE PLANETS THROUGHOUT THE EDZAR GALAXY TO ENSURE CONTINUATION OF THE RIGEL SUPERSOCIETY.

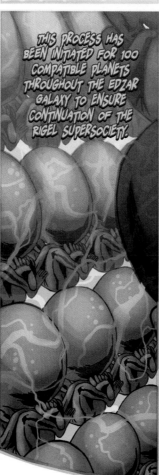

SO THEY **WERE** COLONIZING.

THEIR CIVILIZATION HAD LIKELY NOT DEVELOPED FASTER-THAN-LIGHTSPEED TRAVEL AT THE TIME, SO THEY DEVELOPED A LONGFORM METHOD.

AS WE KNOW, THE RIGELLIANS TRIED IN PERSON MUCH LATER.

THE POD **REACHED** EARTH. SO WHY ISN'T THE WORLD **RUN** BY RIGELLIANS NOW?

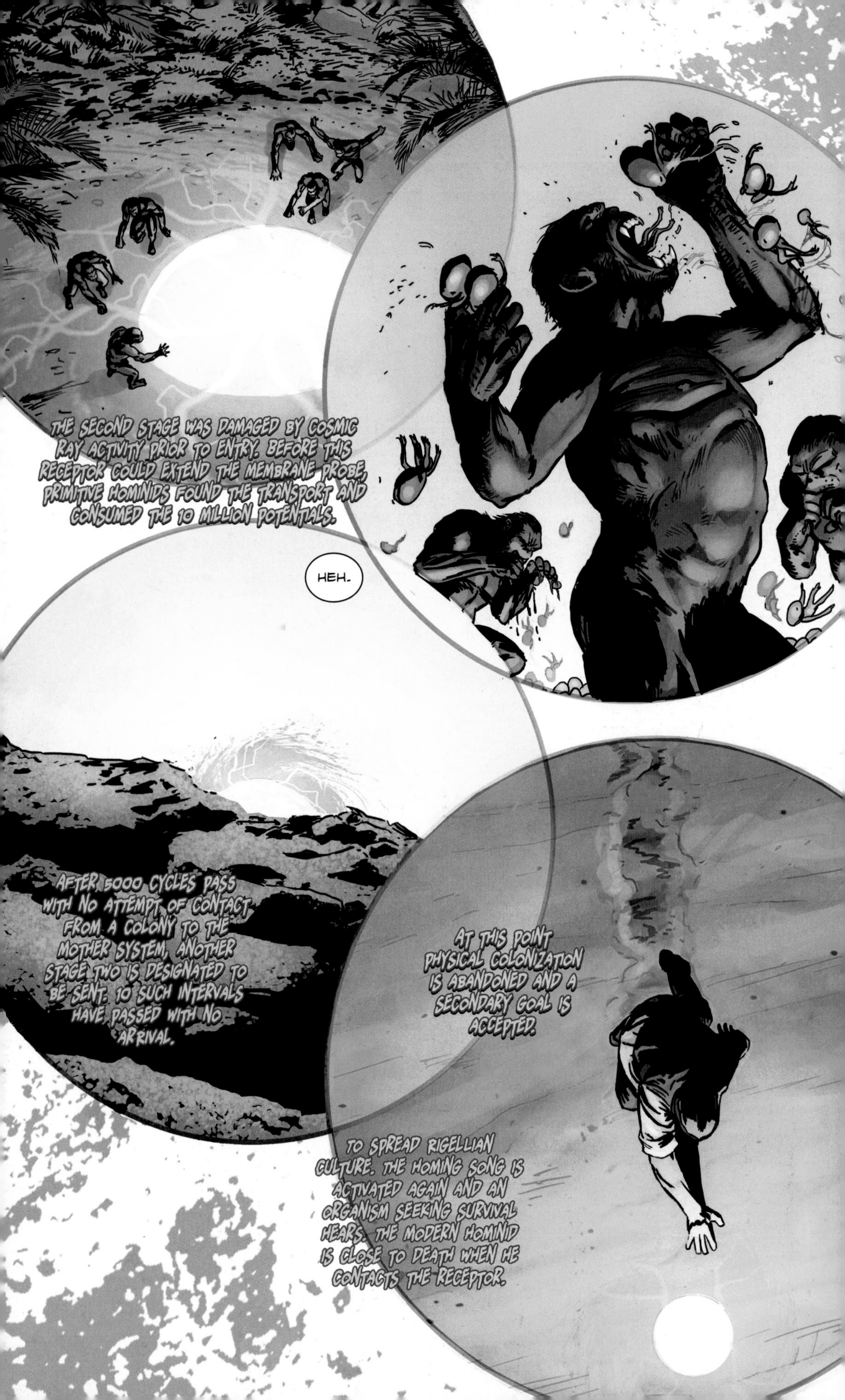
THE SECOND STAGE WAS DAMAGED BY COSMIC RAY ACTIVITY PRIOR TO ENTRY. BEFORE THIS RECEPTOR COULD EXTEND THE MEMBRANE PROBE, PRIMITIVE HOMINIDS FOUND THE TRANSPORT AND CONSUMED THE 10 MILLION POTENTIALS.
HEH.
AFTER 5000 CYCLES PASS WITH NO ATTEMPT OF CONTACT FROM A COLONY TO THE MOTHER SYSTEM, ANOTHER STAGE TWO IS DESIGNATED TO BE SENT. 10 SUCH INTERVALS HAVE PASSED WITH NO ARRIVAL.
AT THIS POINT PHYSICAL COLONIZATION IS ABANDONED AND A SECONDARY GOAL IS ACCEPTED.
TO SPREAD RIGELLIAN CULTURE. THE HOMING SONG IS ACTIVATED AGAIN AND AN ORGANISM SEEKING SURVIVAL HEARS. THE MODERN HOMINID IS CLOSE TO DEATH WHEN HE CONTACTS THE RECEPTOR.

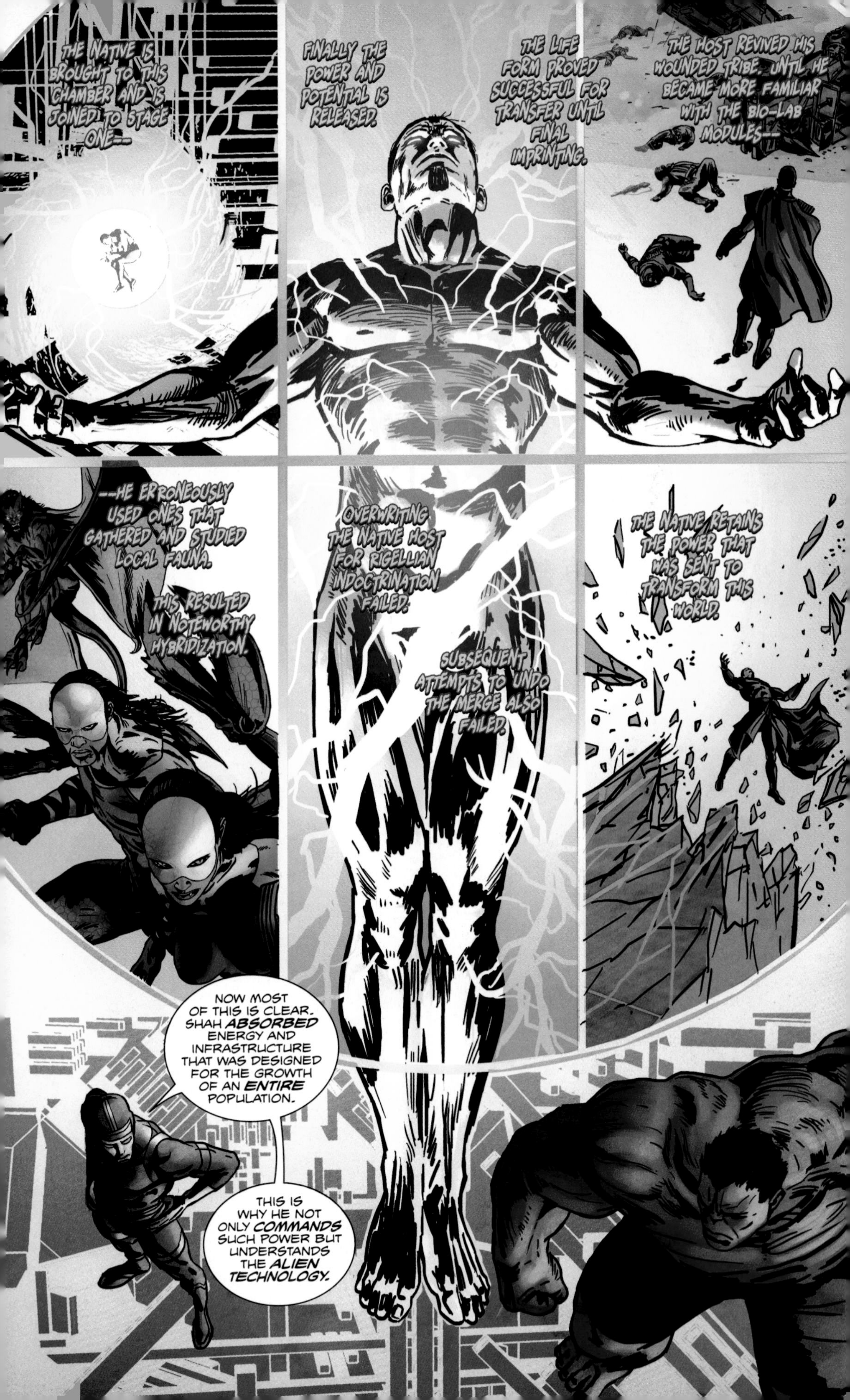
THE NATIVE IS BROUGHT TO THIS CHAMBER AND IS JOINED TO STAGE ONE--
FINALLY THE POWER AND POTENTIAL IS RELEASED.
THE LIFE FORM PROVED SUCCESSFUL FOR TRANSFER UNTIL FINAL IMPRINTING.
THE HOST REVIVED HIS WOUNDED TRIBE. UNTIL HE BECAME MORE FAMILIAR WITH THE BIO-LAB MODULES--
--HE ERRONEOUSLY USED ONES THAT GATHERED AND STUDIED LOCAL FAUNA.
THIS RESULTED IN NOTEWORTHY HYBRIDIZATION.
OVERWRITING THE NATIVE HOST FOR RIGELLIAN INDOCTRINATION FAILED.
SUBSEQUENT ATTEMPTS TO UNDO THE MERGE ALSO FAILED.
THE NATIVE RETAINS THE POWER THAT WAS SENT TO TRANSFORM THIS WORLD.
NOW MOST OF THIS IS CLEAR. SHAH ABSORBED ENERGY AND INFRASTRUCTURE THAT WAS DESIGNED FOR THE GROWTH OF AN ENTIRE POPULATION.
THIS IS WHY HE NOT ONLY COMMANDS SUCH POWER BUT UNDERSTANDS THE ALIEN TECHNOLOGY.

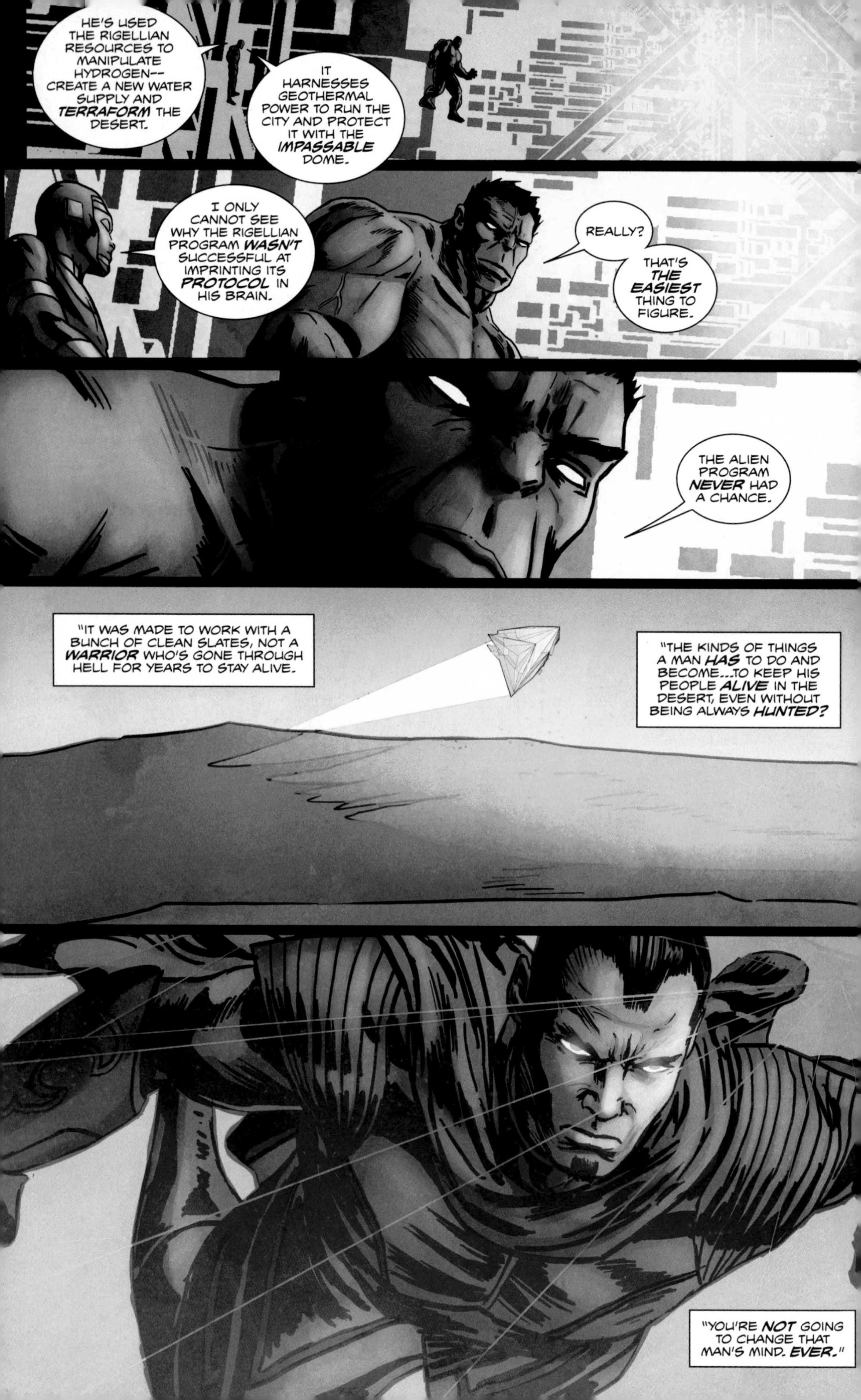
HE'S USED THE RIGELLIAN RESOURCES TO MANIPULATE HYDROGEN-- CREATE A NEW WATER SUPPLY AND TERRAFORM THE DESERT.
IT HARNESSES GEOTHERMAL POWER TO RUN THE CITY AND PROTECT IT WITH THE IMPASSABLE DOME.
I ONLY CANNOT SEE WHY THE RIGELLIAN PROGRAM WASN'T SUCCESSFUL AT IMPRINTING ITS PROTOCOL IN HIS BRAIN.
REALLY?
THAT'S THE EASIEST THING TO FIGURE.
THE ALIEN PROGRAM NEVER HAD A CHANCE.
"IT WAS MADE TO WORK WITH A BUNCH OF CLEAN SLATES, NOT A WARRIOR WHO'S GONE THROUGH HELL FOR YEARS TO STAY ALIVE.
"THE KINDS OF THINGS A MAN HAS TO DO AND BECOME...TO KEEP HIS PEOPLE ALIVE IN THE DESERT, EVEN WITHOUT BEING ALWAYS HUNTED?
"YOU'RE NOT GOING TO CHANGE THAT MAN'S MIND. EVER."

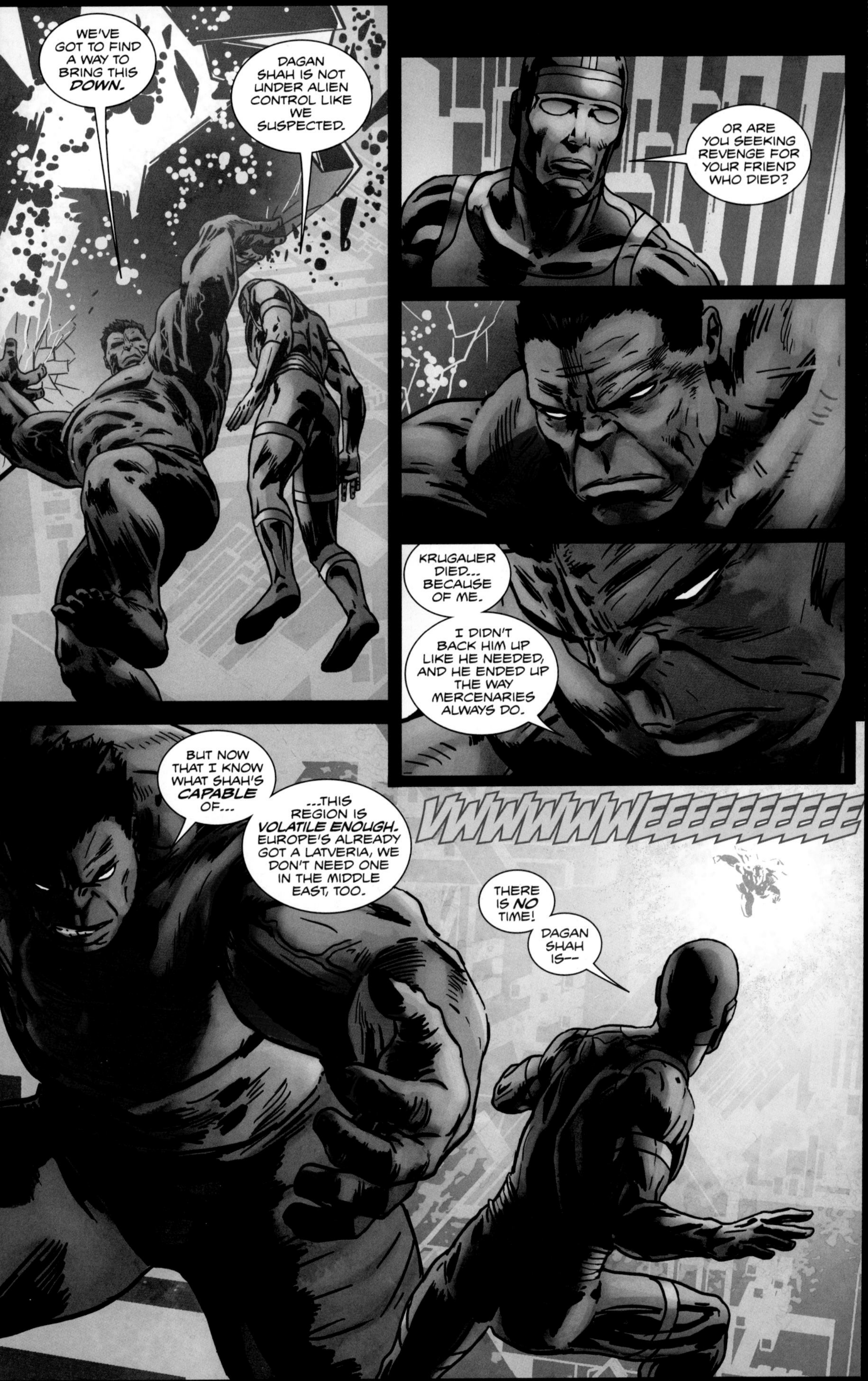
WE'VE GOT TO FIND A WAY TO BRING THIS DOWN.
DAGAN SHAH IS NOT UNDER ALIEN CONTROL LIKE WE SUSPECTED.
OR ARE YOU SEEKING REVENGE FOR YOUR FRIEND WHO DIED?
KRUGAUER DIED... BECAUSE OF ME.
I DIDN'T BACK HIM UP LIKE HE NEEDED, AND HE ENDED UP THE WAY MERCENARIES ALWAYS DO.
BUT NOW THAT I KNOW WHAT SHAH'S CAPABLE OF...
...THIS REGION IS VOLATILE ENOUGH. EUROPE'S ALREADY GOT A LATVERIA, WE DON'T NEED ONE IN THE MIDDLE EAST, TOO.
VWWWWWWEEEEEEEEEE
THERE IS NO TIME!
DAGAN SHAH IS--

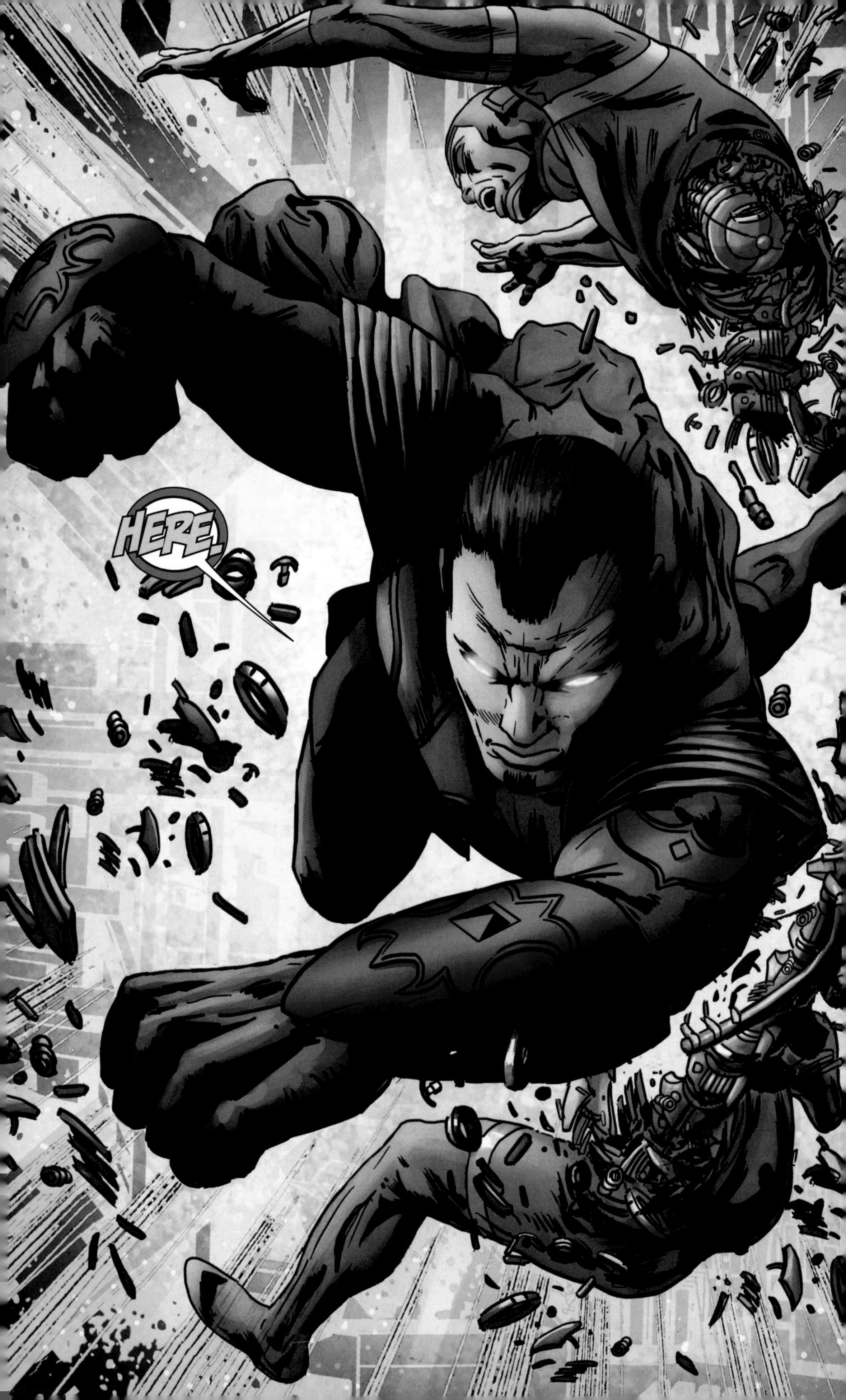
HERE.

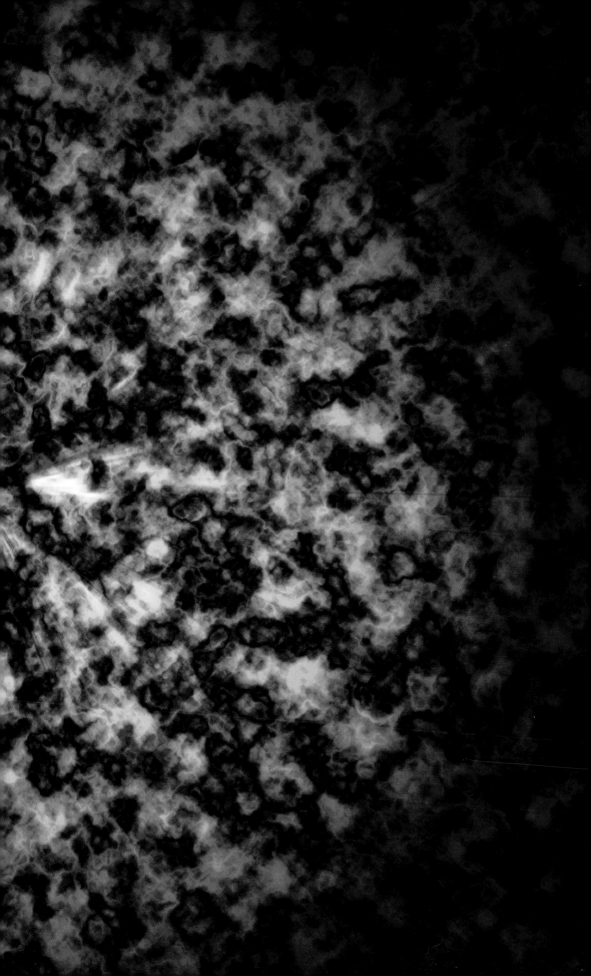

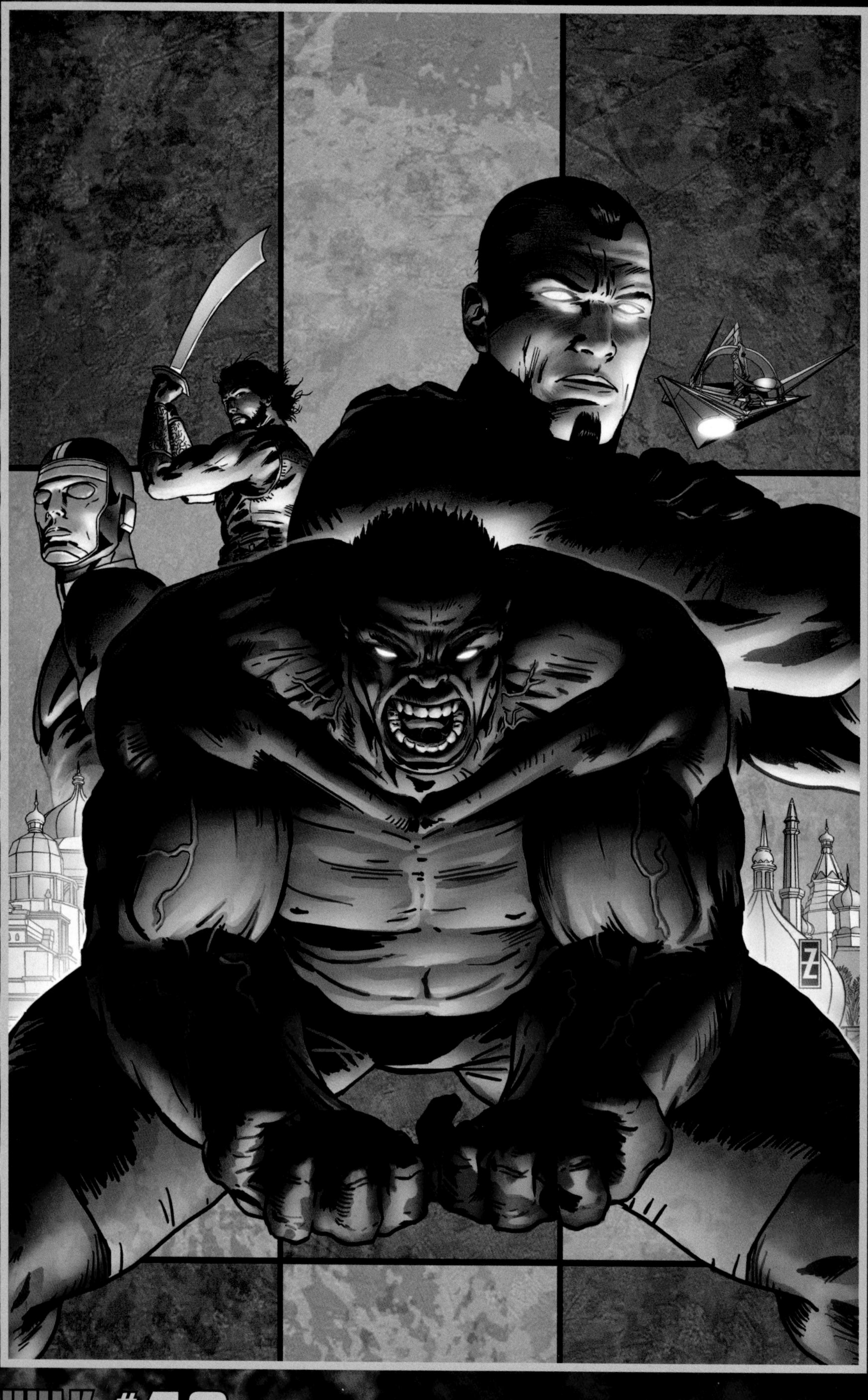
Z

HULK #46

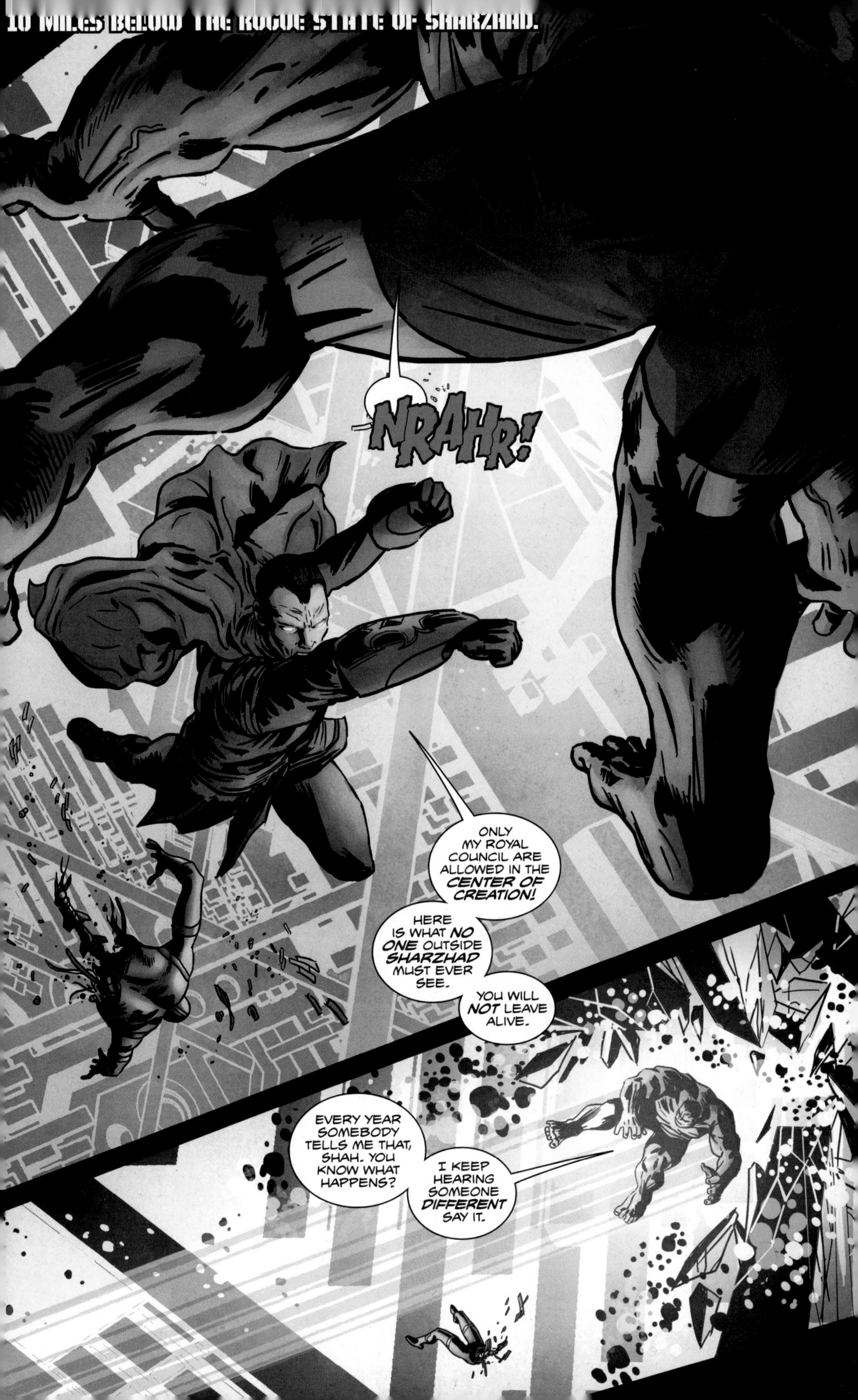

10 MILES BELOW THE ROGUE STATE OF SHARZHAD.
NRAHR!
ONLY MY ROYAL COUNCIL ARE ALLOWED IN THE CENTER OF CREATION!
HERE IS WHAT NO ONE OUTSIDE SHARZHAD MUST EVER SEE.
YOU WILL NOT LEAVE ALIVE.
EVERY YEAR SOMEBODY TELLS ME THAT, SHAH. YOU KNOW WHAT HAPPENS?
I KEEP HEARING SOMEONE DIFFERENT SAY IT.

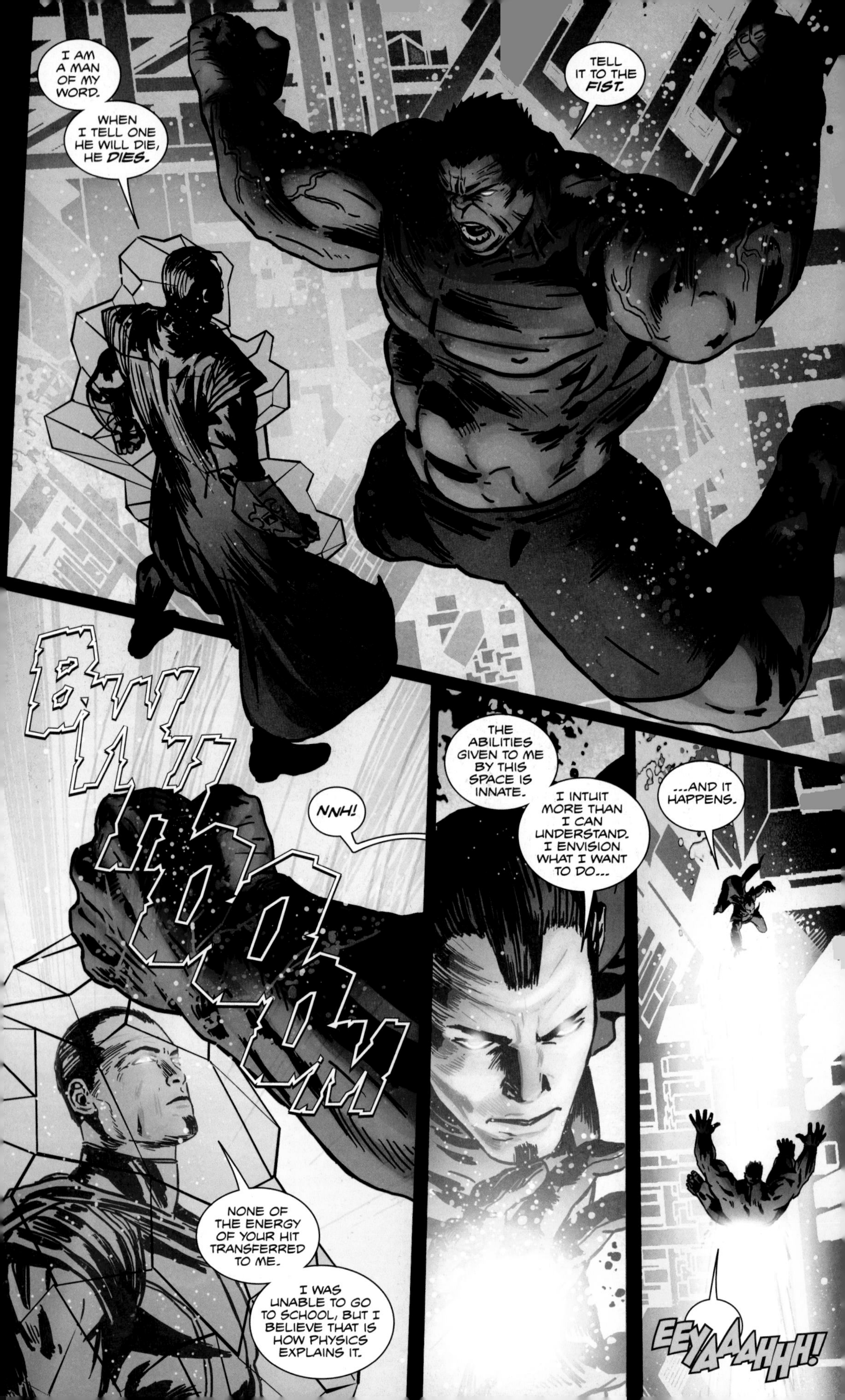
I AM A MAN OF MY WORD.
WHEN I TELL ONE HE WILL DIE, HE DIES.
TELL IT TO THE FIST.
NNH!
THE ABILITIES GIVEN TO ME BY THIS SPACE IS INNATE.
I INTUIT MORE THAN I CAN UNDERSTAND. I ENVISION WHAT I WANT TO DO...
...AND IT HAPPENS.
NONE OF THE ENERGY OF YOUR HIT TRANSFERRED TO ME.
I WAS UNABLE TO GO TO SCHOOL, BUT I BELIEVE THAT IS HOW PHYSICS EXPLAINS IT.
EEYAAAHHH!

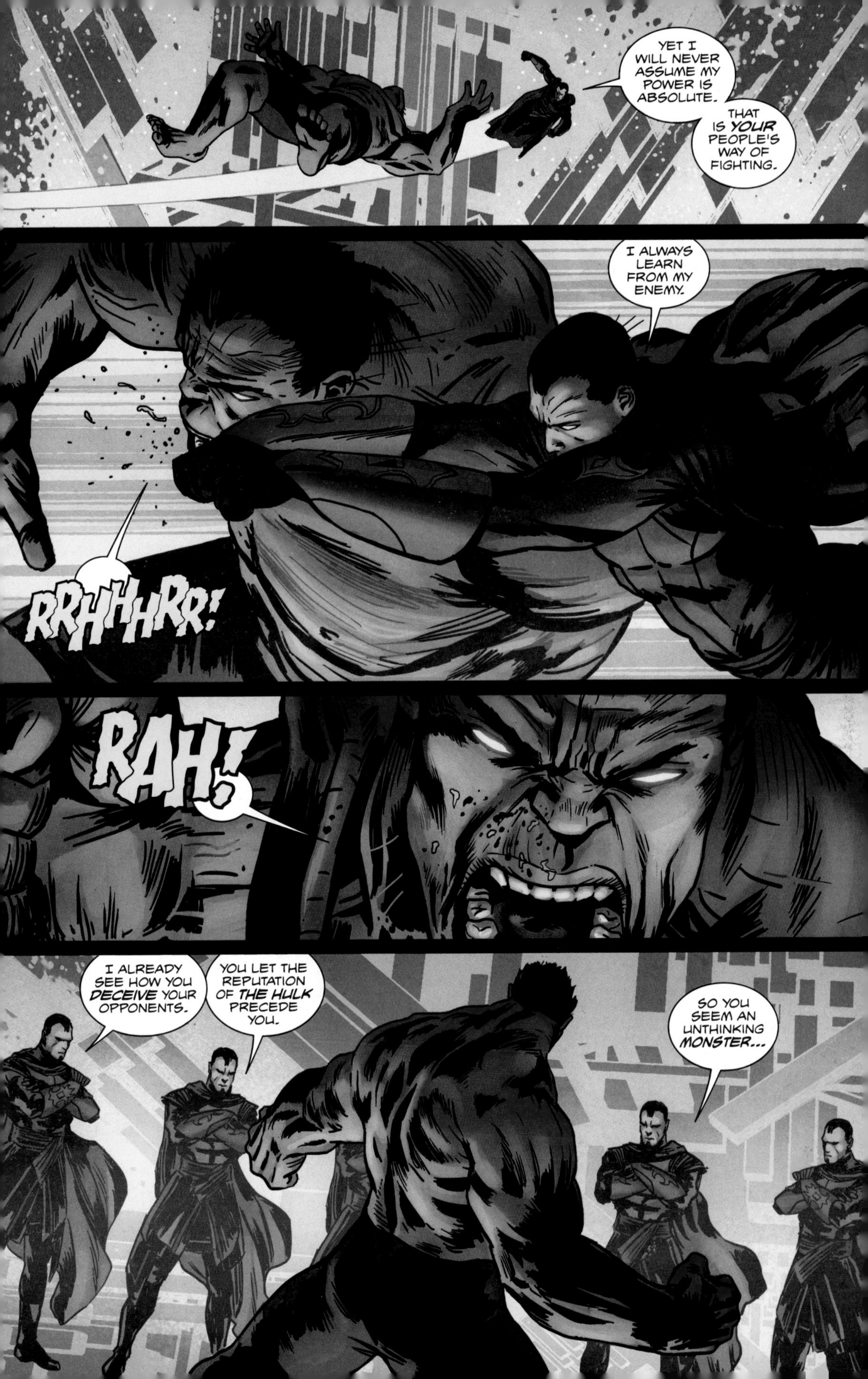
YET I WILL NEVER ASSUME MY POWER IS ABSOLUTE.
THAT IS YOUR PEOPLE'S WAY OF FIGHTING.
I ALWAYS LEARN FROM MY ENEMY.
RRHHHRR!
RAH!
I ALREADY SEE HOW YOU DECEIVE YOUR OPPONENTS.
YOU LET THE REPUTATION OF THE HULK PRECEDE YOU.
SO YOU SEEM AN UNTHINKING MONSTER...

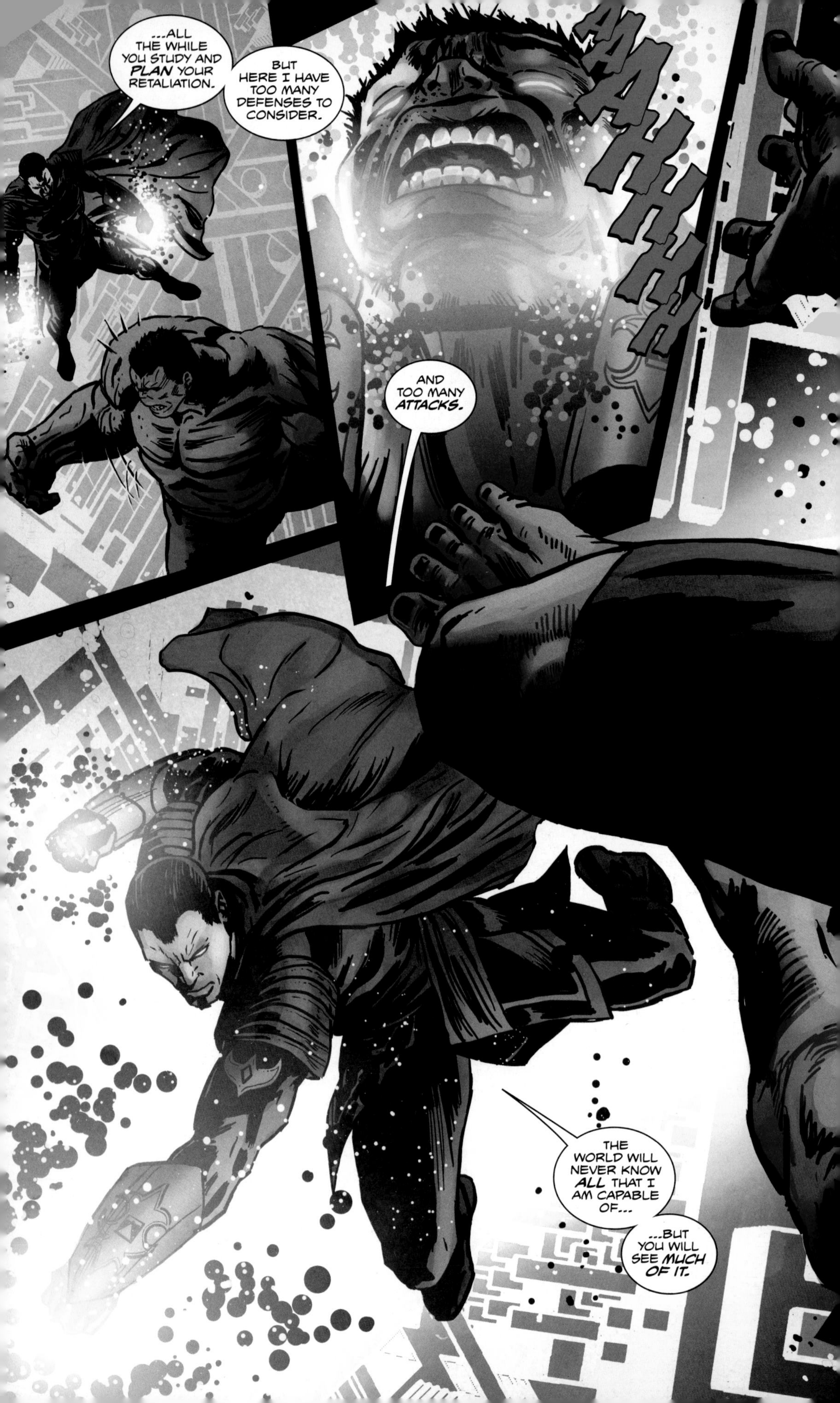

...ALL THE WHILE YOU STUDY AND PLAN YOUR RETALIATION.
BUT HERE I HAVE TOO MANY DEFENSES TO CONSIDER.
AAAHHHHH
AND TOO MANY ATTACKS.
THE WORLD WILL NEVER KNOW ALL THAT I AM CAPABLE OF...
...BUT YOU WILL SEE MUCH OF IT.

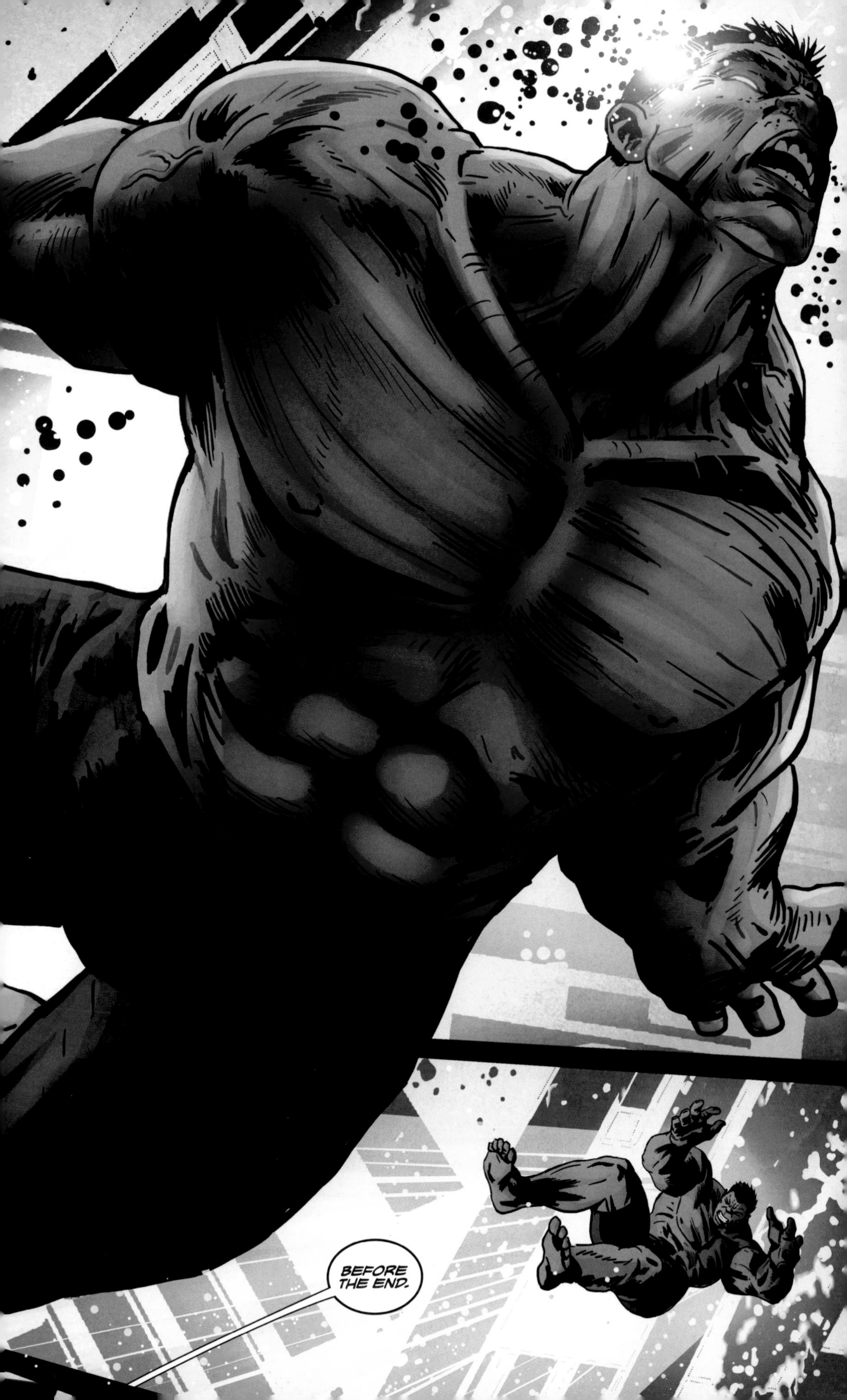
BEFORE THE END.

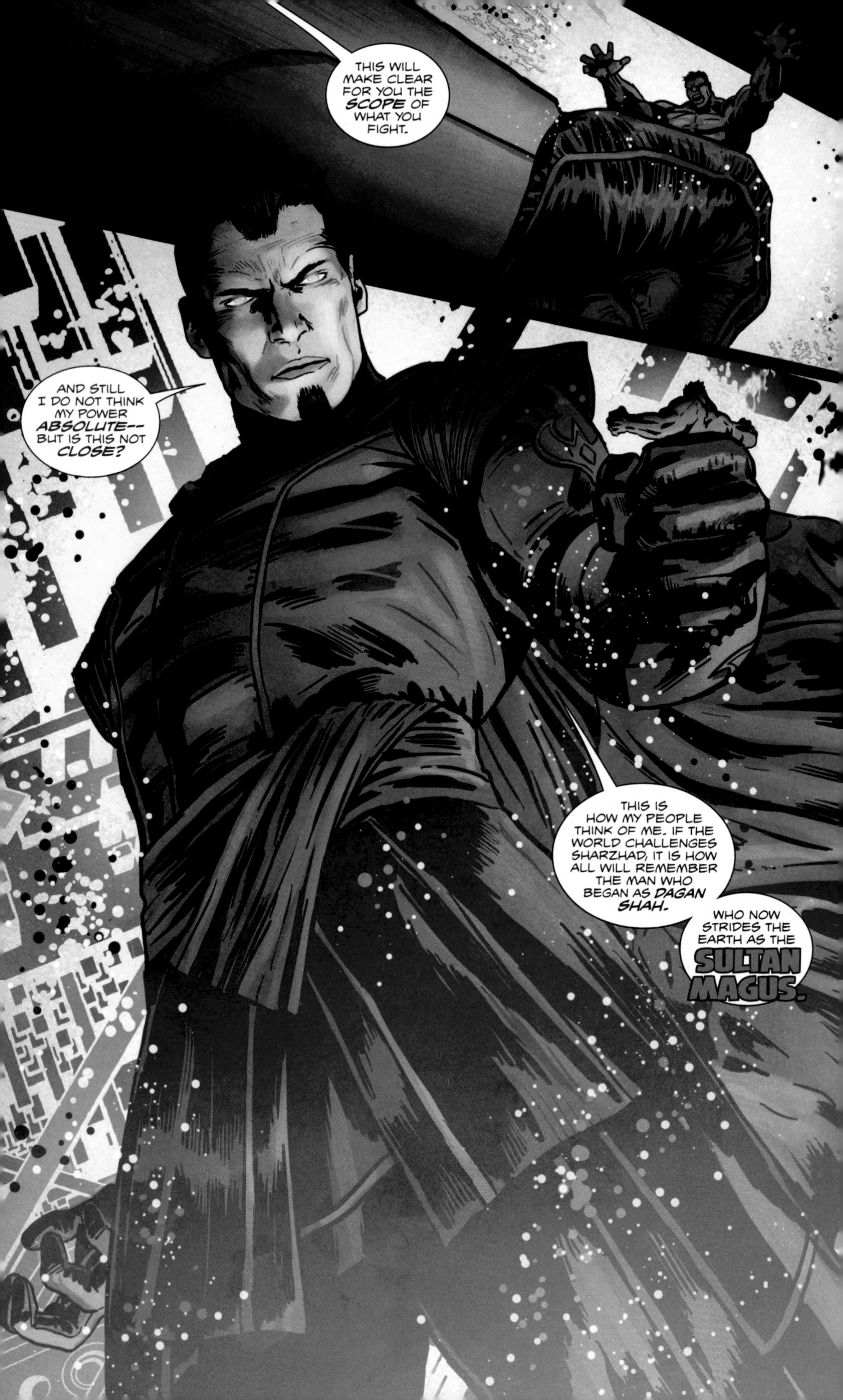
THIS WILL MAKE CLEAR FOR YOU THE SCOPE OF WHAT YOU FIGHT.
AND STILL I DO NOT THINK MY POWER ABSOLUTE-- BUT IS THIS NOT CLOSE?
THIS IS HOW MY PEOPLE THINK OF ME. IF THE WORLD CHALLENGES SHARZHAD, IT IS HOW ALL WILL REMEMBER THE MAN WHO BEGAN AS DAGAN SHAH.
WHO NOW STRIDES THE EARTH AS THE SULTAN MAGUS.

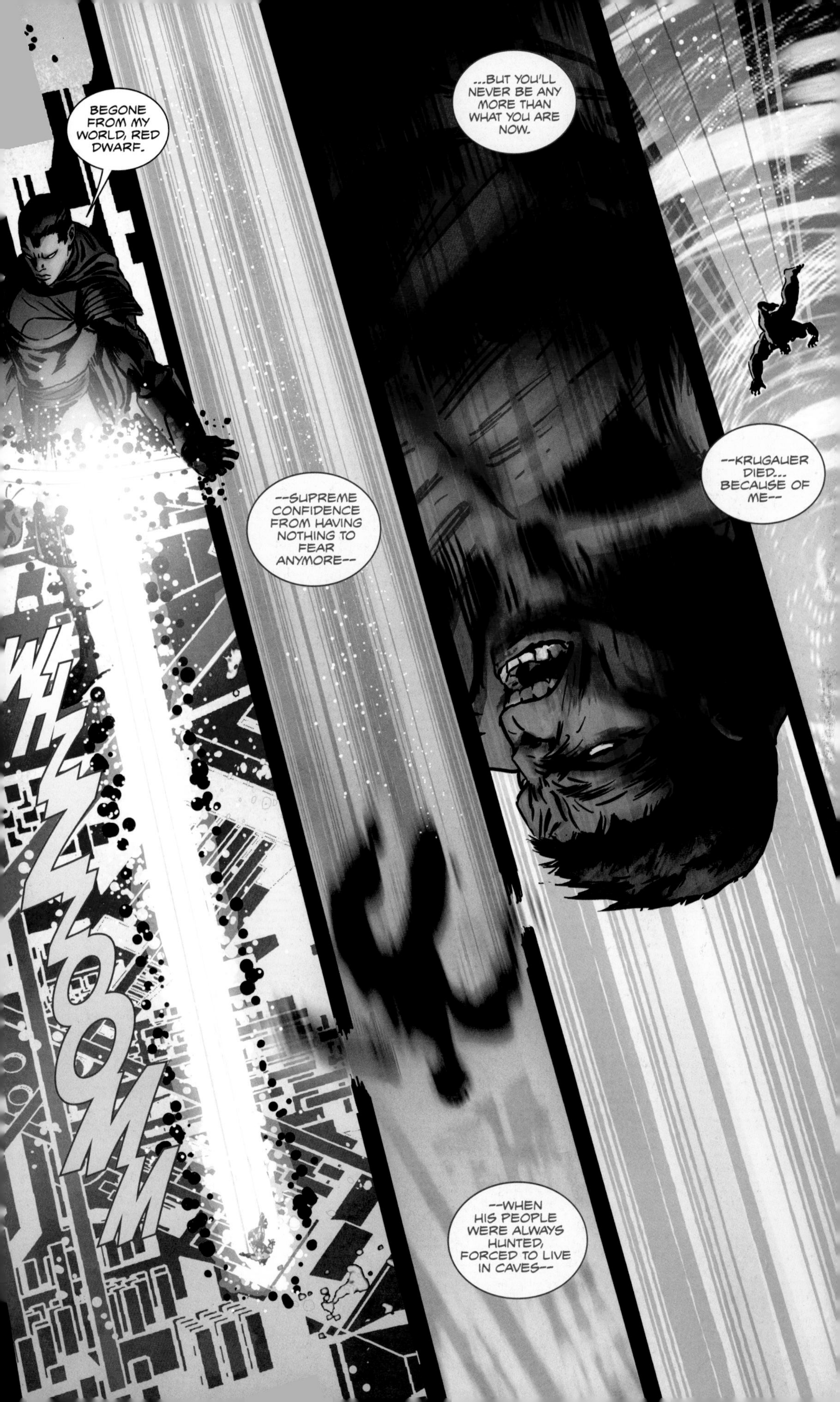
BEGONE FROM MY WORLD, RED DWARF.
WHHOOM!
--SUPREME CONFIDENCE FROM HAVING NOTHING TO FEAR ANYMORE--
...BUT YOU'LL NEVER BE ANY MORE THAN WHAT YOU ARE NOW.
--WHEN HIS PEOPLE WERE ALWAYS HUNTED, FORCED TO LIVE IN CAVES--
--KRUGAUER DIED... BECAUSE OF ME--

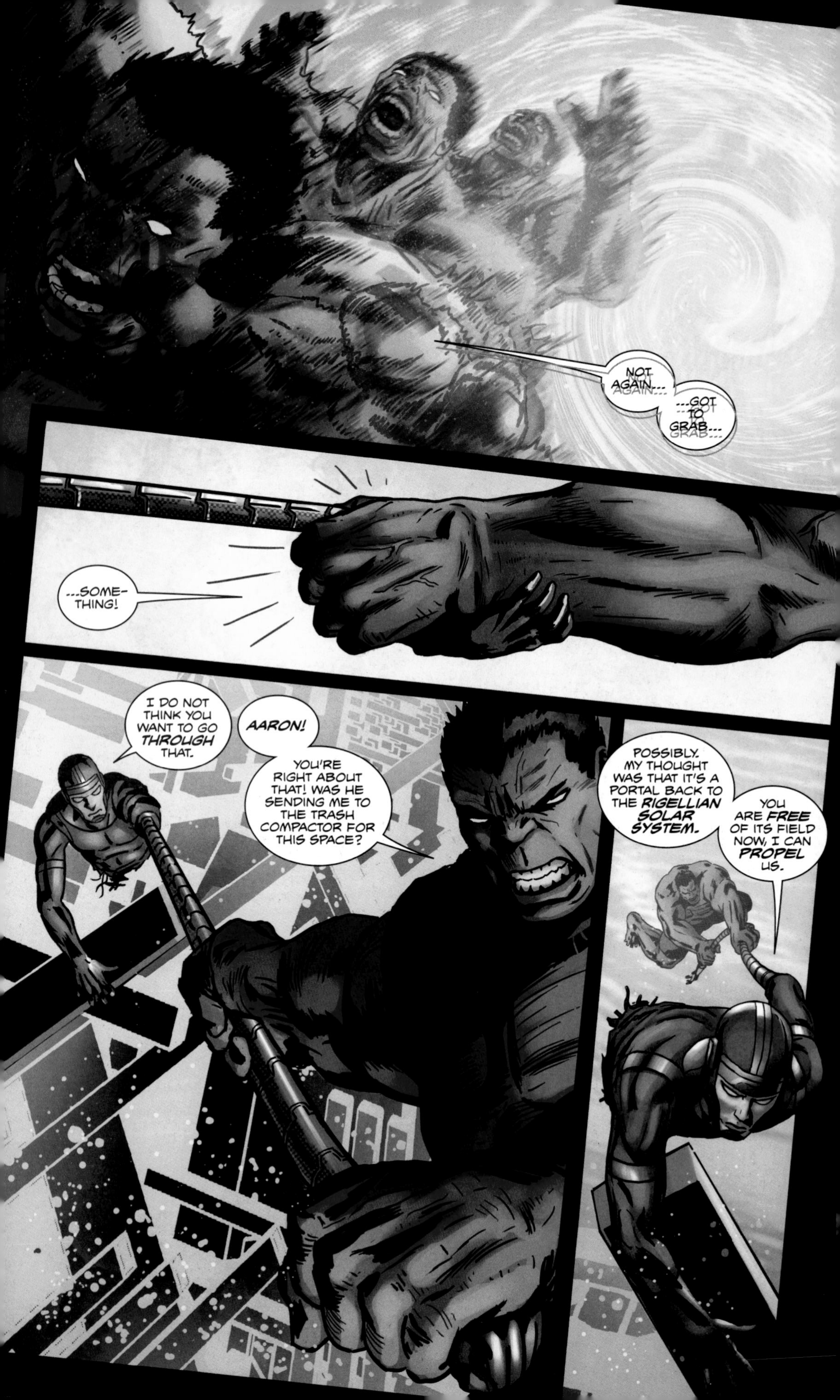
NOT AGAIN...
...GOT TO GRAB...
...SOME-THING!
I DO NOT THINK YOU WANT TO GO THROUGH THAT.
AARON!
YOU'RE RIGHT ABOUT THAT! WAS HE SENDING ME TO THE TRASH COMPACTOR FOR THIS SPACE?
POSSIBLY. MY THOUGHT WAS THAT IT'S A PORTAL BACK TO THE RIGELLIAN SOLAR SYSTEM.
YOU ARE FREE OF ITS FIELD NOW, I CAN PROPEL US.

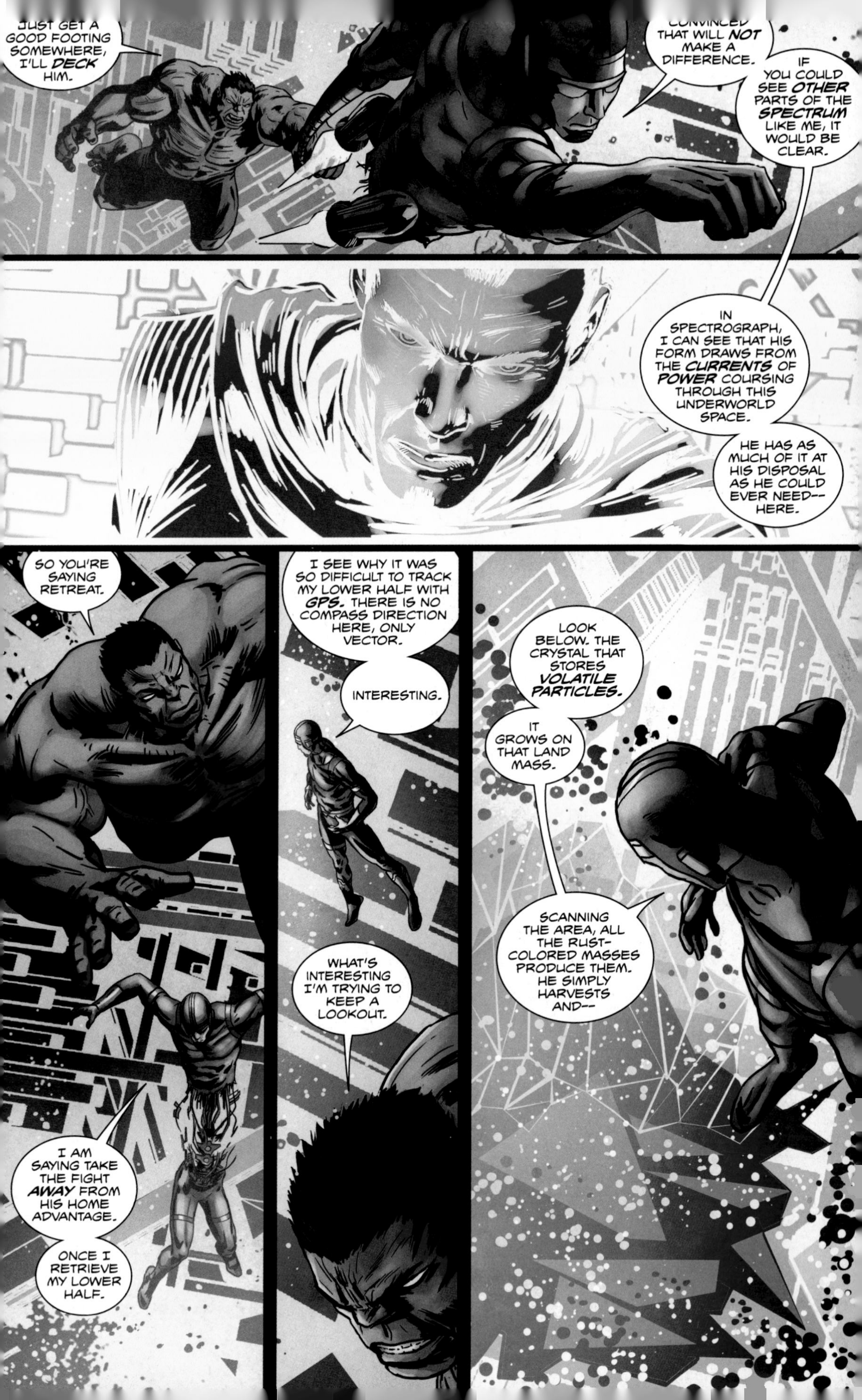
JUST GET A GOOD FOOTING SOMEWHERE, I'LL DECK HIM.
CONVINCED THAT WILL NOT MAKE A DIFFERENCE.
IF YOU COULD SEE OTHER PARTS OF THE SPECTRUM LIKE ME, IT WOULD BE CLEAR.
IN SPECTROGRAPH, I CAN SEE THAT HIS FORM DRAWS FROM THE CURRENTS OF POWER COURSING THROUGH THIS UNDERWORLD SPACE.
HE HAS AS MUCH OF IT AT HIS DISPOSAL AS HE COULD EVER NEED-- HERE.
SO YOU'RE SAYING RETREAT.
I AM SAYING TAKE THE FIGHT AWAY FROM HIS HOME ADVANTAGE.
ONCE I RETRIEVE MY LOWER HALF.
I SEE WHY IT WAS SO DIFFICULT TO TRACK MY LOWER HALF WITH GPS. THERE IS NO COMPASS DIRECTION HERE, ONLY VECTOR.
INTERESTING.
WHAT'S INTERESTING I'M TRYING TO KEEP A LOOKOUT.
LOOK BELOW. THE CRYSTAL THAT STORES VOLATILE PARTICLES.
IT GROWS ON THAT LAND MASS.
SCANNING THE AREA, ALL THE RUST-COLORED MASSES PRODUCE THEM. HE SIMPLY HARVESTS AND--

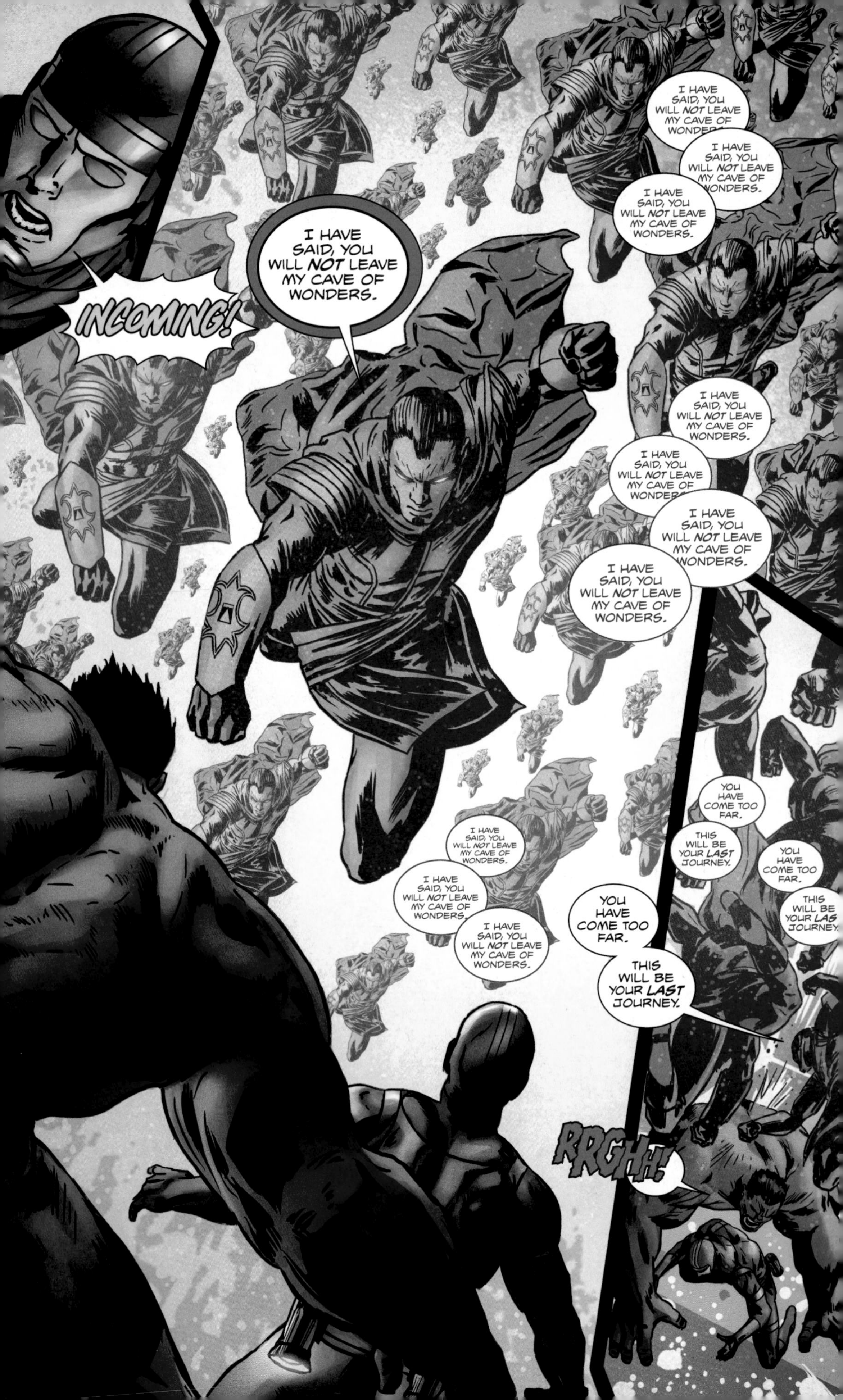

INCOMING!
I HAVE SAID, YOU WILL NOT LEAVE MY CAVE OF WONDERS.
I HAVE SAID, YOU WILL NOT LEAVE MY CAVE OF WONDERS.
I HAVE SAID, YOU WILL NOT LEAVE MY CAVE OF WONDERS.
I HAVE SAID, YOU WILL NOT LEAVE MY CAVE OF WONDERS.
I HAVE SAID, YOU WILL NOT LEAVE MY CAVE OF WONDERS.
I HAVE SAID, YOU WILL NOT LEAVE MY CAVE OF
I HAVE SAID, YOU WILL NOT LEAVE MY CAVE OF WONDERS.
I HAVE SAID, YOU WILL NOT LEAVE MY CAVE OF WONDERS.
I HAVE SAID, YOU WILL NOT LEAVE MY CAVE OF WONDERS.
I HAVE SAID, YOU WILL NOT LEAVE MY CAVE OF WONDERS.
I HAVE SAID, YOU WILL NOT LEAVE MY CAVE OF WONDERS.
YOU HAVE COME TOO FAR.
THIS WILL BE YOUR LAST JOURNEY.
YOU HAVE COME TOO FAR.
THIS WILL BE YOUR LAST JOURNEY.
YOU HAVE COME TOO FAR.
THIS WILL BE YOUR LAS JOURNEY.
RRGHH!

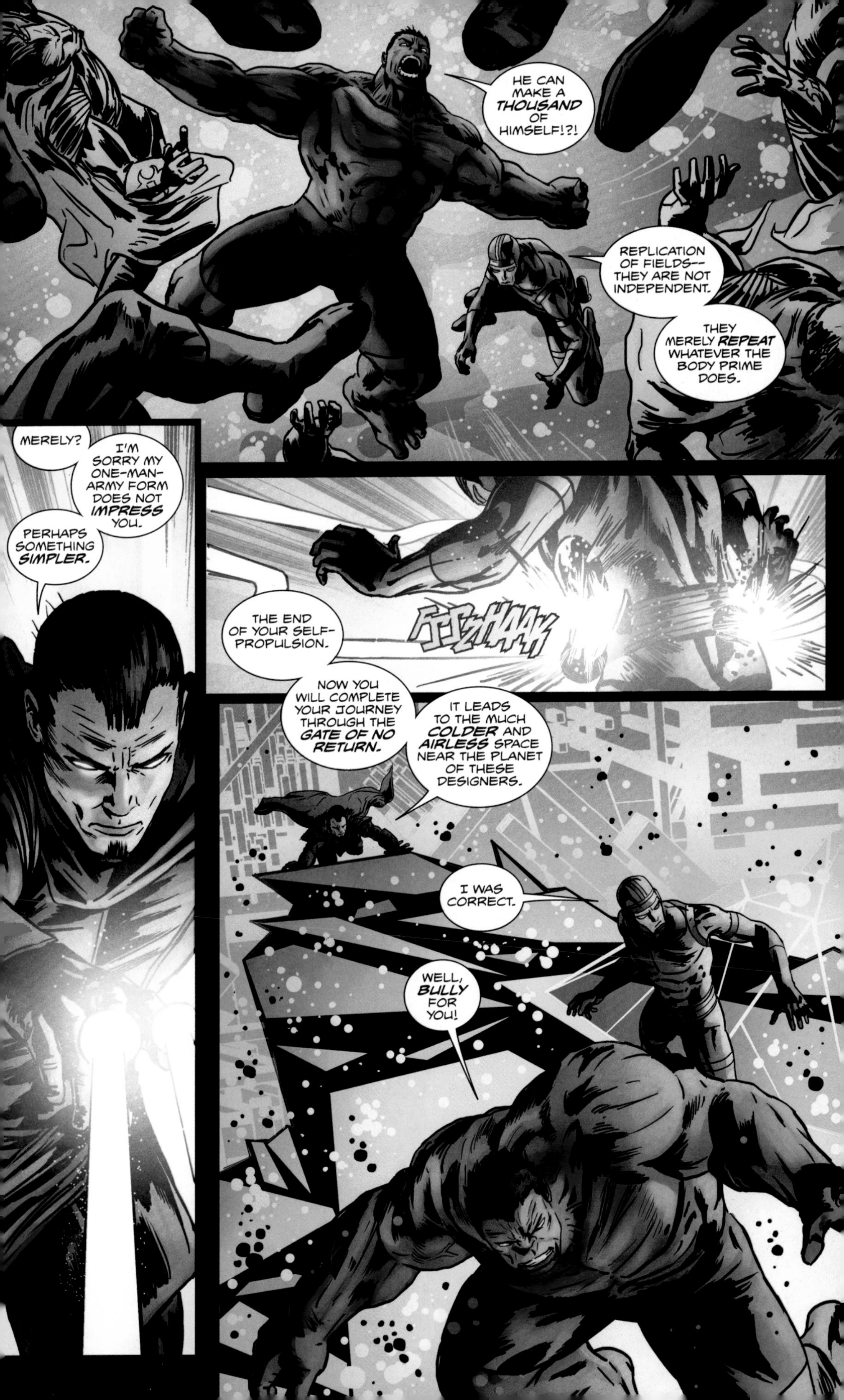
HE CAN MAKE A THOUSAND OF HIMSELF!?!
REPLICATION OF FIELDS-- THEY ARE NOT INDEPENDENT.
THEY MERELY REPEAT WHATEVER THE BODY PRIME DOES.
MERELY?
I'M SORRY MY ONE-MAN-ARMY FORM DOES NOT IMPRESS YOU.
PERHAPS SOMETHING SIMPLER.
THE END OF YOUR SELF-PROPULSION.
FTTZHAAK
NOW YOU WILL COMPLETE YOUR JOURNEY THROUGH THE GATE OF NO RETURN.
IT LEADS TO THE MUCH COLDER AND AIRLESS SPACE NEAR THE PLANET OF THESE DESIGNERS.
I WAS CORRECT.
WELL, BULLY FOR YOU!

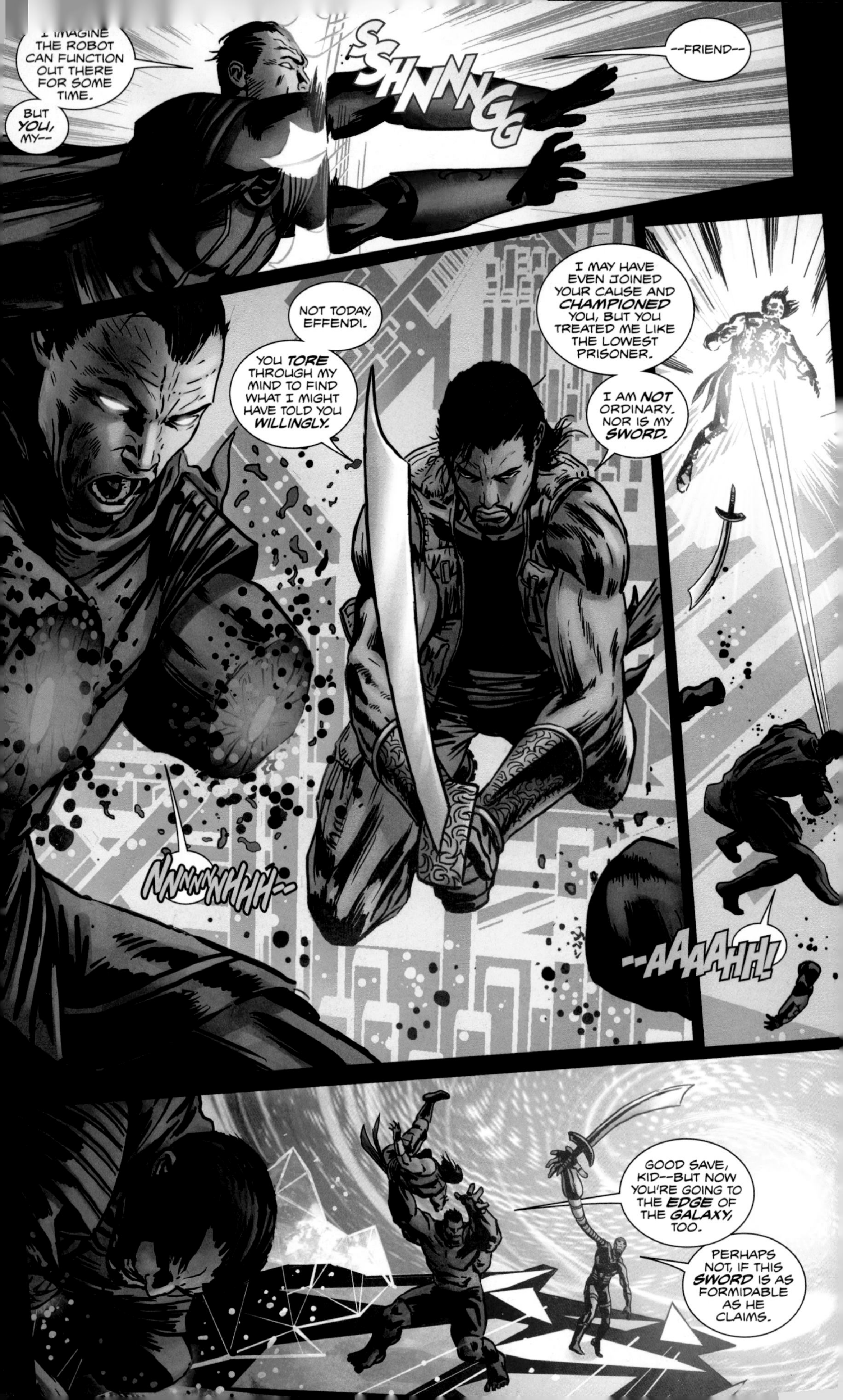
I IMAGINE THE ROBOT CAN FUNCTION OUT THERE FOR SOME TIME.
BUT YOU, MY--
SSHNNNGG
--FRIEND--
NOT TODAY, EFFENDI.
YOU TORE THROUGH MY MIND TO FIND WHAT I MIGHT HAVE TOLD YOU WILLINGLY.
I MAY HAVE EVEN JOINED YOUR CAUSE AND CHAMPIONED YOU, BUT YOU TREATED ME LIKE THE LOWEST PRISONER.
I AM NOT ORDINARY. NOR IS MY SWORD.
NNNNNNHHH--
--AAAAHH!
GOOD SAVE, KID--BUT NOW YOU'RE GOING TO THE EDGE OF THE GALAXY, TOO.
PERHAPS NOT, IF THIS SWORD IS AS FORMIDABLE AS HE CLAIMS.

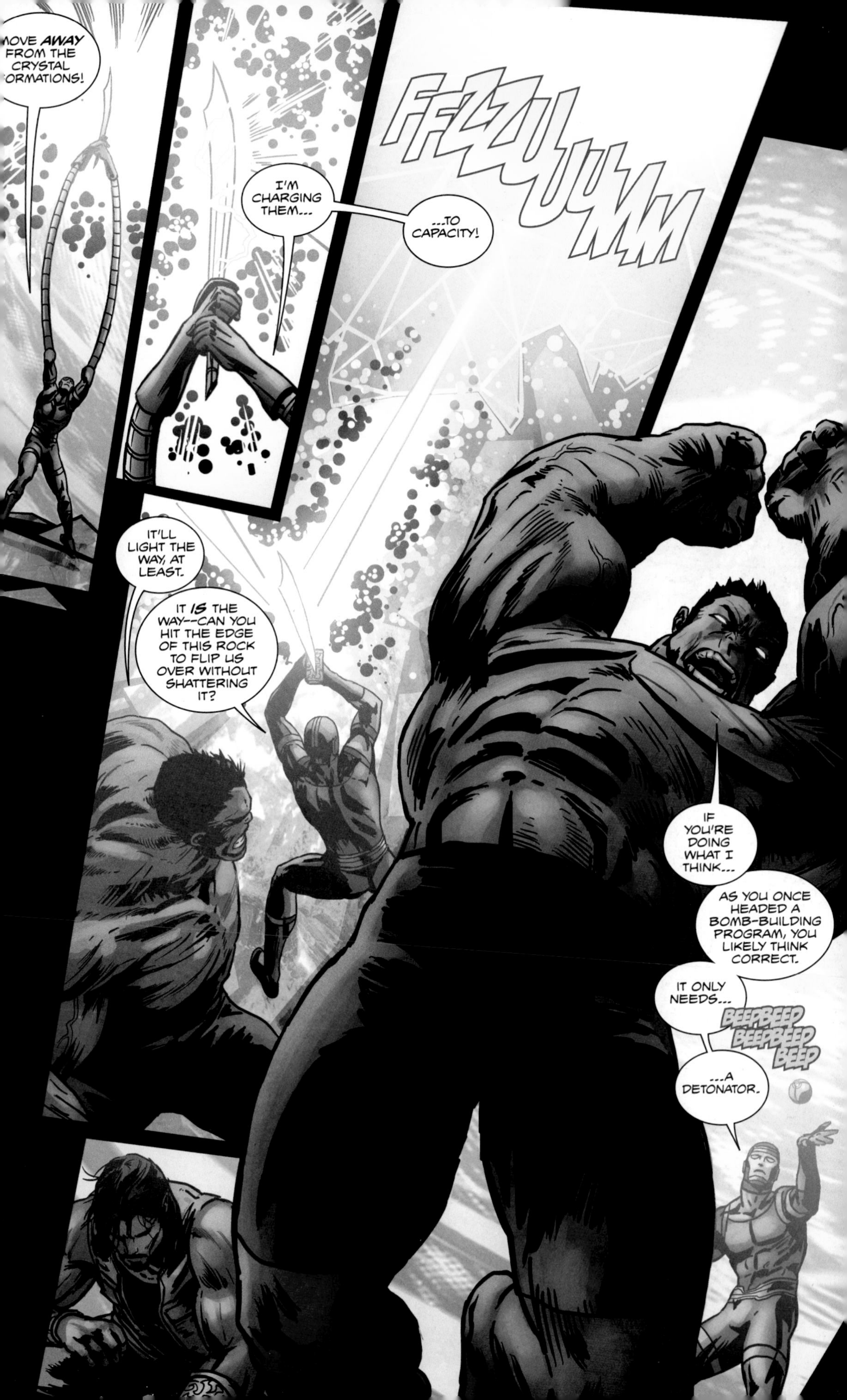
MOVE AWAY FROM THE CRYSTAL FORMATIONS!
I'M CHARGING THEM...
...TO CAPACITY!
FFZZUUUMM
IT'LL LIGHT THE WAY, AT LEAST.
IT IS THE WAY--CAN YOU HIT THE EDGE OF THIS ROCK TO FLIP US OVER WITHOUT SHATTERING IT?
IF YOU'RE DOING WHAT I THINK...
AS YOU ONCE HEADED A BOMB-BUILDING PROGRAM, YOU LIKELY THINK CORRECT.
IT ONLY NEEDS...
BEEPBEEP BEEPBEEP BEEP
...A DETONATOR.

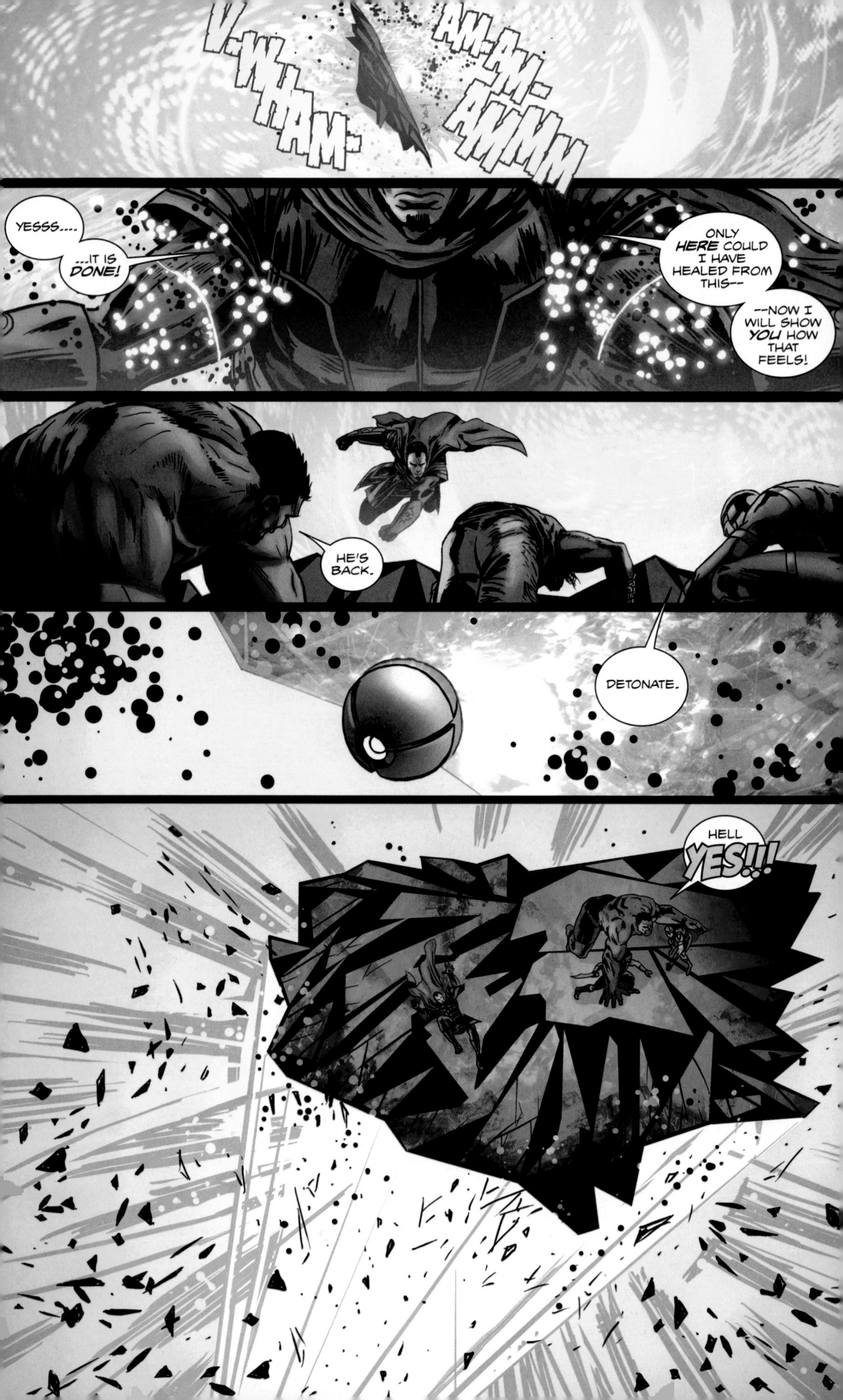
V-WHAM-
AM-AM-AMMM
YESSS....
...IT IS DONE!
ONLY HERE COULD I HAVE HEALED FROM THIS--
--NOW I WILL SHOW YOU HOW THAT FEELS!
HE'S BACK.
DETONATE.
HELL YES!!!

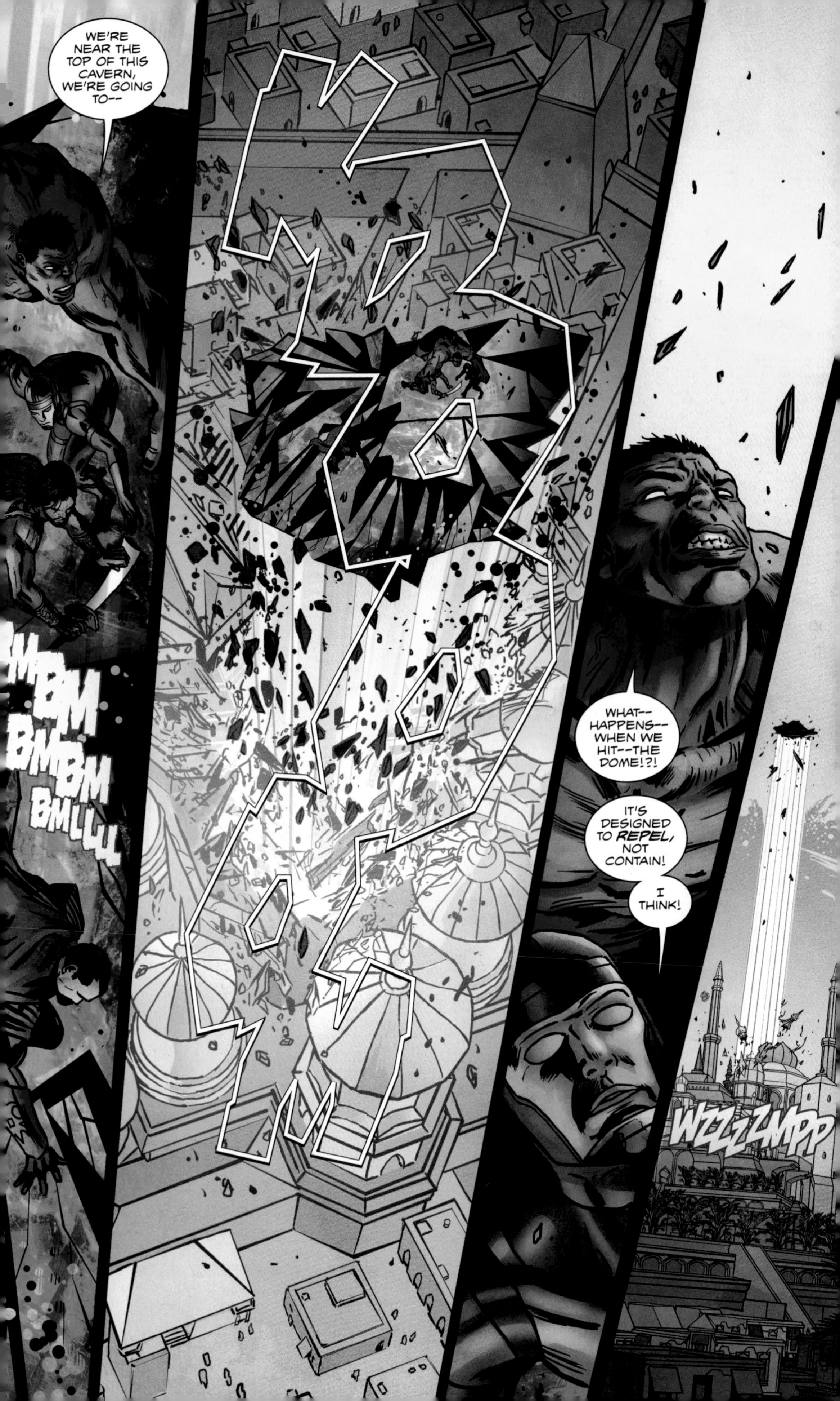

WE'RE NEAR THE TOP OF THIS CAVERN, WE'RE GOING TO--
BMBM BMBM BMLLL
WHAT-- HAPPENS-- WHEN WE HIT--THE DOME!?!
IT'S DESIGNED TO REPEL, NOT CONTAIN!
I THINK!
WZZZZMPP

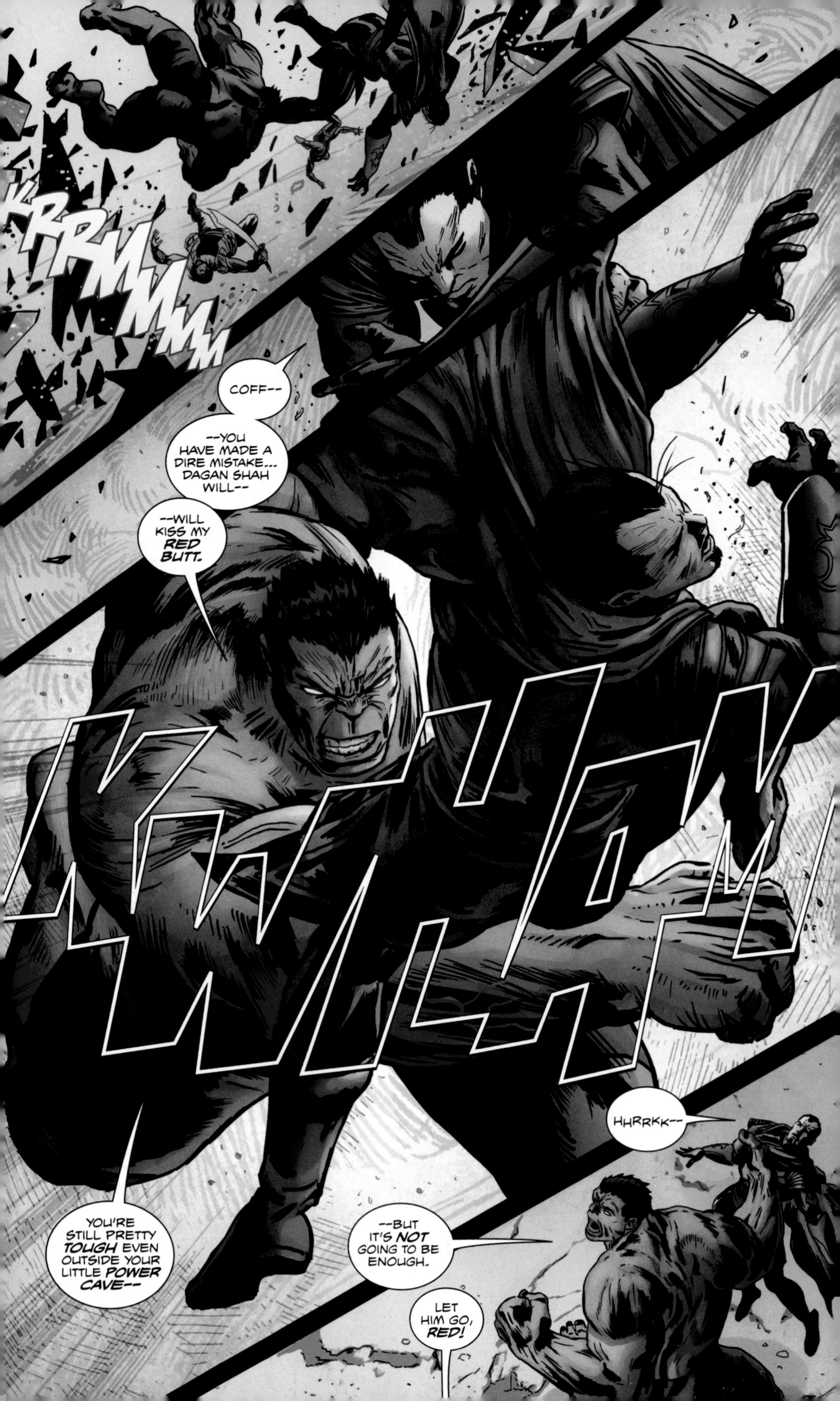
KRRMMMMM
COFF--
--YOU HAVE MADE A DIRE MISTAKE... DAGAN SHAH WILL--
--WILL KISS MY RED BUTT.
KWHOM
YOU'RE STILL PRETTY TOUGH EVEN OUTSIDE YOUR LITTLE POWER CAVE--
HHRRKK--
--BUT IT'S NOT GOING TO BE ENOUGH.
LET HIM GO, RED!

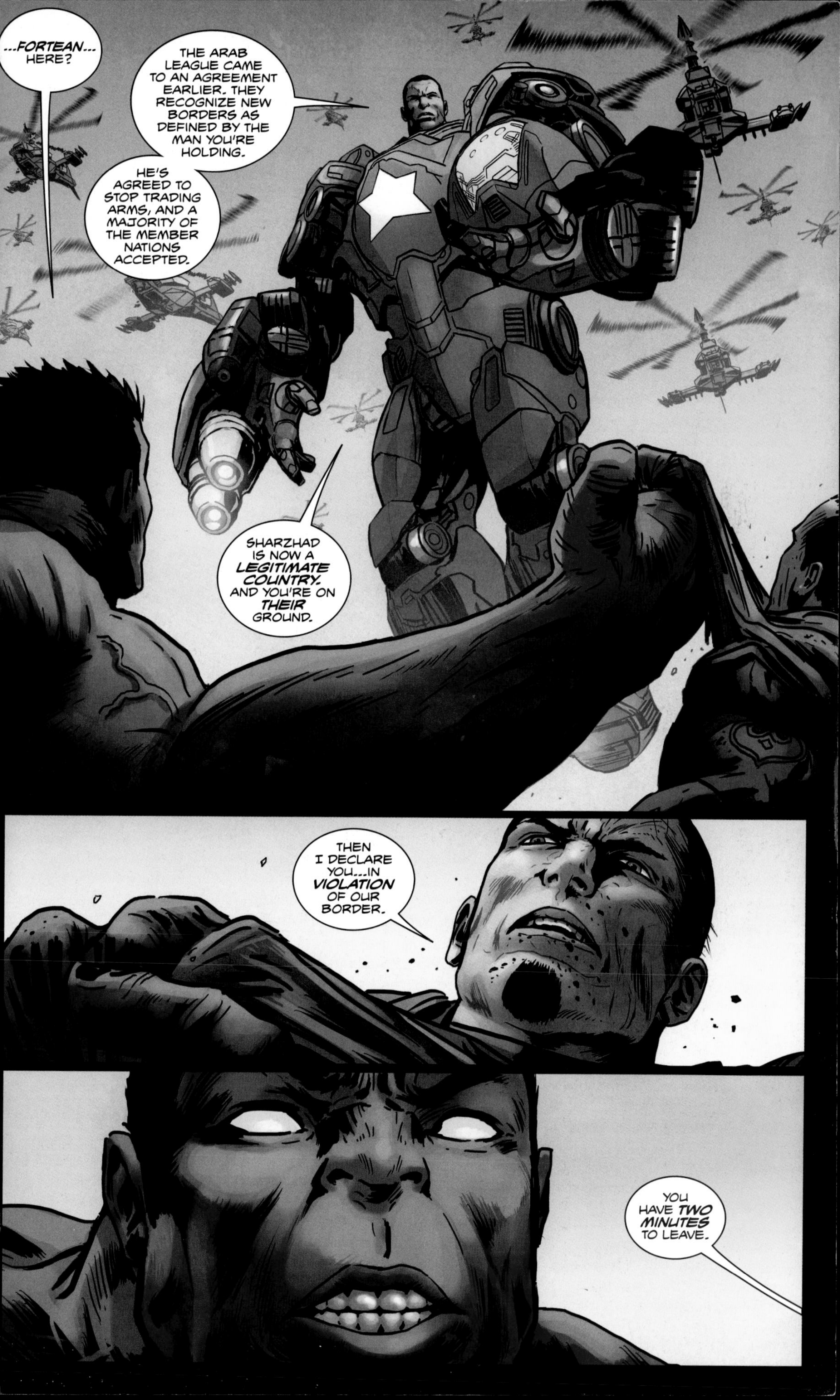
...FORTEAN... HERE?
THE ARAB LEAGUE CAME TO AN AGREEMENT EARLIER. THEY RECOGNIZE NEW BORDERS AS DEFINED BY THE MAN YOU'RE HOLDING.
HE'S AGREED TO STOP TRADING ARMS, AND A MAJORITY OF THE MEMBER NATIONS ACCEPTED.
SHARZHAD IS NOW A LEGITIMATE COUNTRY. AND YOU'RE ON THEIR GROUND.
THEN I DECLARE YOU...IN VIOLATION OF OUR BORDER.
YOU HAVE TWO MINUTES TO LEAVE.

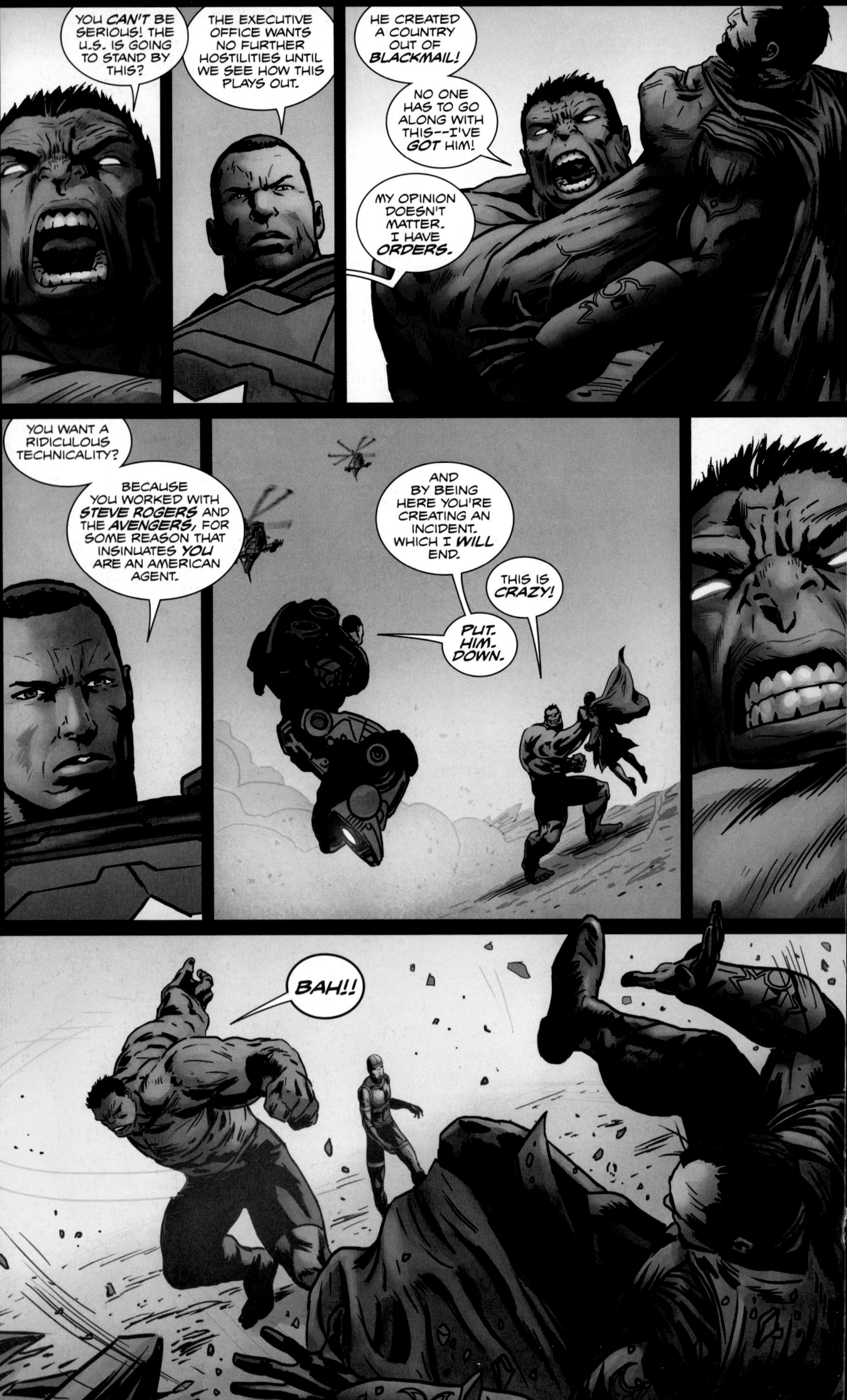

YOU CAN'T BE SERIOUS! THE U.S. IS GOING TO STAND BY THIS?
THE EXECUTIVE OFFICE WANTS NO FURTHER HOSTILITIES UNTIL WE SEE HOW THIS PLAYS OUT.
HE CREATED A COUNTRY OUT OF BLACKMAIL!
NO ONE HAS TO GO ALONG WITH THIS--I'VE GOT HIM!
MY OPINION DOESN'T MATTER. I HAVE ORDERS.
YOU WANT A RIDICULOUS TECHNICALITY?
BECAUSE YOU WORKED WITH STEVE ROGERS AND THE AVENGERS, FOR SOME REASON THAT INSINUATES YOU ARE AN AMERICAN AGENT.
AND BY BEING HERE YOU'RE CREATING AN INCIDENT. WHICH I WILL END.
THIS IS CRAZY!
PUT. HIM. DOWN.
BAH!!

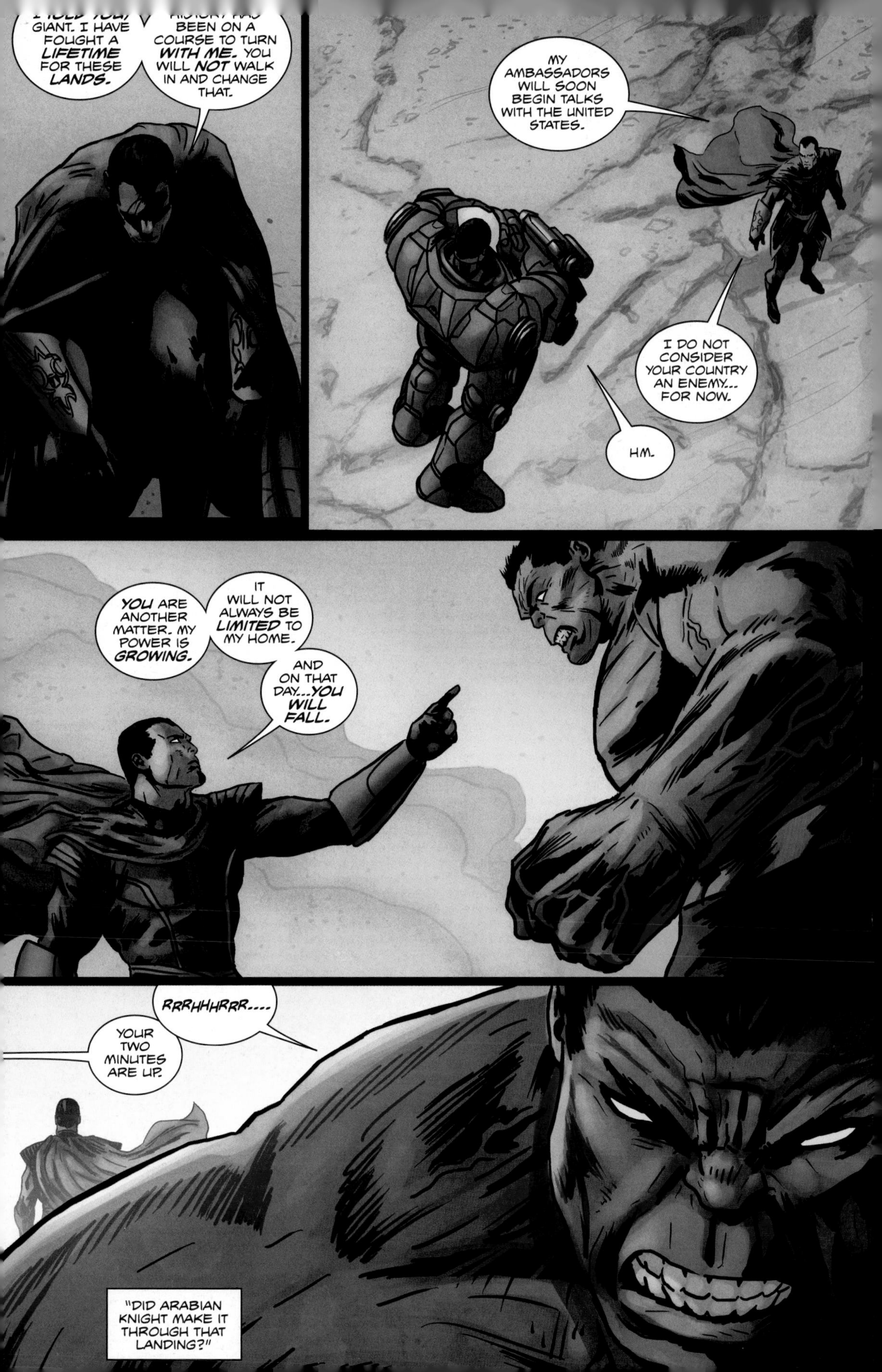
GIANT. I HAVE FOUGHT A LIFETIME FOR THESE LANDS.
BEEN ON A COURSE TO TURN WITH ME. YOU WILL NOT WALK IN AND CHANGE THAT.
MY AMBASSADORS WILL SOON BEGIN TALKS WITH THE UNITED STATES.
I DO NOT CONSIDER YOUR COUNTRY AN ENEMY... FOR NOW.
HM.
YOU ARE ANOTHER MATTER. MY POWER IS GROWING.
IT WILL NOT ALWAYS BE LIMITED TO MY HOME.
AND ON THAT DAY...YOU WILL FALL.
RRRHHHRRR....
YOUR TWO MINUTES ARE UP.
"DID ARABIAN KNIGHT MAKE IT THROUGH THAT LANDING?"

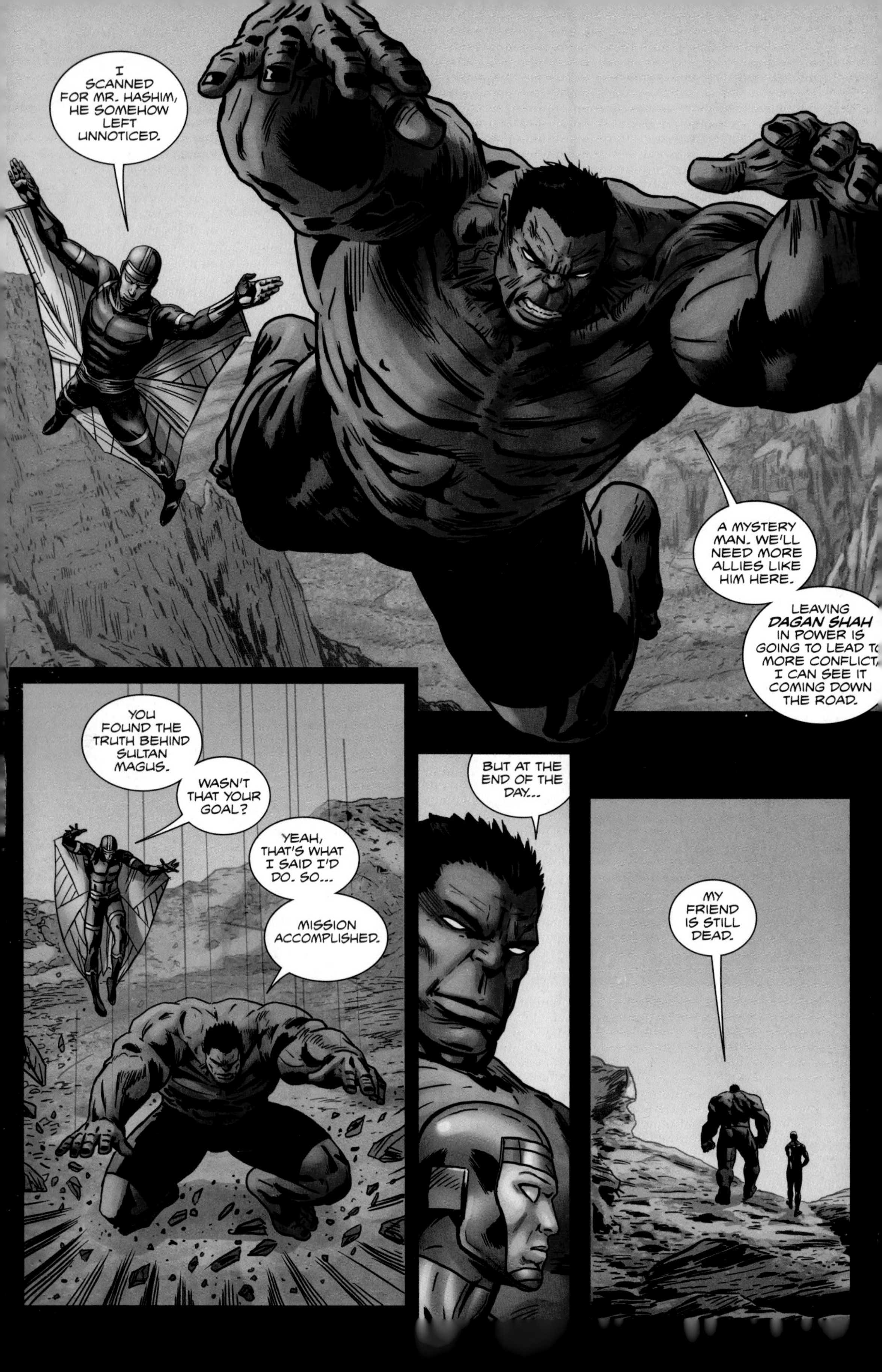
I SCANNED FOR MR. HASHIM, HE SOMEHOW LEFT UNNOTICED.
A MYSTERY MAN. WE'LL NEED MORE ALLIES LIKE HIM HERE.
LEAVING DAGAN SHAH IN POWER IS GOING TO LEAD TO MORE CONFLICT, I CAN SEE IT COMING DOWN THE ROAD.
YOU FOUND THE TRUTH BEHIND SULTAN MAGUS.
WASN'T THAT YOUR GOAL?
YEAH, THAT'S WHAT I SAID I'D DO. SO...
MISSION ACCOMPLISHED.
BUT AT THE END OF THE DAY...
MY FRIEND IS STILL DEAD.